Bloom's Literary Themes

Alienation
The American Dream
Civil Disobedience
Dark Humor
Death and Dying
Enslavement and Emancipation
Exploration and Colonization
The Grotesque
The Hero's Journey
Human Sexuality
The Labyrinth
Rebirth and Renewal
Sin and Redemption
The Sublime
The Taboo
The Trickster

THE TRICKSTER

Bloom's Literary Themes

THE TRICKSTER

Edited and with an introduction by
Harold Bloom
Sterling Professor of the Humanities
Yale University

Volume Editor
Blake Hobby

BLOOM'S
LITERARY CRITICISM
An imprint of Infobase Publishing

Bloom's Literary Themes: The Trickster

Copyright ©2010 by Infobase Publishing
Introduction ©2010 by Harold Bloom

Bloom's Literary Criticism
An imprint of Infobase Publishing
132 West 31st Street
New York NY 10001

Library of Congress Cataloging-in-Publication Data
   Bloom's literary themes : the trickster / edited and with an introduction by Harold Bloom ; volume editor, Blake Hobby.
      p. cm.
   Includes bibliographical references and index.
   ISBN 978-1-60413-445-2 (hc : alk. paper)   1. Tricksters in literature.   2. Fools and jesters in literature.   I. Bloom, Harold.   II. Hobby, Blake.   III. Title.
   PN56.5.T74B56 2010
   809'93352—dc22

                                        2009038088

You can find Bloom's Literary Criticism on the World Wide Web at
http://www.chelseahouse.com

Text design by Kerry Casey
Cover design by Takeshi Takahashi
Composition by IBT Global, Inc.
Cover printed by Yurchak Printing, Landisville, Pa.
Book printed and bound by Yurchak Printing, Landisville, Pa.
Printed in the United States of America

This book is printed on acid-free paper.

Contents

Series Introduction by Harold Bloom: Themes and Metaphors

1. TOPOS AND TROPE

What we now call a theme or topic or subject initially was named a *topos*, ancient Greek for "place." Literary *topoi* are commonplaces, but also arguments or assertions. A topos can be regarded as literal when opposed to a trope or turning which is figurative and which can be a metaphor or some related departure from the literal: ironies, synecdoches (part for whole), metonymies (representations by contiguity) or hyperboles (overstatements). Themes and metaphors engender one another in all significant literary compositions.

As a theoretician of the relation between the matter and the rhetoric of high literature, I tend to define metaphor as a figure of desire rather than a figure of knowledge. We welcome literary metaphor because it enables fictions to persuade us of beautiful untrue things, as Oscar Wilde phrased it. Literary *topoi* can be regarded as places where we store information, in order to amplify the themes that interest us.

This series of volumes, *Bloom's Literary Themes*, offers students and general readers helpful essays on such perpetually crucial topics as the Hero's Journey, the Labyrinth, the Sublime, Death and Dying, the Taboo, the Trickster and many more. These subjects are chosen for their prevalence yet also for their centrality. They express the whole concern of human existence now in the twenty-first century of the Common Era. Some of the topics would have seemed odd at another time, another land: the American Dream, Enslavement and Emancipation, Civil Disobedience.

I suspect though that our current preoccupations would have existed always and everywhere, under other names. Tropes change across the centuries: the irony of one age is rarely the irony of another. But the themes of great literature, though immensely varied, undergo transmemberment and show up barely disguised in different contexts. The power of imaginative literature relies upon three constants: aesthetic splendor, cognitive power, wisdom. These are not bound by societal constraints or resentments, and ultimately are universals, and so not culture-bound. Shakespeare, except for the world's scriptures, is the one universal author, whether he is read and played in Bulgaria or Indonesia or wherever. His supremacy at creating human beings breaks through even the barrier of language and puts everyone on his stage. This means that the matter of his work has migrated everywhere, reinforcing the common places we all inhabit in his themes.

2. CONTEST AS BOTH THEME AND TROPE

Great writing or the Sublime rarely emanates directly from themes since all authors are mediated by forerunners and by contemporary rivals. Nietzsche enhanced our awareness of the agonistic foundations of ancient Greek literature and culture, from Hesiod's contest with Homer on to the Hellenistic critic Longinus in his treatise *On the Sublime*. Even Shakespeare had to begin by overcoming Christopher Marlowe, only a few months his senior. William Faulkner stemmed from the Polish-English novelist Joseph Conrad and our best living author of prose fiction, Philip Roth, is inconceivable without his descent from the major Jewish literary phenomenon of the twentieth century, Franz Kafka of Prague, who wrote the most lucid German since Goethe.

The contest with past achievement is the hidden theme of all major canonical literature in Western tradition. Literary influence is both an overwhelming metaphor for literature itself, and a common topic for all criticism, whether or not the critic knows her immersion in the incessant flood.

Every theme in this series touches upon a contest with anteriority, whether with the presence of death, the hero's quest, the overcoming of taboos, or all of the other concerns, volume by volume. From Monteverdi through Bach to Stravinsky, or from the Italian Renaissance through the agon of Matisse and Picasso, the history of all the arts demonstrates the same patterns as literature's thematic struggle with itself. Our country's great original art, jazz, is illuminated by what the great creators called "cutting contests," from Louis Armstrong and Duke Ellington on to the emergence of Charlie Parker's Bop or revisionist jazz.

A literary theme, however authentic, would come to nothing without rhetorical eloquence or mastery of metaphor. But to experience the study of the common places of invention is an apt training in the apprehension of aesthetic value in poetry and in prose.

Volume Introduction by Harold Bloom

The figure of the Trickster is all but universal in the world's cultures, and generally emerged from shamanistic origins. Folklore and anthropology are essential to the study of the Trickster, and I particularly recommend the religious historian Mircea Eliade's seminal study, *Shamanism*.

This though is a volume about the *literary* theme of the trickster, and so I will remark here upon some of that wily figure's transformations in Homer's Odysseus (Ulysses), Chaucer's Pardoner and Wife of Bath, Shakespeare's clowns, fools, sprites, and villains. Later come the trickster's ongoing fortunes in Melville, Mark Twain, and Franz Kafka. The list could be extended, but these will suffice.

All "practical jokesters" are tricksters, but the converse scarcely is true. Odysseus-Ulysses is the archetype of the survivor, and you do not want to be in the same boat with him. He will reach the shore, you will drown. The Trojan Horse is his most notorious trick, yet there are many more. In his final incarnation he is Joyce's endlessly amiable Leopold Bloom, but Poldy is a sport in the annals of Ulysses. Shakespeare's scurvy politician Ulysses in *Troilus and Cressida* is the more representative figure.

The evil trickster in the highest degree in Shakespeare is Iago, the truest *diabolos* in all of literature. The clowns and fools in the Shakespearean cosmos are too wise to be innocent but also too benign to be harmful. Shakespeare balances his clowns and sprites between the Chaucerian models of the likeable but ambiguous Alice, the Wife of Bath, and the uncanny Pardoner, who is suspended between cupidity and faith.

In American literature the trickster stars as Melville's *Confidence Man* and in a sophisticated second innocence as the magnificent

Huckleberry Finn, ancestor of Hemingway himself and of his Nick Adams. The master of the trickster theme in modern literature, Franz Kafka, is a link to its long history in Yiddish culture, including on the stage and in prose fiction. After Kafka, we are all tricksters, evading our doom as best we can.

THE ADVENTURES OF HUCKLEBERRY FINN
(MARK TWAIN)

"The Trickster Tricked: Huck Comes Out of the Fog in Mark Twain's *The Adventures of Huckleberry Finn*"
by Robert C. Evans

Mark Twain's great novel *Huckleberry Finn* is a book brimming with tricks, trickery, and tricksters. Tom Sawyer, for instance, is obviously one of the latter; so are the Duke and the Dauphin; and so, to a lesser extent, is Huck himself. Tricks provide much of the hilarity we associate with this book, as when young Tom (pretending to be a newly arrived stranger), without warning or permission, suddenly and boldly kisses Sally Phelps, a much-older relative whom he has only just met: "he reached over and kissed aunt Sally right on the mouth, and then settled back again, in his chair, comfortable, and was going on talking, but she jumped up and wiped it off with the back of her hand, and says: 'You owdacious puppy!'" Tom, instead of apologizing in the face of the woman's now-ignited wrath, only digs the hole deeper by explaining, "I didn't mean no harm. I—I—thought you'd like it." When an exasperated Aunt Sally then calls him a "born fool" and picks up a nearby stick, Tom pushes the joke even further by explaining that he had been told by "everybody" that she would like to be kissed, but then he promises, "I won't ever do it again. Till you ask me." By this time Aunt Sally is about to explode: "Till I *ask* you! Well, I never see the beat of it in my born days! I lay you'll be the Methusalem-numbskull of creation before ever *I* ask you—or the likes of you!" (*HF* 287). Tom

1

continues to push the gag further and further until he finally explains that he is in fact the young relative whose arrival she has long been expecting. When a now-joyful Aunt Sally rushes to embrace and kiss him, Tom gives the joke one last twist: "No, not till you've asked me, first" (HF 288).

Tricks of this sort help make *Huckleberry Finn* enormously funny, but sometimes the tricks have a darker and more disturbing effect. This is especially true of the tricks played on black characters, and it is particularly true of the trick played by Tom on Jim in the final chapters of the novel. Tom is the only person at the Phelps farm who knows that Jim has already been freed from slavery in the will of the now-dead Miss Watson, Jim's former owner, but Tom, instead of announcing Jim's liberty as soon as he arrives, instead contrives an elaborate and often dangerous plot to "free" Jim from the small shack in which he is now imprisoned. The closing chapters thus have the ironic effect of only helping to emphasize how far, in fact, Jim remains from true freedom, even after the details of Miss Watson's will are finally revealed. Tom's trick on Jim, like many of the tricks played by white characters on black characters in this book, leaves a bad taste in one's mouth, partly because the tricks remind us of how truly vulnerable the black characters are. Practical jokes between friends help highlight, affirm, and strengthen pre-existing friendships. Practical jokes played on persons with less power than oneself, however, can seem crude, thoughtless, demeaning, and even mean. Reading about such tricks can therefore be disturbing. Twain, in a sense, thus plays a massive trick on any reader who picks up *Huckleberry Finn* and expects it to be a book as full of innocence and lighthearted fun as *The Adventures of Tom Sawyer*. The story of Huck is a far more disconcerting, perplexing, and thought-provoking book than its predecessor, in part because so much of its trickery involves such dark overtones.

One of the best examples of Twain's crafty use of trickery occurs in Chapter 15, when Huck, in a canoe, becomes temporarily separated from Jim, who remains on their raft, as the two make their way down the Mississippi River. For a long time the two remain separated as their crafts speed along the swiftly moving water, enveloped by a thick fog. Huck becomes increasingly afraid, and at one point he tries to explain and justify his agitated emotions by directly addressing the reader: "If you think it ain't dismal and lonesome out in the fog that way, by yourself, in the night, you try it once—you'll see" (*HF* 101).

Huck appeals to the reader's sense of sympathy, suggesting that if we could only imagine ourselves in his place, we would understand and forgive his fears. He later mentions that after fighting the river for hours in search of Jim, he became exhausted and that, although he did not want to fall asleep, "I was so sleepy I couldn't help it" (*HF* 102). When he finally woke up to find that the fog had cleared, "I thought I was dreaming, and when things begun to come back to me, they seemed to come up dim out of last week" (*HF* 102). Fortunately, however, he now spots the raft and makes his way toward it.

When Huck arrives at the raft, he sees Jim "setting there with his head down between his knees, asleep, with his right arm hanging over the steering oar. The other oar was smashed off, and the raft was littered up with leaves and branches and dirt. So she'd had a rough time" (*HF* 102). Huck sees, in other words, an image of Jim that should instantly remind him (and the reader) of himself and of his own quite recent experiences in the canoe. Like Huck a few moments before, Jim is exhausted and now asleep; he is alone; and he is probably frightened. However, just when we might expect Huck to sympathize with Jim and embrace him joyfully, to treat Jim with the same kind of empathetic understanding that Huck himself had so recently sought from the reader, Twain plays a trick on us by having Huck play a trick on Jim. Without any warning or explanation, Huck immediately adopts the attitude and behavior of a trickster: "I made fast and laid down under Jim's nose on the raft, and began to gap, and stretch my fists out against Jim" (*HF* 103). Huck, that is, pretends to be awaking from sleep, and the practical joke on Jim has now begun. The novel seems, suddenly, to have reverted to an earlier, more light-hearted tone, and the dark, "dismal and lonesome" atmosphere of the past few pages seems about to evaporate and instead be replaced by some good fun at Jim's expense. Yet the joke, thanks to Twain the trickster, will soon be on both Huck and the reader.

The paragraphs that now follow are among the most famous and most important in the novel: They mark a significant moment of transformation, a crucial stage in Huck's moral maturation and in his development toward ethical adulthood. What begins as a trick on Jim, designed to make him look and feel foolish, soon evolves into an episode in which it is Huck who not only behaves like a fool but eventually feels far worse than one. The tone of the episode moves rapidly from apparently good-natured fun to something far more profound and serious, as Twain shows his capacity to move far beyond the lighthearted but somewhat meaningless high jinks of *Tom Sawyer*. Huck, in this episode, becomes the trickster tricked, but the trick is also partly played by Twain on the unassuming reader. Anyone who begins reading this episode by identifying with Huck's spirit of apparently innocent play ultimately has the rug pulled out from under him. Likewise, anyone who starts reading this passage by expecting that Jim, the supposedly foolish "darky," will be the object of hilarious laughter is soon disabused of that notion. Twain, in a splendid twist, manages to turn the admittedly superstitious Jim—the stereotypically naïve, ignorant, and untutored slave—into a figure of almost tragic dignity, a figure who seems far more worthy of our respect than anyone else in the novel. By the end of this chapter, it is Huck who feels foolish, as should any reader who may have shared Huck's assumptions about Jim. Huck, at least, has the excuse of youth to help explain his juvenile attitudes and thoughtless conduct in this chapter (he is only thirteen). The society surrounding Huck (and Twain), however, has no similar justification.

To read the conclusion of Chapter 15 for the first time is to feel a bit of a shock; to read it a second or third time is to experience a kind of revelation, as the double-edged subtleties and ironic implications of Twain's phrasing rise to the surface. For instance, the fact that Huck initially stretches his "fists out against Jim" seems at first to be merely a gesture of pretended awakening. It is possible to argue that there may be a hint of veiled or unconscious aggression in Huck's fisted gesture, but the fact that he does indeed *touch* Jim seems to be the most significant aspect of this detail. That touch symbolizes the level of intimacy that has developed between the two, a white boy and an older black man—a man who has now become a kind of father figure to Huck. Although the mischievous Huck is about to injure the bond that is signified by that touch, the temporary damage done to their relationship will soon ironically result in an even stronger tie—a tie that might never have formed if Huck had not learned a valuable lesson through his trickery. Paradoxically, then, the trick that threatens to break Huck's ties with Jim actually strengthens them. At the beginning of this episode, Huck only pretends to awaken, but by the end of the chapter he will in fact have awakened in a far more serious and consequential sense.

Jim's deep delight that Huck has returned safely ("It's too good for true, honey, it's too good for true") should already begin to make the reader feel uncomfortable. Jim is so clearly a good, kind, and caring man that the idea of playing a trick on him (especially at this point of heightened emotion, when he feels so vulnerable) already seems unsettling. When Jim welcomes his young friend back as "de same ole Huck—de same ole Huck," we can already see that his phrasing is partly right and partly wrong. Huck, by beginning his deception, has indeed begun to behave like the "de same ole Huck" who has teased and tricked Jim in the past, but he is also departing from the "Huck" whom Jim thinks he knows intimately and can trust. Huck, for the sake of a cheap laugh, is in the process of violating the bond that has thus far developed between the two during their trip down the river. Thus, when Jim welcomes back "de same ole Huck, thanks to goodness" (*HF* 103), there is a darkly ironic undertone to his final word.

Huck, however, refuses—at least for now—to openly reciprocate the love Jim showers upon him. Instead, he pursues his trick, asking Jim if he has been drinking. Jim is incredulous: "Drinkin'? Has I ben a drinkin'? Has I had a chance to be a drinkin'?" (*HF* 103). Huck thus plays a trick on Jim by pretending to think that Jim must be inebriated, but Twain cleverly turns the trick on Huck by repeating the word "drinkin'" so insistently that the reader is inevitably reminded of an earlier episode in the book in which Jim actually *was* shown to be drinking. In this episode, memorably emphasized in the first edition of the book by an illustration drawn by E.W. Kemble (*HF* 64) in which a bug-eyed Jim is shown hopping up and down on one leg, draining a bottle of whiskey, Jim plays a trick on Jim that ends up being very dangerous. Readers will remember Huck, knowing Jim's fear of snakes, has killed a rattlesnake and "curled him up on the foot of Jim's blanket, ever so natural, thinking there'd be some fun when Jim found him there" (HF 64). Here again, Twain tricks the trickster. Unfortunately, Huck not only forgot about the snake, but he also forgot that "wherever you leave a dead snake, its mate always comes there and curls around it" (*HF* 64–65). Jim is therefore bitten by the dead snake's mate, and he grabs the whiskey to try to help alleviate his considerable pain. Thus, when Huck accuses Jim of having been drinking on the raft, it is hard not to recall this earlier episode when Jim was actually driven to drink as the result of Huck's own pranks. Huck has apparently failed to learn his lesson from his tricks in Chapter 10, and indeed he never admitted his responsibility for the dangerous situation, but in the aftermath of Huck's trick in

Chapter 15, he matures considerably. As a result of Jim's reaction to the second trick, Huck begins to develop into a far more moral and ethically responsible person than he was in previous pages. Twain thus reminds us of the earlier episode partly to emphasize how much Huck has grown up by the end of his trickery in Chapter 15.

As the second episode of trickery unfolds, more and more ironies appear. Huck accuses Jim of talking "wild" (*HF* 103) when it is actually Huck, of course, who is doing so. Even more darkly ironic is the fact that twice in this episode Jim addresses Huck as "boss" (*HF* 103)—a word he never uses elsewhere in referring to his friend. "Boss," as it happens, is a word used only six times in the whole novel, and in two of those cases it is used to refer to Huck's abusive father and his domination of his son (*HF* 26, 29). By calling Huck "boss," Jim may be expressing thinly veiled sarcasm; perhaps he already suspects that he is being subjected to a trick. If that is the case, then his use of the word *boss* is itself a kind of retaliatory trick on Huck—an example of feigned and ultimately subverting defer-ence. Jim's use of the word *boss* may imply that he realizes Huck is treating him not as a friend but as a subservient black man, and indeed Huck does actually call Jim "'a tangle-headed old fool'" (*HF* 103), but by the end of this episode it is Huck who will appear (and feel) genuinely foolish.

Huck begins his trick on Jim by claiming that there never was a dangerous fog. By denying the literal fog, which had made it impossible for Huck and Jim to get their bearings, he tries to create a metaphorical fog that will trap Jim in Huck's deceit and prevent him from seeing the truth. The more Huck deliberately deceives Jim, however, the more Huck ironically enters into his own kind of moral fog. Indeed, Jim's description of the actual fog seems to parallel the symbolic situation in which he and Huck now find themselves: "we got mix' up . . . en one un us got los' en t'other one was jis' as good as los', 'kase he didn' know whah he wuz. . . . Now ain' dat so, boss—ain't it so? You answer me dat" (*HF* 103). The touch of defiance in Jim's final words ("You answer me dat") suggests that Jim is not nearly as foolish, naïve, or compliant as Huck would like to believe. Only by brazenly and repeatedly lying to Jim does Huck finally succeed in making Jim believe him, using his friend's deep trust against him. It is only because Jim trusts Huck so deeply and feels such affection for him that he finally falls for Huck's trick. Indeed, only after Jim has begun to fall for Huck's trickery does he begin to refer to him by name again (rather than as "boss" [*HF* 104]), signifying the shift in his thinking.

Huck, of course, cannot accept a single victory. Instead, having convinced Jim that he dreamed the whole episode about being lost in the fog, he now encourages Jim to make an even bigger fool of himself by urging him to explain and interpret the dream. Jim, with all his defenses down, willingly obliges, and Huck is more than happy to sit and listen to Jim's explanations. Only after Jim finishes does Huck expose his trick and reveal the fool he has made of his friend. Appropriately, the sun has now come up, and so it is now possible for Jim to see clearly some "leaves and rubbish" and a "smashed oar" on the raft—all evidence that Jim had been right all along, that Huck has been lying, and that Jim has been deceived. It seems appropriate that all these revelations should coincide with daybreak, especially since a new day is figuratively about to dawn in the relationship between Jim and Huck. It also seems ironic, however, that day should rise just as the darkness of Huck's deceit becomes apparent.

Jim, in one of the most moving but also one of the most chilling speeches in the entire book, now offers a new interpretation—an interpretation of the "trash" Huck has just revealed. He reiterates the deep love he has come to feel for Huck. He explains how much he missed Huck during his absence, and he says that when he saw Huck again he felt so thankful that he could have gotten down on his knees and kissed Huck's foot. And then he concludes: "En all you wuz thinkin' 'bout, wuz how you could make a fool uv ole Jim wid a lie. Dat truck dah is *trash*; en trash is what people is dat puts dirt on de head er dey fren's en makes 'em ashamed" (*HF* 105). Huck's attempt to make a fool of his friend thus boomerangs as Huck confesses that Jim's pained but dignified response makes Huck feel so "mean" (both hardhearted and low) that "I could almost kissed *his* foot to get him to take it back" (*HF* 105). It was, Huck says, "fifteen minutes before I could work myself up to go and humble myself to a nigger—but I done it, and I warn't ever sorry for it afterwards, neither. I didn't do him no more mean tricks, and I wouldn't done that one if I'd knowed it would make him feel that way" (*HF* 105).

These final words (the concluding words of Chapter 15) are highly significant. They reveal just how far Huck has developed his moral character. In the snakebite trick of Chapter 10, Huck not only failed to confess to Jim his role in the event, but he more importantly failed to express any sense of real guilt or regret over his behavior and the suffering it caused. He called himself "a fool" (*HF* 64) for not remembering that a dead snake's mate comes looking for it, and he announced that "I made up my mind that I wouldn't ever take aholt of a snake-skin again with my hands" (*HF* 65), but never had he voiced any shame or remorse for causing Jim so much pain. (Indeed, in the Kemble drawing, Huck looks on with near fascination, rather than obvious guilt, as Jim jumps up and down with the jug of whiskey [*HF* 64].) In contrast, at the conclusion of Chapter 15, both Huck and the reader feel stunned by the pain Jim expresses, and Huck develops genuine feelings of remorse for his thoughtless actions.

Any reader who began Twain's novel assuming that Jim would simply serve as an object of uncomplicated humor has thus been unforgettably tricked by Twain. By the end of Chapter 15, Jim has already begun to emerge as the central moral character of the book—a characterization that becomes even more obvious when Twain tricks the reader again at the end of Chapter 23 with Jim's surprising self-condemnation for what he considers his own blameworthy behavior toward his small daughter. Ironically, Jim's painful confession there makes him seem an even more admirable figure than he was already. Twain continually surpsises the reader with his depiction of Jim and the layers and depth he gives to a character who might have easily remained a mere stereotype. Ultimately, the greatest trickster in *Huckleberry Finn* is not Huck or Tom or the Duke or the Dauphin; the greatest trickster is and always remains Twain himself.

Works Cited

Twain, Mark. *Adventures of Huckleberry Finn*. Ed. Victor Fischer and Lin Salamo. Berkeley: University of California Press, 2001.

THE WORKS OF SHERMAN ALEXIE

"Futuristic Hip Indian: Alexie"
by Kenneth Lincoln, in *Sing With the Heart of a Bear: Fusions of Native and American Poetry, 1890–1999* (2000)

INTRODUCTION

Kenneth Lincoln calls Sherman Alexie a "Huckster, con man, carny barker, stand-up comedian, Will Rogers to Jonathan Winters, Cheech & Chong to Charlie Hill. The impudence of the anti-poetic Red Rapster." Lincoln, one of the most respected scholars in American Indian studies, outlines the many ways that Alexie himself is a trickster figure. Focusing on Alexie's difficult-to-classify works and also on his public persona, Lincoln sees Alexie as a "stand-up comedian" whose "firecat imagination plays tricks on the reader, for our supposed good, for its own native delight and survival." Lincoln argues that Alexie creates "Indi'n vaudeville, then, stand-up comedy on the edge of despair."

Alexie is not writing the intellectualized masturbation that passes for so much of today's poetry. He is a singer, a shaman,

Lincoln, Kenneth. "Futuristic Hip Indian: Alexie." *Sing With the Heart of a Bear: Fusions of Native and American Poetry, 1890–1999.* Berkeley, Calif: University of California Press, 2000. 267–276.

a healer, a virtual Freddy Fender saying, "Hey baby, que paso? *I thought I was your only vato.*"

—Adrian C. Louis, Foreword to *Old Shirts & New Skins*

But I haven't met an Indian writer out there who isn't arrogant—or a writer in general who isn't arrogant.... don't pretend I'm not.

—Sherman Alexie, *Indian Artist*, SPRING 1998

With Sherman Alexie, readers can throw formal questions out the smoke-hole (as in resistance to other modern verse innovators, Whitman, Williams, Sexton, or the Beats). Parodic antiformalism may account for some of Alexie's mass maverick appeal. This Indian gadfly jumps through all the hoops, sonnet, to villanelle, to heroic couplet, all tongue-in-cheeky. "I'm sorry, but I've met thousands of Indians," he told *Indian Artist* magazine, Spring 1998, "and I have yet to know of anyone who has stood on a mountain waiting for a sign." A reader enters the land of MTV and renascent AIM: a cartoon Pocahontas meets Beavis and Butt-head at the forest's edge, Sitting Bull takes on Arnold Schwarzenegger at Wounded Knee '73. The Last Real Indian has a few last words.

A stand-up comedian, the Indian improvisator is the performing text, obviating too close a textual reading: youngish man, six-foot-two or so, born in 1966 at the height of hippie nativism, from Wellpinit, Washington, now living in Seattle and taking the fin de siècle literary world by storm (an Indian Oscar Wilde?). After a century of benign neglect, Indian literature has hit an inflationary spiral with six-figure book deals and million-dollar movies. New York publishers have been humping this sassy, talk-back satirist as the last essentialist hold-out, a commercially successful Crazy Horse of mass marketing. The "most prodigious" Native American writer to date, Alexie told a Chicago *Sun* reporter asking about his brassy novel, *Indian Killer*, October 1996, to which the reporter queried, "Indian du jour?" Our young hero replied, "If so, it's been a very long day. How about Indian du decade?" Millennial Indian *extraordinaire*? The reporter raised the controversy over *Granta* naming Alexie one of the twenty "Best Young American Novelists" for *Reservation Blues* (not a novel), and Sherman snapped: "To say I was on the list because I'm an Indian is ridiculous: I'm one of the most critically respected writers in the country. So the *Granta* critics ... essentially, fuck 'em" (October 31, 1996, *New City's Literary*

Supplement). Starting with Native American writers, Alexie's competition includes no less than Allen, Erdrich, Harjo, Hogan, Momaday, Ortiz, Silko, TallMountain, Tapahonso, Welch, and Whiteman, among others (not to mention non-Indians like Toni Morrison, Norman Mailer, Cormac McCarthy, or Rita Dove). If "most critically respected" in a specific fictional genre of *Indian Killer* (thriller violence with racial undertones), his closest rivals are Tony Hillerman, Gerald Vizenor, Mickey Spillane, and Stephen King, an acknowledged model, John Steinbeck and the Brady Bunch tossed in. "He's young," says my elder brother back home, "he'll ripen, given time."

A breed Spokane and Coeur d'Alene, not just anybody, but thirteen-sixteenths *blood*, according to his poetry: "I write about the kind of Indian I am: kind of mixed up, kind of odd, not traditional. I'm a rez kid who's gone urban" (*Indian Artist*). What kind of an Indian is this?—a photogenic black mane of hair, dark-framed bifocal glasses, high-school class president, bookworm nose broken six times by bullies (he reminisces), English lit college degree from Eastern Washington State (after passing out as a premed student in his anatomy class; twice). His work is wizened with poetic anger, ribald love, and whipsaw humor. The crazy-heart bear is dancing comically, riding a wobbly unicycle, tossing overripe tomatoes at his audience. "This late in the 20th century," the poet says in *Red Blues*, "we still make the unknown ours by destroying it." His firecat imagination plays tricks on the reader, for our supposed good, for its own native delight and survival. "You almost / believe every Indian is an Indian," the poet swears to Marlon Brando.

Sherman: not so much a rhymer in the old sense, as a circus juggler who can eat apples, he says, while juggling. A college graduate who played basketball sixteen hours a day to keep from boozing with his cronies: Seymour chugging beer as a poet writes poetry (up to the last one that kills you) and Lester dead drunk in the convenience store dumpster. Alexie's sister and brother-in-law, passed out in a trailer, died by fire when a window curtain blew against a hot plate.

The boy mimed everyone in his family and still won't stop talking. "I was a divisive presence on the reservation when I was seven," he told an *LA Times* reporter, December 17, 1996. "I was a weird, eccentric, very arrogant little boy. The writing doesn't change anybody's opinion of me." Promoting his new movie, *Smoke Signals* (coproduced with Cheyenne-Arapaho director Chris Eyre), the writer describes himself today as "mouthy, opinionated and arrogant," a court jester's cross of Caliban, Groucho Marx, and Lear's Fool, but underneath, "I'm a sweetheart" (*Denver Post*, October 20, 1997). He's the best native example yet of Lewis Hyde's wiley hinge-maker, Trickster, the infant Prince of Thieves, Hermes stealing into Olympus to claim legitimacy: "Wandering aimlessly, stupider than the animals, he is at once the bungling host and the agile parasite; he has no way of his own but he is the Great Imitator who adopts the many ways of those around him. Unconstrained by instinct, he is the author of endlessly creative and novel deceptions, from hidden hooks to tracks that are impossible to read."

Artistic grist and ironic survival are inseparable in this verse, tracing a short lifetime of basketball (a team captain "ball hog" in high school), beer, TV, rez cars falling apart, pony dreams, fetal alcohol syndrome (FAS) babies, and fancy-dancing drunks. "You call it geno-cide; I call it economics," Custer snorts. A warm-up for fiction and the movies, poetics are wrapped up in the politics of native poverty, torqued metrics, and ethnic protest: dime store Indi'n princesses and back alley vision questers, 7–11 heroes and Vietnam vets, Marlon Brando and Crazy Horse. No insurance CEO or village doctor, Alexie has the near fatal, comic bravado of surviving an everyday rez, where every day is a blow to the stomach and a blaze of understanding. Being Indian means you're hanging on for dear life, hanging in there with catastrophic humor, kicking back at sunset, staggering through the '49 to dawn, laughing your ass off and on again (the short fiction says), and accepting that bottom line of your neighbor's butt next to you, misplaced, displaced, re-relocated into the present Red reality, so real that it hurts. So unreal in its hurtful beauty, so surreal that it makes you blink and smile to see another dawn. "*How do you explain the survival of all of us who were never meant to survive?*" It's a long walk from Sitting Bull bearing "hard times" to Charlie Blackbird "surviving." Alexie takes to Internet chat rooms for essential defenses of native sovereignty and intercultural access to America's power structures, particularly publishing and the movies.

So, from Momaday's visionary form, through Welch's shamanic rhythm, here's a surreal trickster savage in two-dimensional poetic cartoon. Rather than close reading or parsing the lines, his work elicits charged reaction, critical gut response, positive or negative argument. Reading Alexie's work triggers a recoil from the shock of Indian reality, like looking into the Sun Dance sun, going blind, and slowly regaining sight, stars and blackspots and sunbursts floating across the field of perception, so you know it's your perception, anyway, at last, of reality: "*whiskey salmon absence*," the poem "Citizen Kane" ends. Firewater, relocation, vanishing American. The images, concretely charged as Pound's Vorticist objects, are loaded in disconnections: the poison where food swarms, desperate homing, the absence that starves Indians to death. "Rosebud" is not a child's movie sled but a desperately poor Sioux reservation in the Dakotas.

"But, I mean, I really love movies. I always have," Alexie said in "Making Smoke" (*Aboriginal Voices* May–June 1998). "I love movies more than I love books, and believe me, I love books more than I love every human being, except the dozen or so people in my life who love movies and books just as much as I do." His favorite films are *Midnight Cowboy*, *The Graduate*, and *Aliens*. The writer goes on, "I mean, screenplays are more like poetry than like fiction. Screenplays rely on imagery to carry the narrative, rather than the other way around. And screenplays have form. Like sonnets, actually. Just as there's [sic] expectations of form, meter, and rhyme in a sonnet, there are the same kinds of expectations for screenplays." There are two dimensions in Alexie's work, screenplay to verse, often no more than two characters in the short fiction, *The Lone Ranger and Tonto Fistfight in Heaven*. His work is mostly minimalist drama, back to the first Greek plays, *alazon* to *eiron*, dreamer to realist, fool to cynic. Toss in commedia dell'arte, Punch and Judy, Laurel and Hardy, Amos and Andy, Lewis and Martin, Red Ryder and Little Beaver. The embedded third dimension of this post-holocaustal comedy is cultural landscape, for lack of a better term, devastated native homestead. So a third character might be salvage-surrealist, Old Man absent and implied, as with Welch's winter-in-the-blood Na'pi. The third-dimensional axis then is Indi'n humor, a vanishing point of survival in the canvas of a hidden spirit world, including Trickster mimics, all around and behind us. Alexie takes Welch's foxy shaman a skitter-step forward to tease Mary Austin: "Sweetheart, history / doesn't always look like horses."

Poetry comes on not so much a text as a comic ruse, a razored one-liner, a reader's riff to wake up America. The world is Indian as a coyote magician who makes every ordinary day a trick of survival, a vanishing act, a raw joke. A reader's breath catches in the throat and comes out laughing strange; still . . . a breath it is, of life. It gets you going, brothers and sisters, a buzzing, rattling, weeping, yipping imagination. Cry so hard you begin to laugh: run so fast you lap your shadow: dream so hard you can't sleep: think so hard you startle awake like a child. "Mafia gave birth to a wily boy," the Homeric hymn begins, "flattering and cunning, a robber and cattle thief, a bringer of dreams, awake all night, waiting by the gates of the city—Hermes, who was soon to earn himself quite a reputation among the gods, who do not die." Crossing Ginsberg with Creeley, Hughes's Crow with Berryman's Mistah Bones, Alexie brews a homeboy devil's own humor. The voice makes junkyard poetry out of broke-down reality, vision out of delirium tremens, prayer out of laughter. "When my father first smiled," the poet recalls, "it scared the shit out of me."

Look back at "Seattle, 1987" (appendix to chapter three), an early Alexie poem, first published in *The Jacaranda Review* and tracked to *Old Shirts & New Skins*. It sets up in triads, with one-line answering interstices, but the rhymes are lame (century / lake / it) and the rhythms scattered, three to seven beats. The poet sounds mysteries "beneath" a lake at the century's end: "drowned horses snapping turtles cities of protected bones." The gaps between the old horse-culture icons (*sunka wakan*, the Lakota called horses, "holy" or "super dog"), toothy denizens, and tribal runes space the poem across the page, as a "camera trick" jump-starts the sun on cable TV. "How the heart changes," the poet laments urban strangers, made without totemic "song." No dance, no song, Pound said, no poem. No tradition carries, no metaphor steadies, no structure holds, no tribal village binds. Instead, a clumsy magician gets a dollar bill in his top hat: the poet falls in love with street trickster failure and confesses, à la James Wright's "wasted" life, "There are so many illusions I need to believe." The tone is flat, failed romantic, a touch sardonic, beat. This young Indian is holding out for vision, needing to believe, tricked by MTV and sidewalk magic, laughing up his sleeve. His is more performance than poem, more attitude than art, more schtick than aesthetic. Definitely talented, deeply impassioned, hyphenated American-Indian; but to what end?

Indi'n vaudeville, then, stand-up comedy on the edge of despair. A late-twentieth-century, quasi-visionary clown tells the truth that hurts and heals in one-liners cheesy as the Marx Brothers, trenchant as Lenny Bruce, tricky as Charlie Hill's BIA Halloween "Trick or Treaty." The stand-up poet marvels in dismay, "Imagine Coyote accepts / the Oscar for lifetime achievement." There's an old trickster-teacher role here in a young Indian's hands—jokes draw the line, cut to the quick, sling the bull, open the talk. "White Men Can't Drum," Alexie announced in *Esquire Magazine*, October 1992, roasting the new-age men's movement, all the Wannabe fuss and fustian.

"How do you explain the survival of all of us who were never meant to survive?" asks the verse straight man.

"There is nothing we cannot survive," the poet swears.

Surviving war is the premise. In *The Summer of Black Widows* (1996), Alexie's sixth poetry collection in as many years (composing by computer), "Father and Farther" (also performed on the rock cassette, *Reservation Blues*) recalls a drunken basketball coach and a losing team. "Listen," his father slurs, "I was a paratrooper in the war."

"Which war?" the boy-poet asks.

"All of them," he said. Quincentennial facts: Native Americans as a composite are the only in-country ethnic group that the U.S. has declared war against, 1860–1890. Some existing 560 reservations, 315 in the lower forty-eight states, are natively seen from inside as occupied POW camps. Think of it as the delayed stress of contemporary Indian America: the post traumatic shock of surviving Columbus to Cotton Mather, Buffalo Bill Cody to Andy Jackson, Chivington to Custer. "Goddamn," the general says, again and again, "saber is a beautiful word," in ironic cut against Auden's penchant for "scissors." World War I Indian volunteers, as cited, gained Native Americans dual citizenship in 1924. Code Talkers in World War II made natives national heroes. Korea, Vietnam, and Desert Storm's chemical poisoning brought tribal veterans into millennial terror.

In 1993, the UCLA American Indian Studies Center published *Old Shirts & New Skins* as no. 9 in the Native American Poetry Series. Old shirts, not stuffed new suits: new'skins, Redskins reborn, sloughing "old" skins. There are always two sides to things, bicultural ironies to new-age lies, & the "blessed ampersand," hip shorthand to a coded new tongue, the with-it Indi'n poet. There's no text "set" here as such, but more a radical riff, something spilled over, a virus, a toxin released, a metastasizing anger. It's a "reservation of my mind," the poet says. The opening epithet equates, "Anger x Imagination = poetry," in the amplitude & invention of the angry young Indian. One shot short of death, Seymour says, drink as you write free verse, no matter if "our failures are spectacular." Maverick Trixter talks back, makes a different kind of poetry for people with differences: "it was not written for the white literary establishment," Adrian Louis says in the foreword to *Old Shirts & New Skins*.

A double buckskin language frays the edges of bicultural America, questions the multiple meanings of reservation, red, risk, Cody & Crazy Horse, Marlon Brando & John Wayne, Christ & Custer, who *died for your sins*. The critic is left with notes to bumper-sticker poetics, insult & antagonism, the fractious come-hither. Poetry as disruptive tease, a sideshow of historical truth & poetic hyperbole. Or, to borrow from the social sciences, "privileged license": tribal teasing tests boundaries, deepens resilience, insures survival, bets on renewal. Not without the warrior history of Old English insults, flytyngs, hurled across a river a thousand years ago in "The Battle of Maldon." LA South Central Blacks doin' the dozens, *Yer granmother wears combat boots!* The Last Poets in Harlem chant, *Niggers like to fuck each other. . . .* El Paso Hispanics drive *slow 'n low riders*. Inventories of abuses, imagined & otherwise: hunger of imagination, poverty of memory, toxicity of history, all in the face of cultural genocide and racial misrepresentation and outright extermination, to challenge musty stereotypes of vanishing, savage, stoic, silent, shamanic, stuperous Indians. Poetry is never bread enough & doesn't pay the bills, "damned from beginning to end," Williams says. Who could quibble aesthetics in this setting?

money is free if you're poor enough

Are there any connections with canonical American poetry? Start with Langston Hughes's essentialist pride in the Harlem Renaissance, "I, too, sing America," not just Walt Whitman fingering leaves of grass, or Carl Sandburg shouldering Chicago. Allen Ginsberg howled his native place in the 1950s: the marginalized, dispossessed, discriminated, hipster, homosexual, Jewish, offbeat antihero. It's an old revolutionary American motif, the lost found, the last first, the underdog bites back. Sylvia Plath's rage and exhibitionist daring to die for us as Lady Lazarus: "Out of the ash / I rise with my red hair / And I eat men like air." Ted Roethke's lost son, lyric blues: "Thrum-thrum, who can be equal to ease? / I've seen my father's face before / Deep in the belly of a thing to be." John Berryman's brilliant mad comic pain: *"These songs were not meant to be understood, you understand, / They were meant to terrify & comfort. / Lilac was found in his hand."*

A kind of Indian antipoetry breaks form at the millennial end. Alexie pushes against formalist assumptions of what poetry ought to be, knocks down aesthetic barriers set up in xenophobic academic corridors, and rebounds as cultural performance. He can play technique with mock sonnet, breezy villanelle, unheroic couplet, tinkling tercet, quaky quatrain in any-beat lines. The rhymer trades on surreal images and throwaway metaphors in a drunken villanelle: *Trail of Tears . . . trail of beers.* The rush of his poems is an energy released, stampeding horses, raging fires, stomping shoes: the poet as fast & loose sharpster in accretive repetition. Alexie likes catalogues, anaphoral first word repetitions, the accumulative power of oral traditions. There is something freeing about all this—free to imagine, to improvise, to make things up, to wonder, to rage on. Sharpening wits on quick wit, his poetry runs free of restrictive ideas about Indians, poems, ponies, movies, shoes, dreams, dumpsters, reservations, angers, losses. His lines break free of precious art . . . but free for what, that matters? Do we care? the hard questions come tumbling. Do we remember, or listen closely, or think carefully, or wonder fully, or regard deeply enough?

Readers certainly learn about New Rez Indians who shoot hoop, stroke pool, fancy dance, drink beer, snag girls, hustle, hitch, rap, joke, cry, rhyme, dream, write everything down. These Computer *Rad*'Skins write verse that does not stay contained in formal repose: does not pull away, or shimmer in the night sky, or intimidate the common reader, but comes on full as a poetry that begs visceral response. Often cartoonish, a gag, a point-of-view gimmick, more "like" *Virtual Indian.* "There is no possible way to sell your soul" for poetry, Alexie said in LA (December 17, 1996), "because nobody's offering. The devil doesn't care about poetry. No one wants to make a movie out of a poem." This trickster has made one movie, as mentioned, and cast another from *Indian Killer.*

Call it a reactive aesthetics, kinetic pop art, protest poetics to involve and challenge late-century readers—cajoled, battered, insulted, entertained, humored, angered to respond. A poetry that gets us up off our easy chairs. Tribal jive, that is, streetsmart, populist, ethnocentric, edged, opinionated, disturbed, fired up as reservation graffiti, à la John Trudell's Venice, California, rock lyrics, a Cherokee-breed Elvis as "Baby Boom Che." Alexie joins the brash, frontier braggadocio of westering America, already out west a long time, ironically;

a tradition in itself, shared with Whitman, Lawrence, Stein, Mailer, Kesey, Kerouac, Ginsberg, Vonnegut, Bellow, Heinemann, Mamet. Huckster, con man, carny barker, stand-up comedian, Will Rogers to Jonathan Winters, Cheech & Chong to Charlie Hill. The impudence of the anti-poetic Red Rapster, daring us not to call this poetry. "I'm not a rapper," Russell Means crows of his punk album, *Electric Warrior*, "I'm a Rapaho!"

"You'll almost / believe every Indian is an Indian," Alexie carries on.

Frybread . . . Snakes . . . Forgiveness.

THE CONFIDENCE-MAN: HIS MASQUERADE
(HERMAN MELVILLE)

"The Confidence-Man: The Con-Man as Hero"
by Paul Brodtkorb, Jr., in *Studies in the Novel* (1969)

INTRODUCTION

In his commentary on Herman Melville's last full-length work, Paul Brodtkorb likens *The Confidence-Man* to modern works that challenge accepted notions of what it means to be human, convey a sense of absurdity, play with language and puns, and focus on the meaninglessness of existence. For Brodtkorb, the protean confidence-man acts as a trickster, one who reveals the emptiness behind the world's many masks, the façade of meaning and order that crumbles under his hoaxes. As Brodtkorb argues, the "playful con-man, diffracted into various masquerades, is the hero of the book, its ground and condition, its spirit, and in his very playfulness even its potential saviour. His presence is why the book still speaks to us today." Brodtkorb challenges the reader to see Melville's confidence-man as a trickster whose machinations reveal the human experience as a masquerade: "The book's basic vision is of masks; and underneath, masks, further masks; and under all masks there is more than a chance that there is nothing at all."

Brodtkorb, Paul, Jr. "*The Confidence-Man*: The Con-Man as Hero." *Studies in the Novel* 1.4 (Winter 1969): 421–435.

" ... (but, indeed, where in this strange universe is not one a stranger?)"

> —Mark Winsome to the Cosmopolitan

The late Richard Chase began that line of eminent critics who have looked upon *The Confidence-Man* with interest and nearly whole-hearted approval. R.W.B. Lewis is one of the latest in the line: agreeing with Chase that it ranks "second only to *Moby-Dick*" among Melville's writings, he calls it "the pivotal text in the history of apoca-lyptic literature in America,"[1] with descendants as varied as Twain's *The Mysterious Stranger*, Faulkner's *The Hamlet*, West's *Day of the Locust*, Ellison's *Invisible Man*, Barth's *Sot-Weed Factor*, Heller's *Catch-22*, and Pynchon's *V.* Inflated as such judgments of *The Confidence-Man* may seem, nevertheless, granted their premises, they are not excessive, for what Chase and Lewis see and value in the book, what they find most striking, is first of all its modernity.

Certainly Melville's *contemporaries* didn't like the book. Most of them would have agreed with Lemuel Shaw, Jr. (the half-brother of Melville's wife), who characterized Melville's writing as "pages of crude theory & speculation to every line of narritive [*sic*]—& inter-spersed with strained and ineffectual attempts to be humorous."[2] Time, however, moves on and sensibilities change. For us, Melville's strained humor is camp: it is the strain, not the humor, that amuses. Today, we are quite used to understated visions of the apocalypse, to literary put-ons, to self-cancelling ironies, for modern writers have made these things unremarkable.

Lewis offers the very shrewd observation that though *The Confi-dence-Man* is hard to read, it is easy to re-read. Perhaps a first reading is necessary to free ourselves of our normal plot and character expec-tations about Nineteenth Century American novels; the second time through, we can pick up more of the book's patterns and attitudes, and find them familiar. And if we do this, along with Chase and Lewis, we only do what readers of every age have done, to the *a capella* rage of historical scholars: we read the books of the past in the terms of the present, and thereby, if we conceive of books as having a "correct" reading, distort them. But to do this to them is to help make them live again for us, and is only common sense in common readers.

In what follows, I would like to consider one element of *The Confidence-Man*'s appeal to modern readers: namely, some of that same "crude theory" to which Lemuel Shaw, Jr. objected, specifically theory about human character as related to the book's apparently satirical mode of being.

Much of *The Confidence-Man*'s irony is directed against ordinary unconscious humanity because it blandly assumes that it knows itself when in fact it does not; usually, it is directed against the opposition between the Christian principles mouthed and the un-Christian principles acted. Those genuinely liberated from this unconsciousness are chiefly the various confidence men, satanic and merely human, who are free to be hypocrites and "under an affable air . . . hide a misanthropical heart" (p. 201); who are chained to nothing, not even misanthropy; who are free to be consciously inconsistent. But the book's basic irony is not satirical: it is directed against neither the con-men, nor ordinary human hypocrisy which, presumably, could be changed into "sincerity" by a cognitive act of will. Instead, it seems non-satirically to point out that, given the nature of selfhood, sincerity and consistency of belief are impossible.

The idea of human selfhood advanced by the novel is the one partially elaborated in chapter 14, which defends the inconsistency principle in man.[3] "No writer," writes the narrator, "has produced such inconsistent characters as nature herself has." Because character is so inconsistent,

> all those sallies of ingenuity, having for their end the revelation of human nature on fixed principles, have, by the best judges, been excluded with contempt from the ranks of the sciences—palmistry, physiognomy, phrenology, psychology. Likewise, the fact, that in all ages such conflicting views have, by the most eminent minds, been taken of mankind, would . . . seem some presumption of a pretty general and pretty thorough ignorance of it. (p. 78)

Apart from chapter 14, there are several narrator's asides which unironically make the same point: for example, the one at the beginning of chapter 13, where readers are warned not to be "tempted into a more or less hasty estimate" of John Ringman, the Black Rapids Coal Company agent, in order "that they may not . . . be thereupon betrayed into any surprise incompatible with their own good opinion of their previous penetration" (p. 70). Part of what the narrator means in such asides is summed up by Mark Winsome's disciple, Egbert:

> there is no bent of heart or turn of thought which any man holds by virtue of an unalterable nature or will. Even those

feelings and opinions deemed most identical with eternal right
and truth, it is not impossible but that, as personal persuasions,
they may in reality be but the result of some chance tip of Fate's
elbow in throwing her dice. (p. 251)

Egbert says that man is infinitely mutable; for

he may travel, he may marry, he may join the Come-Outers,
or some equally untoward school or sect, not to speak of other
things that more or less tend to new-cast the character. And
were there nothing else, who shall answer for his digestion,
upon which so much depends? (pp. 250–51)

If *Moby-Dick*, then, panoramically eyes the vastnesses of nature's
varied phenomena, among which are her deceits, reversals, and
metamorphoses, *The Confidence-Man* focuses most sharply on *human*
nature, using narrower satirical conventions to make similar ontological points about it. The book takes issue with normal views of the
"heart of man" (p. 79): that man is a something with characteristics
as an object has qualities, that therefore he can be known in significantly fundamental ways. It is precisely because it sees inconsistency
as the most plausible essence of human nature that the book is nomi-
nally "comic"; it is why the narrator can call his first major digression
on human inconsistency "the comedy of thought," and the narrative
itself, which demonstrates and imitates that "thought," the comedy
of "action" (p. 79).

There are three general character inconsistencies demonstrated in
the narrative. First, and most basic, there is irrational inconsistency,
Egbert's "mutability of . . . humanity" (p. 251): that of the rhapsodic
pessimism of the unknowingly twice-diddled merchant who is opti-
mistic except after wine (and who provides the occasion for the first
inconsistency chapter); that of Orchis, China Aster's antagonist; that
of Moredock, the Indian-hater, who is "an example of something
apparently self-contradicting" in that he has a "loving heart" (p. 175);
that of another Indian-hater, who irrationally throws himself upon
the charity of an Indian ("What is too often the sequel of so distem-
pered a procedure may be best known by those who best know the
Indian" [p. 171]); that of the student with his Tacitus, "pensive" (p. 27)
and stammering and apparently sensitive in chapter 5, self-assured

and philistine in chapter 9. Second, there is rational inconsistency: that of the confidence-men, who are so in order to practice "deception and deviltry" (p. 36) for their own obvious human or obscure satanic purposes (e.g., Charlie Noble, a cynic who pretends to be affable and to like the wine he drinks, which he later calls "elixir of logwood" [p. 211] when he turns churlish, the cosmopolitan having eluded him); that of Charlemont, "the Gentleman madman," who switches his character in order to "be beforehand with the world, and save it from a sin by prospectively taking that sin" to himself (p. 210). Third, there is the inconsistency of those who have been led by a confidence-man into premature revelation of their own irrationalities: that of the religious old man of the end, who wishes to distrust not "the Creature; for that would imply distrust of the Creator," yet keeps his money in a belt because it is "never too late to be cautious" (p. 281); that of Pitch, the Missouri bachelor who claims to stick to what he says (p. 143), but who, because he is too well acquainted with "facts," the metamorphoses of nature, and Calvinistic theology, can despite his suspicions be argued by the agent from the Philosophic Intelligence Office into accepting virtue as potential within any man, as sainthood was potential in sinners like Saint Augustine or the butterfly in the caterpillar.

The diddling of Pitch provides a major instance of the peculiar relation to the book's truths that the definitely satanic characters bear: perhaps because Satan doomed man to knowledge of good and evil, the satanic confidence-men can come closer in many respects to the truth of the book's actuality in certain of their remarks than the other characters do. Always, they will use truth for their own benefit, often ironically reversing it, or merely warping it, as the P.I.O. agent does with Pitch (many of his analogies, as analogies, are quite true). Used in this way, truth has "the operation of falsity" (as the con-man says of Tacitus [p. 28]) because of *why* it is spoken; like the one-legged misanthrope of the early chapters, the con-man speaks so that "even were truth on his tongue, his way of speaking it would make truth almost offensive as falsehood" (p. 34). But once his reasons for and manner of speaking truth are taken into account, much of his irony can be decoded and found to correspond to the actualities of the book's world. Like Melville in his well-known review of Hawthorne,[4] wherein he held that Shakespeare's "dark characters ... Hamlet, Timon, Lear, and Iago" craftily say or insinuate those things "which we feel to be so terrifically true, that it were all but madness for any good man, in his own proper character, to utter, or even hint," the confidence-men have taken the "ugly view" and thereby have seen the "deeper meanings" (p. 28) of life as well as of books.

Because they have seen these deeper meanings, much of what they say, suitably de-ironized, is assumed and demonstrated by this book as probable truth. In respect to the inconsistencies of character, what they say, demonstrate, and imply is usually true as far as it goes. But there is a more basic reason than they normally suggest for human inconsistency. It is implied in the cosmopolitan's injunction to the barber, near the book's end: "You can conclude nothing absolute from the human form" (p. 254). The narrator agrees: "Upon the whole, it might rather be thought, that, he, who, in view of its inconsistencies, says of human nature the same that, in view of its contrasts, is said of the divine nature, that it is past finding out, thereby evinces a better appreciation of it than he who, by always representing it in a clear light, leaves it to be inferred that he clearly knows all about it" (p. 77). Man is past finding out because his mutability is extreme: he is a creature of moods—the Negro cripple confidence-man turns his face "in passively hopeless appeal, as if instinct told [him] that the right or the wrong might not have overmuch to do with whatever wayward mood superior intelligences might yield to" (p. 11). Chapter 23 is titled "In Which the Powerful Effect of Natural Scenery is Evinced in the Case of the Missourian, Who, in View of the Region Roundabout Cairo, Has a Return of His Chilly Fit," and in it Pitch muses upon this aspect of mutability, as

> He bethinks him that the man with the brass plate [one of the confidence-men] was to land on this villainous bank [by a bluff called "The Devil's Joke"], and for that cause, if no other, begins to suspect him. Like one beginning to rouse himself from a dose of chloroform treacherously given, he half divines, too, that he, the philosopher, had unwittingly been betrayed into being an unphilosophical dupe. To what vicissitudes of light and shade is man subject! He ponders the mystery of human subjectivity in general. (p. 147)

Beyond this subjectivity, beyond the confidence-man's exploitation of his knowledge of this subjectivity, can be seen the fundamental ontological reason for human inconsistency: there is finally, no such thing as *character*. One of the most consistent figures in the book is, paradoxically, the confidence-man, who throughout his waltzing shifts of form has a constancy not of appearance but of action: in Francis Fergusson's terms, "to deceive the other" is his stability.[5] Yet such stability is not character but role:

> Society his stimulus, loneliness was his lethargy. Loneliness, like the sea-breeze, blowing off from a thousand leagues of blankness, he [the confidence-man] did not find, as veteran solitaries do, if anything, too bracing. In short, left to himself, with none to charm forth his latent lymphatic, he insensibly resumes his original air, a quiescent one, blended of sad humility and demureness.
>
> Ere long he goes laggingly into the ladies' saloon, as in spiritless quest of somebody. . . . (p. 48)

The confidence-man's mode of being in this book involves necessary relation to others; apart from society, he barely exists. In fact, this is true of most of the other characters, who are seen in societal situations, playing out their parts. The second element of the book's title is "masquerade," and what the book demonstrates about that idea is that posing, role-playing, is a fundamental condition of humanity's existence. "Look [at your business card], and see whether you are not the man I take you for" (p. 20), says the coal company agent.

> "Why ... I hope I know myself," answers his intended victim.
> "And yet self-knowledge is thought by some not so easy," says the agent.

Even in theories of character older and simpler than that of this book, self-knowledge is arrived at through subtle processes and is *not* easy. But in the book's perspective on human inconsistency, a further implication suggests itself: a precondition of knowing oneself would be personal consistency, yet a man could be consistent only if he had an immutable essence, or if he had a static idea of Man good for all occasions to which he could refer as if it were his essence (and thereby play the role of Man). Yet, as chapter 14 minimally asserts, the essence of human nature is probably inconsistency; beyond that, in any case, it has none discoverable.

A sense of the impossibility of self-knowledge as well as knowledge of others underlies Mark Winsome's questions: "What are you? What am I? Nobody knows who anybody is" (p. 216). Incompatible as these questions are with his other doctrines of labels and universal goodness—"Emersonian" doctrines mocked by the entire narrative—Winsome in these questions implies the roots of his own inconsistency. Nobody knows self or other because there is no self or other to know; only roles exist, but roles change, and as they do, so, correlatively, do beliefs, the foundations of "character." When Winsome's disciple, Egbert, speaks of humanity's mutability, he says that unforeseeable circumstances may at times "new-cast the character" (p. 251); but his chief examples—travel, marriage, and religious conversion—offer man new roles more than changed character. That circumstances suggest the role to play has been foreshadowed earlier when the spectators who judged the Negro cripple did so only because the situation suggested, but did not force, them to be judges; the idea had not occurred to them before the situation suggested it, but when it did they "could not resist the opportunity of acting the part" (p. 12). Egbert, in the role of the confidence-man Charlie Noble only because the cosmopolitan suggested it, and Winsome, both of whom glory in their inconsistency, are so excessively mutable precisely because they believe they are. It is the role they have chosen: "to be inconsistent." Thus, even inconsistency itself may not be the ultimate truth about human nature, but it is the best assumption anyone in the book can make.

To sum up: the novel tends to see human reality as confined to appearances. Roles, masquerades, are as far as one can go in determining a man's "reality" at any given moment, and a role is probably the best that a man can be consistent with because, as the misanthropic one-legged man (therefore a one-sided man, according to the confidence-man, but he is more than adequately accurate about what is going on around him) says, "All doers are actors" (p. 35). Despite its apparently biased source, and despite its exploitation of the slight semantic confusion of a pun, the invalid syllogism is true, even tautologous. Every character in the book demonstrates its truth by "acting" in the ordinary sense of playing a set or given role; like "Signor Marzetti in the African pantomime," they play "the intelligent ape" till they seem it (p. 150). Like Frank Goodman and Charlie Noble, they play such parts well; indeed, "to the life" (p. 205), existing for us chiefly as dupers and duped, the gulled and the gulling. Like Egbert, playing Charles, "who . . . seemed with his whole heart to enter into the spirit of the thing [his polemical impersonation of Charlie]" (p. 250), it is not possible to separate man from role, nor does the book try, for at this point the narrative simply calls Egbert "Charlie" without quotation marks. The same principle applies as well to the "sincere" characters: even though the good clergyman of the earlier chapters may believe in his role, he would not know what it (therefore he) was if the idea of clergyman did not exist as a model so that in "being" one he necessarily "acts" (p. 35), just as the one-legged man says of him. This is perhaps something of what the cosmopolitan means when he says to the Missouri bachelor, "Life is a picnic *en costume*; one must take a part" (p. 152); and in this passage the operative word is "must."

With masquerade spreading its meaning to include all the book's characters, a simple attitude of approval or disapproval of hypocrisy becomes, even for the characters themselves, irrelevant. The Missouri bachelor disapproves of masquerade's hypocrisy so much that he despairingly wants to substitute machines for men; yet he is betrayed as his secret, dialectic desire to believe good of man breaks through his chosen role of Timon, when the P.I.O. agent couches that desire in the language of Pitch's valued mechanistic (therefore understandable, therefore safe) science, referring that science to Pitch's experience of nature and theology, and in doing so making science seem as false when applied to humanity as the first "inconsistency" chapter said it was. Nor is conscious masquerading held up as a praiseworthy alternative to self-deceptive role-playing; it isn't even much of a safeguard: the swindlers themselves can be swindled by superior con-men.

Rather, masquerading seems in the book less a question of moral choice than a question of necessity, beyond which it can become a way of testing a dangerous, shifty world to see how it will react to one's posited self: it becomes a mask from behind which to reconnoitre. This testing is by no means absolute: there is no workable guide to the genuineness of symbolic currency, as the old man at the end discovers; in fact to believe the opposite is to dupe oneself most. But if being cheated is universal, perhaps alertness becomes nearly all; perhaps by it and through it one can be cheated just a little less. The argument is in the realm of emotion, not formal logic, which in any case can not deal with absurdity. The book's basic vision is of masks;

and underneath, masks, further masks; and under all masks there is more than a chance that there is nothing at all.[6] The confidence-man takes leave of Egbert with

> a grand scorn . . . leaving his companion at a loss to determine where exactly the fictitious character had been dropped, and the real one, *if any* [italics added], resumed. If any, because, with pointed meaning, there occurred to him, as he gazed after the cosmopolitan, these familiar lines:
>   "All the world's a stage,
>   And all the men and women merely players,
>   Who have their exits and their entrances,
>   And one man in his time plays many parts." (p. 253)

Melville's "if any" glosses Shakespeare more nihilistically than Jacques' speech will perhaps sustain; but if we accept Melville's "pointed meaning" rather than Shakespeare's, masquerading becomes a matter of simple survival: without masks one would be "naked [in] the street" (p. 263), as the cosmopolitan says to the barber in a satanic understatement: one would not exist at all.

The satirical result of this mode of being is the ethical world of *The Confidence-Man*: the world of the "Wall street spirit" (p. 45), where capitalism, philanthropy, and religion are confidence games in which the market falls when confidence wanes.[7] When the confidence-man asks the barber why he contentedly deals in impostures—wigs, false moustaches, cosmetics, hair dyes—and the barber replies, "Ah, sir, I must live," the implications of his answer reach down into the book's ontology, so that in this matter "all the trades and callings of men are much on a par" (p. 264). Because character is really role, it is no exceptional accusation against the confidence-man to say that "he makes dupes," since "many held in honor do the same; and many, not wholly knaves, do it too" (p. 101); nearly all men are included in the further observation that "he is not wholly at heart a knave, I fancy, among whose dupes is himself."

The "Emersonian" philosophy of Egbert and Winsome is doubtless ethically repellent, and parts of it are clearly false, and other parts, though true, are rationalizations as well, but at least its inconsistency principle begins to fit the data of life that the book presents; and in that correspondence is Egbert's protection from the confidence-man;

for although the cosmopolitan "wins" against Charlie Noble (discomfitting him into undesired self-revelation and retreat in chapter 35), against Egbert, in a closely parallel incident, he loses, being himself discomfitted into retiring behind a burst of ill temper, even parting with a contemptuous shilling which, given his odd view of money (he is chiefly interested in outconning others but his success is sufficiently ratified by the smallest amounts of money, as in the barbershop sequence of the end), must be seen as token of his one real defeat in the book.[8] In that correspondence between philosophy and world, the doctrines of Egbert and Winsome pass the confidence-man's truth test, "for any philosophy that, being in operation contradictory to the ways of the world, tends to produce a character at odds with it, such a philosophy must necessarily be but a cheat and a dream" (p. 223). Egbert's story of China Aster tells of the bankruptcy of a man who tries to be ideally consistent, and Egbert draws the proper moral: take human mutability well into account:

> For, not to go into the first seeds of things, and passing by the accident of parentage predisposing to this or that habit of mind, descend below these, and tell me, if you change this man's experience or that man's books, will wisdom go surety for his unchanged convictions? As particular food begets particular dreams, so particular experiences or books particular feelings or beliefs. I will hear nothing of that fine babble about development and its laws; there is no development in opinion and feeling but the developments of time and tide. (p. 251)

To generalize ethical principles from Egbert's philosophy is really to arrive no further than readiness is all. The universal void of *Moby-Dick* has here become focussed into the potential void at the center of personality, yet the cosmic perspectives are at least implied: not man, nor God, nor nature can be trusted; as the cosmopolitan says to the befuddled old man at the end, "in Providence, as in man, you and I equally put trust" (p. 285).

Theologically, *The Confidence-Man* must be read as an expression of its author's despair, a despair that reaches even into the negativism of its prose. Stylistically, negativism recoils upon itself in the extraordinary frequency of double-negative litotes, of which any given chapter will furnish examples like "not unsusceptible," "less unrefined," "not wholly without," "less inexperienced," "not unprovided for." Further, with few exceptions, humanity in this book is reduced to dupers and duped, many figures being both, so that characters come to seem interchangeable to the point where style itself gets confused, as antecedents of personal pronouns become so vague they must be repeated in parentheses (on one page of "The Story of China Aster," for example, this kind of construction occurs three times, and is clearly deliberate). Then there are the ironical chapter headings like "Only a Page or So," and "Worth the Consideration of Those to Whom it May Prove Worth Considering," and "Which May Pass for Whatever it May Prove to Be Worth," and "In Which the Last Three Words of the Last Chapter Are Made the Text of the Discourse, Which Will Be Sure of Receiving More or Less Attention From Those Readers Who Do Not Skip It"—headings which in their irony imply that the reader is reading only because he is bored,[9] that the material being read to assuage boredom is itself boring, that the reader is unlikely to read it through, but that if he did he would be unlikely to understand it. In all this one sees the despair of its author, doubtless, but the style has literary functions. R.W.B. Lewis has pointed out (pp. 64–66, *op. cit.*) the self-cancelling nature of some of the prose: Goneril, described in what seem to be admiring terms ("young, in person lithe and straight") yet the admiration is immediately withdrawn ("too straight, indeed, for a woman" [p. 65]); the good gentleman with gold buttons (p. 40) who somehow, before Melville is through describing his goodness, becomes associated with those who crucified Christ; the faint-hearted abolitionist (p. 127), "the moderate man," therefore "the invaluable understrapper of the wicked man." The tendency of such prose is toward the oxymoronic; characteristically, the book includes a "genial misanthrope" and a "surly philanthropist" (p. 200). The general effect, to quote Lewis, is "to bring into question the sheer possibility of clear thinking itself—of *knowing* anything" (p. 65, *op. cit.*), and particularly, I would add, knowing anything about people. The style thus makes the reader share the cosmopolitan's distrust, which the book at all levels ratifies.

If the ontological basis of the cosmopolitan's universal distrust is firm, his conclusions as they express themselves ethically are repellent. Yet his masquerades do not in themselves seem to be condemned by the book, if only because of how and where one's emotions are likely to be invested. One feels sorry for the dupes who are taken in by the con-man's ubiquitous spirit because of their own good impulses, of course; but I think one is also likely to admire this arch-confidence-man who concludes the book. If one does, it seems to be an indirect consequence of a certain progression in the book, and, as are one's feelings towards the good-hearted dupes, a direct consequence of what can be seen of the principals' motives.

The progression I have in mind is toward apparent stability. Initially, the world of *The Confidence-Man* is shifting and fluid. Its ethical character is unclear: we learn very soon that charity is a failed project, later that hate, as seen in Moredock, is not relevant either. A beneficent or malevolent world would have ethical meaning, but this world seems neither; nor is it quite neutral. Its inhabitants are equally elusive: there is no obvious protagonist, few characters have names, none remains on stage very long. Portentous allusions are made, satanic forces might, or might not, be abroad. There is no suspense, no plot: situations form, dissolve, reform. Irony undermines all, and we tend to get lost. For most readers, this makes tedious going. But after nearly half the book is over, names, at least, begin significantly to appear, They do not characterize much, except ironically, but they do at least identify. The names appear some time after the uncertainty principle—that masks lie, that men are dupes or dupers or both—has been well established; one does not expect too much of the names, but they deliver more than expected: the characters they identify begin to stay in view longer. One can examine these characters at greater leisure, while the characters in turn prove to be worth one's examination. The movement *seems* to have been from an unstable unreality to an almost stable reality, and one is grateful; and since, by its final third, the book has been all but taken over by the cosmopolitan, one's gratitude, rationally or irrationally, goes out to him.

His motives, at least, suggest that he deserves this. Many of the dupes fall victim to the con-man because their motives betray them. Greed, egotism, and so forth operate in them rather mechanically. Such motives, so presented, are not very interesting in themselves and quickly pall. But the cosmopolitan is different. To a brother con-man, he is loyal (when a "prim-looking stranger" threatens the crippled soldier of fortune, the herb-doctor says, "Dare to expose that poor unfortunate, and by heaven—don't you do it, sir!" [p. 111]). Further, in contrast to the dupes, his motives are pure: he cheats for the sake of cheating. Like the crippled soldier he defends he "fights not the

stupid Mexican, but a foe worthy [of] . . . tactics—Fortune!" (p. 111).
If one admires this sort of thing in him, human absurdity has been
raised to something like a noble principle.

Although previous con-men have hinted at similar unpragmatic
motives (which, indeed, were early recognized by the one-legged man:
"Money, you think, is the sole motive to pains and hazard, deception
and deviltry, in this world. How much money did the devil make by
gulling Eve?" [p. 36]), the cosmopolitan most clearly and emphatically demonstrates his comparative purity of heart and the gratuitous
basis of his actions, when, for example, while the reader knows he
has at least fifty dollars on him, he elaborately does the barber out of
pennies. Furthermore, his virtuosity is, as one double-entendre chapter
heading suggests, "Very Charming"; especially his conning that other
skillful confidence-man, Charlie Noble, into self-revelation. Since
there is no moral baggage to tip the equation in favor of either party,
the satisfaction one derives from this encounter is genuinely aesthetic:
it is the pleasure of watching a fine operator operate, the pleasure of a
disinterested interest in sport, or in pantomime, or in circus acts—the
delight in seeing virtually anything done well. It is, in fact, the absurdity inherent in the mature enjoyment of any art; once again, absurdity
has been raised to a Noble principle.

In short, we admire the final confidence-man: we respect his
authority, his mastery, his paradoxical constancy, and what can only
be called (in relation to, say, the greed of many of the others) the
disinterest of his motives.[10] But our admiration is highly detached: it
is manifested in something like amused contemplation, a distanced
emotion. The events of the book, though portentous, even apocalyptic,
come to seem like a game, sinister without doubt but playful too. The
book's universe has become Ishmael's "vast practical joke" wherein
somehow "nothing dispirits" despite the joke's being on us (*Moby-
Dick*, chapter 49); for the playful con-man, diffracted into many
masquerades, has by virtue of his ubiquity become the spirit of the
book: misanthropic but also comic. It is the presence of that spirit that
transmutes the underlying Melvillean despair into a kind of humorous
serenity. In this curious fashion, *The Confidence-Man* comes as close to
being a "testament of acceptance," an ironic one, of course, as "Billy
Budd" is.

If *The Confidence-Man* in this and similar readings of it looks
anachronistically modern, one legitimately historical reason is that

modern ironic modes are the cultural lag of 19th Century romantic philosophies: Kierkegaard would have had no trouble understanding it. The book's apparent, but not actual, formlessness is simply more familiar today than it was in Melville's time, though European writers then could easily match it. Melville wrote no more fiction for publication in his lifetime, but the novel is valedictory for aesthetic as well as personal reasons: not much further formal ground can be covered with its premises; aesthetically, it is close to a dead end. If, like many current writers, Melville had been interested in propagandizing for premises of absurdity he could, like Sartre, have written didactic fiction in conventional form, or, like *nouvelle-vogue* novelists, have played with the paradox of trying to incorporate absurdity within the formal structure of fiction. Although *The Confidence-Man* does this last to a considerable extent, even approaching what has been called the fallacy of imitative form, Melville apparently wasn't much interested in continuing such an experiment. Antinovels and plays like those of Beckett or Genet,[11] the American novels listed by R.W.B. Lewis, movies like those of Godard and Truffaut, would be the decidedly more conscious steps in that direction.

If he was not interested, maybe the reason was that Melville, "dispirited and ill"[12] when he wrote *The Confidence-Man*, mellowed after he finished it, the writing of it having been successful as therapy. Or maybe he simply felt the problem wasn't resolvable in his terms, as perhaps it isn't; perhaps he felt that stating the problem was enough, and that his statement in itself earned him the right to retire to his custom house to follow Voltaire's advice. The *Fidele* is on a river that runs down to the sea; at some time in the definite future the passengers must face the idea of the sea. When they do, something may come of the Masquerade, but that's all, perhaps, tomorrow's worry—at least it might have seemed so in Nineteenth Century America.

As *The Confidence-Man* stands today it demonstrates with tedious thoroughness the proposition that the idea of absurdity can be faced if it is itself allowed to provide at least a small, tentative stability of shiftiness. The novel reflects this as a truth felt at the timeless instant of its writing and weaves it into its structure. Melville may have written the book in regret or bitterness; very likely his "hyena" humor (*Moby-Dick*, chapter 49) arises from despair—yet whether to deplore or applaud its particular vision of truth is not a question the book itself poses.

When the protean confidence-man, constant only in his characteristic action and the fact of his masquerade, is let loose aboard the *Fidele*, he appears as an "original character," which, like the "revolving Drummond light," shines "away from itself all around it—everything is lit by it, everything starts up to it ... so that, in certain minds, there follows upon the adequate conception of such a character, an effect, in its way, akin to that which in Genesis attends upon the beginning of things" (p. 271). Light attends the beginning of things; in illuminating others—giving definition to their inconsistency, their hypocrisy, and, finally, their emptiness—the confidence-man demonstrates his real universality as he confronts and reflects the many, varied, *other* masks of humanity, all of which nevertheless have masquerade and the possibility of change in common with his. When, apocalyptically, he puts out the light of Judaeo-Christian thought, it is, curiously, for the very reason he says: after nearly two thousand years its illumination has turned false, becoming not more heat than light but more smell than either. It did give some light, enough for Melville to see this far, and no doubt its current dimness is regretted; but the arch confidence-man of all leading an old, fearful, summary Man to the undesired illumination of total darkness is what the reader is left with.

The Confidence-Man, besides being a nihilistic gloss on "All the world's a stage," assumes with Ahab in his worst moments that beyond the mask lies the naught. Which is why the playful con-man, diffracted into various masquerades, is the hero of the book, its ground and condition, its spirit, and in his very playfulness even its potential saviour. His presence is why the book still speaks to us today.

NOTES

1. R.W.B. Lewis, *Trials of the Word* (New Haven, 1965), pp. 209–10. Page references in the text to *The Confidence-Man* are to the Hendricks House edition (New York, 1954), edited by Elizabeth S. Foster.

2. Letter of 21 April 1857, quoted in Jay Leyda, *The Melville Log* (New York, 1951), p. 574.

3. There is a second "inconsistency" chapter, but because chapter 33 defends specifically the cosmopolitan's mutability (his "boisterous hilarity ... with the bristling cynic, and his restrained good nature with the boon companion" [p. 207]) it

must be seen as to some degree ironic, for the cosmopolitan chooses his personality to fit his victim.

4. "Hawthorne and his Mosses," *The Literary World*, 17 August 1850, quoted in Leyda, p. 389.

5. The use of an infinitive phrase to encapsulate a dramatic action is developed in Francis Fergusson, *The Idea of a Theatre* (Princeton, 1949).

6. Compare the passage in *Pierre*, Book XXI, 1:

> Far as any geologist has yet gone down into the world, it is found to consist of nothing but surface stratified on surface. To its axis, the world being nothing but superinduced superficies. By vast pains we mine into the pyramid; by horrible gropings we come to the central room; with joy we espy the sarcophagus; but we lift the lid—and no body is there!—appallingly vacant as vast is the soul of a man!

7. J.C. Oates in "Melville and the Manichean Illusion" (*Texas Studies in Literature and Language*, [Spring 1962]) has expressed a parallel view: "What is changeable is the human heart, and from this everything stems." Oates sees the book as disintegrating "into an underlying nihilism which has resulted, within the novel, from the long series of negations which constitute the confidence-man's experience" (p. 127).

8. For an argument that Egbert does not "win" here, see Lawrence Grauman, "Suggestions on the Future of *The Confidence-Man*" (*Papers on English Language and Literature*, 1 (1965), 241–49).

9. This implication is further spelled out in chapter 33 in the course of an argument for fanciful invention in novels: "Yes, it is, indeed, strange that anyone should clamor for the thing he is weary of [i.e., fidelity to real life]; that anyone, who, for any cause, finds real life dull, should yet demand of him who is to divert his attention from it [i.e., the novelist], that he should be true to that dullness" (p. 206).

10. For a reading that maintains with a good deal of plausibility the view that the cosmopolitan is the hero of the book because it is his ideas that are the most defensible morally, pointing the way toward a humanistic attitude free of the contradictions of religion, see Philip Drew, "Appearance and Reality in Melville's *The Confidence-Man*" (*ELH*, XXXI (1964) 418–42).

On the other hand, Malcolm Magaw in "*The Confidence-Man and Christian Deity*" (*Explorations of Literature*, ed. Rima Drell Reck, Baton Rouge, 1966, pp. 81–99) finds the moral nature of the con-man, whom he sees as emblematic of God, to be inscrutable: Men "may *think* that they can see amorality behind his white mask, or evil behind his black mask; but all 'perceptions' in the fantasy of life are illusions. The masks are not removed; they are only replaced by other masks" (p. 87).

11. Saada Ishag in "Herman Melville as an Existentialist" (*Emporia State Research Studies*, XIV (1965), 5–41) points out some structural and thematic affinities between *The Confidence-Man* and the Theater of the Absurd school.

12. Lemuel Shaw, Jr. See footnote 2.

DECAMERON
(GIOVANNI BOCCACCIO)

"Games of Laughter"
by Giuseppe Mazzotta, in *The World at Play in Boccaccio's* Decameron (1986)

INTRODUCTION

Offering a comprehensive approach to Boccaccio's tales, Giuseppe Mazzotta focuses on the way laughter and games function in the *Decameron*. For Mazzotta, "Boccaccio shows both how laughter is a hollow mask which deceives, blinds us to what we lose, and how it is produced by a mask behind which the tricksters try to appropriate the world and . . . enjoy it." Thus, as Boccaccio's stories are filled with tricksters, Boccaccio himself is a trickster, one who never provides a fixed authorial viewpoint from which the reader can begin to interpret his work. By showing how Boccaccio subverts thought and plays with others' ideas, Mazzotta attempts to wrestle the *Decameron* away from medieval notions of reality and reductive critical interpretations, instead presenting it as ultimately irreducible, the masterwork of a playful disassembler.

Mazzotta, Giuseppe. "Games of Laughter." *The World at Play in Boccaccio's* Decameron. Princeton, N.J.: Princeton UP, 1986. 186–212.

The fifth novella of the eighth day features Maso del Saggio who goes to the local law court in the belief that a friend he is looking for may be idling his hours away watching the lawyers' performances and squabbles. As soon as Maso catches a glimpse of the judge who appears "più tosto un magnano che altro a vedere" (more like a coppersmith than anything else, p. 698), he abandons the search for his friend and decides to play a trick on the judge.[1] He feigns a complaint against an imaginary thief and vociferously pleads his case in order to fix upon himself the general attention. In the meantime, an accomplice of his who has secretly crawled beneath the bench where the judge sits, pulls his pants off.

By these simple touches Boccaccio has drawn the classic pattern of the *beffa*—literally a joke, a comic situation—to which we shall repeatedly return. The foolish magistrate, like all fools in the *Decameron*, is mercilessly flouted by the trickster, and by the mockery the very principle of inviolability of the law is subverted.[2] But what on the surface may seem to be merely a somewhat anarchic pleasure of undermining pretenses, of literally divesting the figurehead of his semblance of authority, hides important implications for some comic motifs in the *Decameron*. The oblique target of the *beffa* is the notion that there can ever be a detached perspective snugly sheltering the judge: Maso's trick actually shatters that distance and, through the resulting inversion, the man who sits ostensibly outside the events to judge them is turned into a principal while the spectators take his place. The comical shifts of focus are constant in the *beffa*, and because of them any fresh attempt on the part of the critic to fix the comedy of the *Decameron* with stable definitions may turn out to be a hazard, a way of falling into the author's unconscionable trap and being caught, like the judge, in the spirals of laughter.

But critics have traditionally practiced a calculated prudence when engaged in a definition of Boccaccio's laughter. They have generally eluded the problem or, what amounts to the same thing, have reduced the comical sense of the *Decameron* to a caricature of the social order. Auerbach, to mention a critic who has most powerfully probed the ideological subversiveness of this text, echoes De Sanctis' detached Hegelian stance in his view of Boccaccio's "light entertainment" as the radical perspective from which he is enabled to dismantle the moral relics of medieval Christianity.[3]

Auerbach's critical statement is certainly not wrong; if anything, it is partial or, more precisely, evasive. The evasiveness may be the proper response to the problem of laughter, which, according to an age-old commonplace, eludes all definitions. In any discussion on laughter, the obvious point of reference is tragedy, and it, by comparison, seems all too accountable. We acknowledge rather clearly, for instance, the grief and terror which shape the tragic vision, or at least accept their mystery as the inevitable ingredient of a dangerously alien world. But laughter, for all our familiarity with it, remains impenetrable, and as soon as we ask the question "why do we laugh," we reach a deadlock.

De Sanctis, to be sure, knows why we do not laugh with the *Decameron.* [4] The *Decameron* is a book of consolation for impending death; but it is also an elegy for comedy and a systematic retrenching into the production of games, *beffe*, which might be called emblematic of the loss if the emblem were not in itself a problem for Boccaccio.

Maso's trick on the judge seems to originate spontaneously and erupt unpremeditated into the ordinary business of life, transforming its texture into a playground, a theatrical space where Maso impersonates both the role of the defendant and the lawyer's cavils. By so doing, he brings into the open the inherent theatricality of the situation, in which a crowd was already idly watching the debates and the judge was as deceptive as the thieves whose cases he tried. [5] In effect, Maso's own trick (and the implication of this statement will be evident later on) is a weapon in that it appropriates the spectacle; more cogently to our concern, it discloses the mimetic quality of the text. Mimesis is conventionally seen as the rational, Aristotelean principle of imitating the fragmentation of reality. This traditional definition is encompassed, in a fundamental way, within a view of mimesis as impersonation—the actor's specific craft, the deceptive emblem of the play which sustains the world of the *Decameron.*

It is through this shifty metaphor that Boccaccio persistently and obliquely raises the question "why do we laugh" every time the *brigata* laughs at each funny story. For there is a sense in which the *brigata*'s laughter is willed just as the choice of the comical perspective in the *Decameron* is deliberate. The general Introduction to the tales bears an unmistakable tragic focus: the city of Florence is infected by the plague; laws and familial bonds are shattered; medical science cannot purge the city of its evil. No sooner, however, has Boccaccio conjured this tragic horror than he turns his back to it. The catharsis can occur by moving to a *locus amoenus*, the playground where the burdens of life are lifted by the *brigata*'s indulgence in dances, games and storytelling. Here the young people even tell tragic stories which possibly betray the symbolic hold that death has over their imagination and suggest that laughter is flanked by a fear of death. How the thought of death and comedy will encroach upon each other's borders remains to be seen. The *brigata*, nonetheless, seems untroubled by darker visions and its somber stories, untypical of the mood of the *Decameron*, are part and parcel of the world of play.

The company's play cannot be dismissed *a priori* as a simple experience of nonsense: it aspires, rather, to be a utopia, a totally inverted image of the chaotic world left behind. And ostensibly, by moving to a marginal rest spot, the company constructs a realm of fantasy which suspends the purposive structure of ordinary life and envelops it within the form of the ritual.[6] The conclusion to the seventh day and the brief introduction to the eighth—a day on which this chapter largely focuses—emphasizes this point.

The *brigata*, we are told, resumes storytelling on a Sunday after observing a suspension of two days in memory of Christ's death. As Boccaccio specifies the Sunday, he seems to stress the sense of time off, the holy-day spirit which shapes the *Decameron*. The juxtaposition of religious ritual and storytelling, however, deserves a special comment. It may be taken to be a sign of Boccaccio's confused morality, the absurd coherence of piety and worldliness. But in their contiguity the two experiences stand in an ironic self-reflection: as each is cut loose from the other, the ritual purification is emptied of any content, and storytelling, in turn, is drawn within the boundaries of pure ritual. Yet the characters' own sense of utopia, of the imagination entirely self-enclosed, is not very sure of itself. As they tell stories of *beffe*, symbolically sitting by the fountain, they are, in effect, engaged in an act of self-reflexiveness in which their desire for an imaginative utopia is asserted and its possibility is questioned. It is as if by the *beffe*, to anticipate, they localize their imagination and in the process utopia is lost.

Fundamental to the motif of the *beffa*, a prank by which a schemer is unmasked and repaid in kind, is a paradigm of exchange, the quid pro quo; and as such it mimes both the law of the market, a recurrent motif in the *Decameron*, and the narrative structure of the text. Stories are recalled and exchanged by the *brigata* and this circuit of exchange simultaneously depends on, and constitutes the bond of community between narrators and listeners.

The law of exchange and its mobile structure is the explicit theme of the *beffa* in the first story of the eighth day. Gulfardo, a German mercenary soldier, falls in love with Ambrogia, a merchant's wife, and asks her to be "del suo amore cortese" (gracious to his love, p. 671). Ambrogia will comply with his request on two conditions, first that secrecy, a basic requirement of the courtly love transparently evoked in the story, be maintained; secondly that he pay her two hundred florins. If the point of departure of the novella is the metaphoric exchange, conventional in medieval love literature, from *ars bellandi lo ars amandi*, the metaphoric movement is undermined by the very emblem of exchange, money.[7]

Ambrogia's demand transgresses the code of "courtly" love: what for Gulfardo is a purely gratuitous giving is to her a transaction, an occasion of barter. Deeply humiliated by her commerce (meretricious love can find no place in Andreas Capellanus' system), Gulfardo turns his love to hatred and contrives his *beffa*.[8] He borrows the two hundred florins from her husband, gives it to her but later tells her husband that, having had no need of the money, he handed it back to Ambrogia.

From the point of view of Neifile, the storyteller, Gulfardo's *beffa* is an expedient of retributive justice, the just counterpart for Ambrogia's greed.[9] Her demand, it would seem, violates the free exchange of love, draws it within the law of the marketplace, while the *beffa* punishes her wrongdoing. Neifile's pattern, however, is at odds with a more fundamental motif of the novella. What Gulfardo reacts against is precisely a threat to his very identity. The price which has been fixed gives a fixed value to him and to his desire; more importantly as Ambrogia asks for money she turns into a mercenary, deals with him on his own terms. The *beffa* Gulfardo devises is the weapon by which he establishes a difference: he casts Ambrogia as a worthless item and himself as her intellectual superior.[10]

There are, thus, two perspectives on the *beffa*: on the one hand, the storyteller assigns to it a value of retributive justice against the law of the market which has disrupted the fairyland of courtly love. On the other hand, Gulfardo sees in it the means by which a hierarchy of intelligence is asserted. The double perspective designates the interest, the movement of appropriation which is inherent to the *beffa*. The very notion of free entertainment that underlies the *brigata*'s escape is undercut by the investment that each character and the storyteller have at stake and because of this the *beffa* enters the world of commerce.

This motif carries thematic weight throughout the *Decameron*, where money lenders and crafty merchants are the characters that to some extent eclipse the medieval romances of lovers and heroes. The merchants are the true tricksters who manipulate events and are in full possession of rationality. Critics, unsurprisingly, have always noted how keenly Boccaccio looks into men's affairs and their ability to deal with the dangers that lurk behind all transactions.[11] It would be easy to remark that the critics, flattered in their own sense of intellectual self-importance, are like merchants fixing a value on their own superior wisdom. Yet, by the *beffa* the world of rationality and self-possession, ostensibly celebrated in the *Decameron*, is subjected to a fierce critique and Boccaccio has a way of insinuating that the fool, dispossessed of value, is always somehow right. We must turn to the story of Calandrino's quest for the heliotrope (VIII, 3) in order to explore this structure.

The primary trait of Calandrino is to be forever the same, unchanged by his experiences and, like the masks of the *commedia dell'arte*, eminently predictable.[12] By the quest of the heliotrope, he seeks an absolute autonomy and pursues his own fantasy to become transcendent and invisible, and gain the invulnerable standpoint from which he can govern and control the world. His steady reappearance as a fool in the *Decameron*, however, shows that he is doomed to be visible and that his desire is shattered. His recurrence, no doubt, is the core of the comical: as the two painters Bruno and Buffalmacco endlessly contrive plots by which Calandrino is forced into his space of self identity, we know that nothing irrevocable happens to him. At the same time, Bruno's and Buffalmacco's repeated *beffe* at his expense bespeak the pleasure inherent in the impulse to repeat: the *beffa* is the weapon to master even if it may betray the masters' insecurity in the presence of Calandrino's foolishness.

For he is very much a fool: not the fool in motley who cloaks himself in simulated inferiority to best ridicule his masters, the clown such as those one finds on the Elizabethan stage. Calandrino's foolishness is banal and his banality is profoundly disturbing. For in the measure in which he is a fool, he asserts the value of the imagination and at the same time sanctions its inevitable failure to create vital resemblances.

As the novella opens, Calandrino—himself a painter—is looking at the paintings and *bas-relief* of the tabernacle which has recently been erected above the high altar in the church of San Giovanni. While he is enthralled by the artifice, Maso contrives a trick against him. He pretends to confide to a friend, loudly enough so that Calandrino may hear, the secret of the land of Cockayne, the place where vines are tied with sausages and mountains are made of Parmesan cheese.[13] Calandrino, the maker of images to which he is provisionally bound, is quickly ensnared by the tale and takes Maso at his word. But he is not a Don Quixote who will wander over the vastness of the world to test and find the reality of his fiction. The horn of plenty Maso evokes is distant and out of reach, and Calandrino will settle on the heliotrope, the fabulous stone which, according to the lapidaries, gives the bearer invisibility and which he thinks he can find along the banks of the Mugnone river.[14] The heliotrope, as the wise Maso of course knows, does not exist: it is only a name, literally the "utopian" center of gravity of the novella and around this absence, this word without content, the vault of the story is built.

It could be argued that in the measure in which Calandrino believes he can find the magic stone along the local river, the myth of utopia has already collapsed. Yet the implied contraction of his vision also suggests that Calandrino lives in a world of confused unreality where all that is familiar is at the same time strange, the near-at-hand mysterious. He is, after all, a foreigner displaced in Florence, and to him Florence is the realm of the marvelous where the impossible quest can occur.

The quest marks both a logical extension and a radical departure from the world of painting. If painting is the fictional space of semblances, the quester seeks reality and sheer invisibility.[15] But there is a special dramatic force in Boccaccio's detail at the beginning of the story where Calandrino is gazing at the "dipinture e gl'intagli del tabernacolo" (the paintings and carvings of the tabernacle, p. 682). In the liturgy of the Church the tabernacle is God's dwelling, the place where the invisible Godhead is given a sacramental visibility. In patristic exegesis, more cogently, the tabernacle is uniformly glossed as "aedificatio terrenae felicitatis" because it symbolizes the promise of the messianic millennium.[16] At the same time, the tabernacle is the typological sign of the transfiguration, the event of the manifestation of the Messiah and the prophecy that like Moses and Christ on Mount Tabor the faithful will experience the glory of divinity and attain to the knowledge of the invisible realm.[17]

From one point of view, Calandrino's adventure is a brilliant parody of the traditional spiritual associations with which the emblem of the tabernacle is burdened. The promise of the millennium is inverted into the quest for earthly pleasures; the mystery of the transfiguration is comically turned into a mad desire to be invisible so that he can rob the banks of their riches. But above and beyond these parodic reversals of the biblical and Christian motif, something very serious takes place. Calandrino, in effect, attempts to charge with an immediate reality both the world of symbolic constructs and Maso's fable. Whatever is just a pure image is valueless to him. The myth of formal, esthetic self-enclosure, in which even the *Decameron* ostensibly partakes, is dismissed by Calandrino's sublime artlessness. And as he tries to seduce both Bruno and Buffalmacco into joining him in his search for the heliotrope, he trivializes the import of their paintings:

> *"Compagni, quando voi vogliate credermi, noi possiamo divenire i più ricchi uomini di Firenze: perciòche io ho inteso da uomo degno di fede che in Mugnone si truova una pietra, la quale chi la porta sopra non è veduto da niuna altra persona; . . . Noi la troverem per certo, per ciò che io la conosco; e trovata che noi l'avremo, che avrem noi a far altro se non . . . andare alle tavole de' cambiatori, le quali sapete che stanno sempre cariche di grossi e di fiorini, e torcene quanti noi ne vorremo? Niuno ci vedrà; e così potremo arricchire subitamente, senza avere tutto dí a schiccherare le mura a modo che fa la lumaca."*

> Believe me, friends, we can become the richest men in Florence, for I have heard from a man who is to be believed that along the Mugnone there is a certain kind of stone, and when you carry it you become invisible; . . . We'll find it without a doubt, because I know what it looks like; and once we have found it, all we have to do is . . . go to the money changers, whose counters, as you know, are always loaded with groats and florins, and help ourselves to as much as we want. No one will see us; and so we'll be able to get rich quick, without having to whiten walls all the time like a lot of snails. (p. 684)

It is at this point that the *beffa* reaches its climax. On a Sunday before sunrise, Bruno and Buffalmacco pretend to join him on his venture but secretly engineer a spectacle whereby the city of Florence is a stage on which Calandrino, believing himself unseen, is the visible occasion for general laughter. Calandrino never reaches the object of his search, for the point where the word and its reality coincide is nonexistent, truly utopian. Nevertheless, the illusion that he has found the stone is to him an exhilarating experience: he is provisionally freed from the tyranny of the others' gaze, unaware that his illusion of being autonomous, to put it in the terms of the profound insight of the *commedia dell'arte*, masks the fact that he is more than ever an automaton.

Nor does the final fall from his fantasy, when on reaching home he is seen by his wife, bring any sobering self-awareness to him. In the best misogynistic tradition, he attributes the loss of the stone's virtue to his wife and fiercely beats her.[18] This is possibly for Boccaccio a way of saying that there is no deception which is ever quite as powerful as self-deception: more cogently, this is his expedient for releasing Bruno's and Buffalmacco's hoax into the domain of the inessential.

For their trick is dwarfed by Calandrino. Ostensibly, they occupy a world of sense, of orderly and meaningful patterns. They are makers of images who can tell fiction from reality and reason from unreason, and who know that the heliotrope is an arbitrary sign without any reference outside of itself. Calandrino, by contrast, is involved in a quest over the trails of the imagination. This imagination is not to be understood as the esthetic faculty that duplicates the world or funnels its experiences into a stable picture. It marks, rather, a purely visionary venture which blurs the line of separation between illusion and reality.[19] On Sunday, the *dies solis*, he seeks the heliotrope, literally the conjunction with the sun.[20]

This impossible hope depends on his act of faith that objects must exist because words for them exist and this, in a real sense, is his folly to which the text twice has oblique but certain allusions. The first time, when the two friends feign not to see Calandrino, Buffalmacco says: "Chi sarebbe stato sì *stolto* che avesse creduto che in Mugnone si dovesse trovare una così virtuosa pietra, altri che noi?" (Who in his right mind, other than we, would ever have believed all that talk about finding such a powerful stone along the Mugnone? p. 687). The second time madness is Calandrino's direct attribute: as he is seen by his wife, "*niquitoso* corse verso la moglie, e presala per le treccie la si gittò a piedi" (Like a madman he rushed toward his wife and catching her by the tresses hurled her to the ground, p. 688). As a fool and madman, he lives in a world of pure exchange in the sense that everything can be mistaken for everything else, and a word, literally nothing, can give

access to the whole world.[21] By mistaking what are only words for
reality, Calandrino ultimately obliterates the value of words. Asked by
Buffalmacco the name of the stone they would be looking for, he simply
replies: "Che abbiam not a far del nome, poi che, sappiamo la vertù?
A me parrebbe che noi andassomo a cercare senza più" (What do we
care about the name, when we know its power? I think we should go
looking for it without wasting any more time, p. 685).

Calandrino's foolishness is his chief liability but also his strongest
asset. As he is visible, he opens our eyes to a world which is too small,
to a vision which is too narrow; and his story is a veritable romance
of which he is the mad hero. He travels the distance that separates
words from things, trying to fill that gap and knowing that the value
of fictions does not lie in their self-enclosures; as such, he is the
boundary line within which Bruno and Buffalmacco are contained.
In a way, even Boccaccio himself can be said to be contained within
Calandrino's imaginative powers, in the same manner in which, say,
Cervantes is contained by Don Quixote. In both cases the writer is
confined to elaborate parables about characters who are not bound by
any laws of logic or reality: in contrast to the freedom of their own
characters, these writers will at best take refuge in the safety of ironic
distance or what could be called a mixture of fascination and skepti-
cism toward the dreams of the characters. In this sense, Calandrino is
something of a threat to the ironies of the artists who give up, a priori
as it were, the possibility of finding utopia and accept its irrevocable
absence within the world.

Calandrino's wondrous imagination surfaces also in the third
story of the ninth day. The narrative focuses once again on Bruno's
and Buffalmacco's extraordinary invention that Calandrino is preg-
nant so that Calandrino, in order to get well without giving birth, will
have to make available some of the money he had just inherited. With
the help of Master Simon, the trick works out fine. And yet, while we
can't but admire the two painters' craftiness, we are equally struck by
Calandrino's belief that he can experience the marvelous adventure
of crossing the boundaries of natural difference, that biology itself
is not a fixed system. Calandrino's stupidity makes everybody roar
with laughter, but stupidity is an *imaginative* value against which
the tricksters' intelligent, ironic plans unavoidably stumble. What is,
then, involved in our laughter either in this story or in the one about
the heliotrope?

For the storytellers join Bruno and Buffalmacco and the Floren-
tine public in laughing at Calandrino. But as they laugh with "gran
piacere" (p. 691), they betray their uneasiness over their own utopian
quest, over their belief that by moving to the *locus amoenus* they have
found the hiding place from the convulsion of the times. Their laughter
seems to draw attention to the fact that their own utopia—far from
being a self-enclosed totality—is a play, a put-on like Bruno's and
Buffalmacco's tricks; and for all their frivolity, the games of laughter
are a necessary retrenching from madness.

Madness, to be sure, constantly menaces the stability of the world
in the *Decameron*. Witness, for instance, the story of Cimone (v, 1).
Cast as an epyllion, the tale focuses on Cimone's redemption from
beast (the *significance* given his name by Boccaccio) to man through
the love for Ifigenia. Cimone sees Ifigenia asleep—discovers, that
is to say, his own spiritual lethargy—and inflamed by love for her
wakes up to virtue. The stilnovistic dream that love ennobles man is
flagrantly parodied as Cimone's newly acquired virtue turns into a
veritable madness of love. The narrative (one is reminded of *Othello*)
takes place in Cyprus, the island of the mad Venus, and Cimone's
love succeeds only after generating mighty wars.[22] This story of
madness is controlled by the frame of order, is part of the experience
of storytelling; yet, as an object of persistent fascination, madness is
the border line of fiction, the temptation that threatens to erode the
edifice of order and occasions, just as Calandrino does to Bruno and
Buffalmacco, the world of representation.

We must turn to another novella (viii, 9) where Bruno and Buffalmacco once again come forth as the zany fabricators of the *beffa* in
order to probe further the question of the value of the trick. The joke
this time is contrived against a foolish physician, Master Simon, with
the ostensible purpose of unmasking his pretenses of learning: from
the outset, in fact, Simon is introduced as dressed in scarlet robes and
"con un gran batalo, dottor di medicine, secondo che egli medesimo
diceva" (with a fine-looking hood, and calling himself doctor of medicine, p. 744).

The carefree life of both Bruno and Buffalmacco arouses his curiosity and he decides to befriend them to find out the reason for their
merry lives. Bruno pretends to share with him an imaginary secret
and weaves the fiction that they are members of a society founded
by the necromancer Michael Scott which assembles twice a month

and by magic practices enjoys the pleasures of banquets, music, and midnight revels.

Simon, like Calandrino earlier, is unable to decipher the transparent lie and is wistfully seduced by it. He believes that the world of appearances pulsates with occult life, that a mythic bond exists between appearances and the beyond. Eager to experience those imaginary pleasures, he begs to join what Bruno defines as a "paradiso a vedere" (paradise itself, p. 748), so that he might enjoy the most beautiful woman in the world.[23] In this sense, the story comically conjures the motif of the Saturnalia, the golden age of revelry where restraints are abolished and one's fantasies are realized.[24] When finally the night appointed for the meeting arrives, Simon is instructed to wear his most sumptuous robe and go to the cemetery of Santa Maria Novella. Of course, neither otherworldly prodigies nor erotic fulfillments take place.

The tale actually turns into a masque, a literal carnival which, as its etymology suggests, is the ironic counterpoint of the erotic expectations.[25] While Simon waits in fear, Buffalmacco disguised as a bear and wearing the mask of a devil comes to take the physician to share in the delights of the magic paradise but, after a few moments, throws him into a ditch of excrement. Bruno and Buffalmacco are hardly able to contain their laughter at their own trick. The morning after, with their bodies painted to simulate tortures received on account of Simon's cowardice, they visit him to complain for the troubles he has caused them. Fearful of becoming a public laughing stock, the doctor from that day forth pampers the two friends more than ever before.

Simon's fall into the mire marks a symbolic degradation, the manipulation by which he is defined as an inferior to the two tricksters. Above and beyond this apparent pretext, the degradation implies that laughter is linked with a fall from Paradise. But for Boccaccio the fall has no theological focus: Paradise is an illusory misnomer and what is really lost by the fall is Hell.

The novella, I submit, features a deliberate Dantesque design, as if Boccaccio were directly involved in a parody of Dante's Hell. The allusion to Michael Scott is an overt recall of *Inferno* XX, the canto of contorted shades where divination and necromancy are expiated;[26] the ensuing description of the assembly's entertainment, "Costoro adunque servivano i predetti gentili uomini di certi loro innamoramenti e d'altre cosette liberamente; . . . poi . . . preserci di grandi e strette amistà con alcuni, più gentili che non gentili" (These two men freely assisted the above-mentioned nobles in certain love affairs and other little escapades of theirs ... and afterwards they acquired a good number of intimate friends, without caring whether they were nobles or plebeians, p. 747) is a paraphrase of Iacopo della Lana's commentary on that canto.[27] The painted bodies of Bruno and Buffalmacco, simulating the tortures, echo the description of the hypocrites as "gente dipinta" (painted people) in *Inferno* (xxiii, 58). And just as in Dante between the world of the sorcerers in *Inferno* xix (the canto of *Simon magus*) and the world of the simulators there stands the so-called *commedia dei diavoli*, in Boccaccio's text we find its playful reenactment.

By staging the *commedia dei diavoli*, Dante primarily dramatizes the common medieval conception of Hell as the place of tricks and frauds. At the same time, he implies that laughter has a demonic property and is in touch with the dark powers. Like the Christian apologists, Tertullian, Cyprian and Boccaccio himself in the *Genealogy of the Gods*, Dante sees mimes and spectacles as arts of the devil, distracting man from his heavenward ascent.[28] He even goes further than this: the devils' comedy enacts a steady danger of spiritual degradation of self. Unsurprisingly the pilgrim, at this stage of the poem, is directly threatened by the devils. Commentators have tried to explain the impasse by resorting to raw autobiography, the suspicion that Dante in his own life may have been guilty of barratry.[29] In effect, the world of comedy is seen as black magic, a fraudulent game in this area where "Michele Scotto, fu, il veramente / de le magiche frode seppe 'l gioco" (Michael Scott it was, who truly knew the game of magic frauds, *Inferno* xx, 116–117). Dante dismisses this ludic moment because it is an illusory instrument by which the world can be shaped and radically juxtaposes to it his own *Commedia*.[30]

What for Dante is an experience of moral terror, Boccaccio displaces into sheer buffoonery. Part of the fun, no doubt, lies in the fact that Boccaccio, a serious commentator of Inferno, is here involved in a deliberate misreading of it. Historically it will be left to Pico and the Hermetic tradition to reverse altogether Dante's perspective and regain magic as a high wisdom, the imaginative realm of man's autonomy whereby the possibilities of angelic perfection or descent into matter are made available to him.[31]

For Boccaccio, Simon literally falls into matter in what seems to be an overt mockery of spiritual falls. In this context there is a further detail that deserves comment: the front wall of Simon's hospital bears the emblem of Lucifer.[32] By the detail, Boccaccio casts the physician as an ineffectual sorcerer and portrays medicine as a practice of black magic.[33] At the same time he exposes the lunacy in his belief both in the uncanny marvels of the Saturnalia and in mysterious bonds between symbolic representation and hidden essences.

Nor are the tricksters molders of worlds: to fashion themselves is simply a travesty, the wearing of a mask to make fun of, and gain ascendancy over, the gullible Simon. In the *Genealogy of the Gods*, Boccaccio still vindicates the value of the poet as a creature who forges and wields the illusion of new worlds. But in this story the imagination, the power by which man is the chameleon, is parodied. Bruno and Buffalmacco are the wizards who conjure the other world, who bring fictions into life and change life into fiction; but the process is contracted into play, a frivolous exercise which has renounced any claim to be vital.

By so doing, Boccaccio silences Dante's tragic sense of laughter in Hell and is far removed from Pico's belief in myth-making through the arcana of magic. In a sense, he purifies the ground, as it were, of the supernatural and valorizes the world of play and *beffe*. The masque is the hub of play and we must look closely at it. For both Bruno and Buffalmacco, the mask is the sign of their superiority, the means of unmasking Simon's own self-deceit. By wearing the mask and simulating tortures they appear, however, as actors. Isidore of Seville gives a definition of the hypocrite which is cogent to our point: hypocrisy, he writes, is the practice of actors who paint themselves in order to deceive.[34] If Simon's appearance is false and hides an essential vacuity, Buffalmacco's impersonation of the devil is a pure fiction, a figure of substitution for nothing. As he wears the mask, he slips into Simon's very world of false appearance; more paradoxically, as he manages to frighten Simon he vindicates his belief that the world of appearance veils occult realities. Not one of them steps out of the bounds of illusion.

The young people of the *brigata*, gratified by the story, laugh at Simon just as they laughed at Calandrino and empathize with the tricksters. We surely understand why the physician is the object of laughter. After all, the introduction to the *Decameron* makes explicit the point that the art of Hippocrates is superfluous, has no restorative power from the threat of death.[35] The masque, which is significantly acted out in the cemetery—the place of death—can hardly conquer death and is, in this sense, equally redundant. Yet, it seems to be a necessary alternative to mad visionaries, a style of mediocrity by which the tricksters always gain a superiority and the storytellers find temporary relief from their anxieties.

But can the game really be such a comforting fiction? Can we really make the world our own at the expense of fools or believe that nobody is ever laughing at us? We must turn back to the second day of the *Decameron* to find some possible answers to these questions.

The thematic burden of the day is the world of Fortune, which, in the introduction to the third story, appears as the Intelligence of God, the rational order that subtends and presides over the chaos of the fallen world of change.[36] This view of Fortune as the providential agency governing the economy of the world recalls explicitly, as has often been remarked, Dante's digression in the canto of the avaricious and prodigals. Dante's discourse casts human rationality as a precarious construct, beset on the one hand by the unintelligibility of Pluto, the god of wealth, and on the other by Fortune's providential but inscrutable designs. The sinners who in their lives transgressed the economy of exchange by overvaluing or dissipating common goods now ironically exchange insults and move in a gloomy circle that parodies the perfect circularity of Fortune's wheel. From man's temporal standpoint, Fortune's movement does not follow any discernible plan: man, however, can still conquer Fortune by the exercise of virtue and by the acknowledgment that she reigns over the things of the world and that there is nothing which really belongs to us.[37]

Boccaccio's extensive rephrasing of Dante's view of Fortune is comically altered later on in the day when the adventures of Andreuccio da Perugia (II, 5) are recounted. This story, in fact, is a parody of the spiritual allegory of man's confrontation with, and binding of, Fortune. Andreuccio, as the etymology of the name implies, is the little man caught in the world of change.[38] He is a merchant, a horse dealer who on a Monday (a detail that suggests that his destiny is linked to the phases of the moon and that he belongs to the sublunary world of change and corruption) appears in the marketplace of Naples to strike his deals.[39] While he uncautiously shows off his money, he is seen by Fiordalisi, a woman who, in flagrant inversion of her name, is a prostitute. She invites him to her house in Malpertugio, which means, in Boccaccio's own etymologizing, a place of ill affair. Andreuccio has no *virtue* and actually mistakes his manhood for *virility*. He accepts her invitation only to have his erotic fantasies deluded. Fiordalisi tells him that she is his natural sister, entertains him for the whole evening in a room which suggests the garden of love, and finally robs him of his money.[40] Only when Andreuccio has fallen into the excrement does he seem to realize that he has been tricked.

As he is fallen, he is involved in what is a transparent parody of the spiritual dark night: the city of Naples is a ghostly labyrinth from which there seems to be no exit. Andreuccio falls once again into a well where he cleanses himself As he is betrayed by his accomplices, he comes forth as *homo sibi relictus*. Finally, with the two thieves he goes to the church to steal the ring off the archbishop who has been buried that day. The church, far from being the place of moral regeneration, is literally transformed into a den of thieves. Yet here he finds his conversion, a figurative death and resurrection comically inverted. He steals the ring and gets caught in the crypt; but then, by an unexpected reversal of the wheel of Fortune and an acquired virtue to exploit the coincidence, he gets out of the crypt, gaining both a new lease on life and the archbishop's ring.

The name of the archbishop, we are told, is Filippo, literally a lover of horses. By this etymological resonance and the fact that the ring is worth more than the florins he lost, the movement of the story both mimes the circulation of Fortune and suggests that there is a gain for Andreuccio.[41] Whereas for Dante, Fortune is conquered by not clinging to earthly goods, Boccaccio inverts Dante's moral paradigm by showing how the very opposite takes place. These reversals are not simply techniques of Boccaccio's art; they are, as we shall now see, the very core of the story.

Rather than being the order of a providential agency, the world is the empire of *alea* [*alea* literally means die (as in dice, a game of chance) and also refers to a Greek soldier credited for inventing the dice game *tabula*] . . . where things are not ever what they seem to be.[42] This view of Fortune sustains the ambiguities, constant inversions, falls and reversals of the novella: three times does Andreuccio fall and rise; by the extensive use of etymologies, Boccaccio seems to suggest that there are names which are "proper," stable receptacles of a univocal sense and identity. But the names appear as deceptive masks: Fiordalisi, regardless of her name, is a prostitute; Andreuccio's own name wavers between virtue and virility. More generally, he possesses, loses, and regains; there is a sister who turns out not to be a sister; the city of Naples is ironically twisted into a disorienting space where all directions are confused.

This land of unlikeness is triggered by Andreuccio's vainglory, concupiscence of the eyes, and concupiscence of the flesh.[43] But as this conventional moral scheme is hinted at, it is quickly discarded. In this perspective, allegory—voided of its moral structure and parodied—is the poetics of dissemblance, for it represents a condition whereby things are not what they mean.[44] By parodying the allegory, Boccaccio seems to be on the side of Bruno and Buffalmacco in showing that the gap between the semblance of things and their meaning can never be bridged.

The only order in such a world of dissemblance and instability is the regularity of Fortune's shifts. If the marketplace is the metaphor of traffic, the space where goods are brought to be exchanged and assessed at their proper value, the wheel of Fortune mocks the merchant's efforts. It is Fortune who is the true trickster of the world. For Dante she is the distant spectator of the "corta buffa" (brief mockery, *Inferno* vii, 61) who "beata si gode" (rejoices in her bliss, 96); for Boethius she behaves dissemblingly like a play actor, "sic illa ludit ... hunc continuum ludum ludimus." She teases man's power to dispose of goods and assigns them in a constant and irrational exchange.[45] In this sense, she enacts Calandrino's very madness in his changing one order of reality for another and in his desire to rob the bank, the place where exchange occurs. This view of Fortune tells us that human mastery, gain and hierarchy—that which is embodied by the *beffa*—are always provisional and contingent, just as the identity between the proper name of Filippo and its sense for Andreuccio is sheer chance, an ironic undercutting of any notion of providentiality.

When Andreuccio's adventure ends happily, the *brigata* laughs, pleasantly relieved at the last twist and turn of the wheel of Fortune. But in spite of the happy ending of the story, there is no real closure: the steady rotation of the wheel asserts the open-endedness of events. Andreuccio wins, but we are asked to extend the trajectory and realize that his fall may happen all over again because even as he is at the top of the wheel, he is always on its shifty curve. What is more, the virtue by which he wins over chance is an act of thievery: the ruby into which his money was metamorphosed may have permanence, but ironically, because of its permanence, it is the more coveted and its possession ever endangered by other thieves.

Both Andreuccio's constant predicament and the *brigata*'s relief disclose the central oddness of the games of laughter—the comical tendency, that is, to mistake provisional appearances for the whole reality. This ambiguity informs the novella genre in the *Decameron*. The novella is a deliberate fragment, a cross section of a totality which, if it exists at all, can never be fully grasped. Boccaccio repeatedly tries to impose on his kaleidoscopic range of stories a unified design and cohesion: the frame, the thematic movement of the text from the chaos of the plague to the difficult order in Griselda's tale, the transitional passages, the topics by which stories are duly placed within given fields of signification, the symbolic numbers of totality (ten days and one hundred novelle). All are expedients which suggest how the sequence can be constructed as a unified totality.

Much like Petrarch's *Canzoniere*, the *Decameron* aspires to be a whole of parts but, at the same time, declares the impossibility of its being arranged as a total and coherent pattern. In the *Canzoniere*, the principle of repetition—as each poem begins anew, it inexorably ends up echoing what has already been said—shows that totality is an illusory mirage.[46] Nonetheless, the Canzoniere has had, and continues to have, readers who are taken in by the esthetic simulation of order; the *Decameron*, I might add, has had exactly the same destiny. Auerbach's close analysis of a passage of a tale, for instance, depends on the assumption that each part reflects the totality and by the synecdoche one knows a fragment and, thus, one can grasp the whole. In a real sense, Auerbach is like the *brigata* in the garden which seizes on the provisional and the partial and wistfully extends it to cover the whole.

Wistfulness is the heart of laughter. It betrays the desire for sense and relief which governs the life of the characters and, for that matter, of the critics. For Boccaccio the metaphor of totality, the project of both Calandrino and Simone, is madness and hence unspeakable. Dissolving their pretenses and borrowing from them there is the world of *beffe*, the play which discloses the illusoriness of the metaphor and which has laughter as its proper response.

In the wake of Aristotle, Thomas Aquinas and Dante speak of laughter as precisely the activity proper to man. [...] Boccaccio shows both how laughter is a hollow mask which deceives, blinds us to what we lose, and how it is produced by a mask behind which the tricksters try to appropriate the world and, like the *brigata*, enjoy it.

The *Decameron* constantly moves between the dream of utopia and the pleasure of the representation: laughter is the precarious point where these polarities intersect and at the same time pull apart. This constant movement discloses laughter as the domain of the imaginary which seeks pretexts and occasions to become "real" and is always a put-on. The rhetorical name for this movement is catachresis, the figure of a borrowed property, the elusive borderland of madness where all efforts at sense are defied.

NOTES

1. This tale of "giudici e notari" (p. 698) logically belongs to the discussion of the theme of law [...]. Here I choose to emphasize the satire of the profession.
   [All quotations from the *Decameron*, unless otherwise stated, are taken from *Tutte le opera di Giovanni Boccaccio*, Vol. IV, *Decameron*, ed. Vittore Branca (Milan, 1976). I have used Roman and Arabic numerals in the body of the text to indicate respectively the day and the novella discussed. For the sake of clarity I have given the page number, which always refers to Branca's edition, for each quotation. The translations from the *Decameron* are mine.]

2. For an important perspective on the trickster, cf. Karl Kerenyi's introduction to Paul Radin, *The Trickster* (London: Routledge and Kegan Paul, 1956).

3. Erich Auerbach, *Mimesis: The Representation of Reality in Western Literature*, trans. Willard R. Trask (New York: Anchor Books, 1957), pp. 197–203.

4. [To him, the *Decameron* represents "un mondo della commedia (cui) manca quell'altro sentimento del comico che nelle sue forme umanistiche e capricciose gli darà l'Ariosto." Its precise meaning notwithstanding, De Sanctis' insight is capital for it captures, as we plan to show, Boccaccio's singular impasse.] Francesco De Sanctis, *Storia della letteratura italiana*, ed. Niccoló Gallo (Turin: Einaudi, 1958), I, p. 383.

5. "E come spesso avviene che, bene che i cittadini non abbiano a fare cosa del mondo a Palagio, pur talvolta vi vanno, avvinne che Maso del Saggio una mattina, cercando d'un suo amico, v'andò; e venutogli guardato là dove questo messer Nicola

sedeva, parendogli che fosse un nuovo uccellone, tutto il venne considerando" (*Decameron*, pp. 698–699).

6. [. . .] There are two general works that I would like to recall for the benefit of the reader as cogent to the point I am making. One is by Johan Huizinga, *Homo Ludens: A Study of the Play Element in Culture* (London: Routledge and Kegan Paul, 1949). For a philosophical approach to the question of play, see Eugen Fink, *Spiel als Weltsymbol* (Stuttgard: W. Kohlhammer, 1960). [. . .] I would also like to point out a passage from *The Art of Courtly Love* on the sense of "time off" (bk. vi, and dialogue): "But where can one find greater effrontery than in a man who for the space of a whole week devotes all his efforts to the various gains of business and then on the seventh day, his day of rest, tries to enjoy the gifts of love and to dishonor Love's commands and confound the distinctions of classes established among men of old?" (trans. Parry, p. 46). In Boccaccio's text there is an inversion of the situation envisaged by the woman in the dialogue with the man of the middle class.

7. The *topos* of love and war, commonly used by Petrarch, for instance, among others, is studied by Denis de Rougemont, *Love in the Western World*, trans. Montgomery Belgion (Greenwich, Conn.: Fawcett Publications, 1966), pp. 257–286.

8. [. . .] I shall add here the passage by Andreas Capellanus, *The Art of Courtly Love* (bk. 1, chap. 9): "Now let us see whether real love can be got with money or any other gift. Real love comes only from the affection of the heart and is granted out of pure grace and genuine liberality, and this most precious gift of love cannot be paid for at any set price or be cheapened by a matter of money. If any woman is so possessed with a feeling of avarice as to give herself to a lover for the sake of pay, let no one consider her a lover, but rather a counterfeiter of love, who ought to join those shameful women in the brothel. Indeed the wantonness of such women is more polluted than the passion of harlots who play their trade openly, for they do what one expects them to, and they deceive no one since their intentions are perfectly obvious" (trans. Parry, p. 144). See also bk. I, chap. 12 (Parry, p. 150) for a further dismissal of the "love of prostitutes."

9. "Avvegna che, chi volesse più propriamente parlare, quello che io dir debbo *non si direbbe beffa anzi si direbbe merito . . .*" (*Decameron*, p. 670; italics mine).

10. A recent statement on comedy in terms of identity and difference has been provided by René Girard, "Perilous Balance: A Comic Hypothesis," *Modern Language Notes*, 87 (1972), pp. 811–826. See also C.L. Barber, *Shakespeare's Festive Comedy* (Princeton: Princeton University Press, 1959).

11. Vittore Branca, *Boccaccio medievale* (Florence: Sansoni, 1956), pp. 71–99. See also Guido Pugliese, "*Decameron*, II, 3: un caso di contingenza causale," *Esperienze letterarie* 5 (1980), 4, pp. 29–41.

12. Ireneo Sanesi, *La Commedia* (Milan: Vallardi, 1935), II, pp. 1–109. For an updating of the questions of the *commedia dell'arte*, see also Roberto Tessari, *La Commedia dell'arte nel seicento* (Florence: Olschki, 1969).

13. A history of this utopian motif from antiquity down is provided by Arthur O. Lovejoy and George Boas, *Primitivism and Related Ideas in Antiquity* (New York: Octagon Books, 1973).

14. The specific virtue of the heliotrope is described by Marbodus, *Liber de gemmis, PL* 171, col. 1757; Pliny, *Natural History*, x, xxxvii, p. 165. Cf. also *Inferno* xxiv, 93.

15. The link between appearance and identity is featured in VI, 5. [. . .]

16. The definition is given by Garnerius de S. Victore, *Gregorianum, PL* 193, col. 396. It is also echoed in *Allegoriae in universam sacram scripturam, PL* 112, col. 1062. The work, which Migne attributed to Rabanus Maurus, is now doubtfully attributed to Garner of Rochefort or Adam Scotus. Cf. also Adam Scotus, *De tripartito tabernacolo, PL* 198, col. 746. The biblical place where the tabernacle is alluded to as a prefiguration of the paradisiac order on earth is Isaiah 32:18 and Haymo's brilliant gloss on the verse in Isaiah, *PL* 116, col. 876. The motif of the feast of the tabernacles is studied with great care by Jean Danielou, *Bible et liturgie* (Paris: Les Editions du Cerf, 1958), pp. 449–469.

17. The scene of the Transfiguration is described by Matthew 17:1; Mark 9:2; Luke 9:28. The typological link between the feast of the tabernacles and the Transfiguration is established by the

apostle Peter's proposal to build the tents for Moses and Elijah. 2 Peter, 1:18, puts forward the view of the Transfiguration as the prophetic sign of the Parousia. Cf. also Origines, *Homelies sur l'Exode*, trans. P. Fortier, intr. and notes H. De Lubac (Paris: Editions du Cerf, 1947), sec. xii, pp. 244–255. Noteworthy are the documented remarks by Danielou, *Bible et liturgie*, pp. 457–461 especially.

18. The myth of the woman as the devil ("questo diavolo di questa femina maladetta mi si parò dinanzi e ebbemi veduto, per ciò che, come voi sapete, le femíne fanno perderla vertù a ogni cosa: . . . *Decameron*, viii, 3, p. 690) echoes a solid patristic tradition about the woman as Eve, on account of whom man, like Calandrino in the novella, loses Paradise. Cf. Tertullian: "Tu es diaboli ianua, . . . tu es quae suasisti . . . tu imaginem dei, hominem Adam, facile elisisti" (*Du cultu feminarum*, I, 1, in *Corpus Christianorum, Series Latina*, lxx, pp. 59–60). See also Jerome, *Adversus Iovinianum*, *PL* 23, cols. 211–338. For a general sketch of the tradition, see F. L. Utley, *The Crooked Rib* (Columbus: Ohio State University Press, 1944). See also Katharine M. Rogers, *The Troublesome Helpmate: A History of Misogyny in Literature* (Seattle: University of Washington Press, 1966).

19. This notion of the imagination can be found in Dante's *Purgatorio* xvii, 13ff. In this central canto of the *Divine Comedy*, Dante suggests how the imaginative faculty, far from duplicating the world of reality or originating from the perception of outside events, *steals* us away from the experience of familiar reality. Cf. the still important survey by M.W. Bundy, *The Theory of the Imagination in Classical and Medieval Thought*, University of Illinois Studies in Language and Literature, no. 12, 2–3 (Urbana: University of Illinois Press, 1927). A valuable reading of this novella, even if in terms entirely different from mine, has been given by Luigi Russo, *Letture critiche del Decameron* (Bari: Laterza, 1977), pp. 245–274; Mario Baratto, *Realtà e stile nel Decameron* (Vicenza: Pozza, 1970), pp. 309–318. See also the remarks by Marga Cottino-Jones, "Magic and Superstition in Boccaccio's *Decameron*," *Italian Quarterly*, 18 (1975), pp. 5–32; and by Millicent Joy Marcus, *An Allegory of Form* (Saratoga, Calif.: Anma Libri, 1979) pp. 79–92.

20. It may be of interest to remark that Calandrino's quest takes place on a Sunday and that the story is told on the eighth day, also a Sunday, as if Boccaccio were obliquely hinting that Calandrino's hope for a utopia is the specular and distorted reflection of the storytellers' *locus amoenus*. The motif of Sunday as the *dies solis* and as the typological eighth day (the day of the spiritual recreation of which Boccaccio gives its frivolous counterpart) is explored by Danielou, *Bible et liturgie*, pp. 328–387. Cf. also Jean Danielou, "La Typologie millenariste de la semaine dans le Christianisme primitive," *Vigiliae Christianae*, 2 (1948), pp. 1–16.

21. For this notion of foolishness and madness see Michel Foucault, *Histoire de la folie* (Paris: Librairie Plon, 1961).

22. For this mythographic motif, see Dante, *Paradiso*, viii, 1–9.

23. The comical role of parasites that Bruno and Buffalmacco play in the story is imaginatively yoked to the role of "corsari" (p. 749), those who steal the property that belongs to others. In this sense the two friends fulfill Calandrino's own desires. More than that, Boccaccio is lining up Calandrino, Bruno and Buffalmacco, and the pirates (for which see ii, 10) as figures that disrupt, in fact or in thought, the economic order. Socially they may well be "useless" or outright harmful, but they are *interesting*, in the full sense of the word, from an imaginative viewpoint.

24. See, for one, Macrobius, *Saturnalia*, ed. Jacobus Willis (Leipzig: Teubner Verlagsgesallschaft, 1970), I, vii, 37ff., p. 34. Cf. also A. Lovejoy and G. Boas, *Primitivism and Related Ideas*, especially pp. 65ff.

25. Paolo Toschi, *Le origini del teatro italiano* (Turin: Edizioni scientifiche Einaudi, 1955). Toschi focuses on the motif of the carnival and in passing alludes (p. 173) to this story of Boccaccio as a "document" proving the use of demonic masks in the late Middle Ages. Cf. also Mikhail Bakhtin, *Rabelais and His World*, trans. Helen Iswolsky (Cambridge, Mass.: The M.I.T. Press, 1965). The literary connection between representation and masking is explored by Angus Fletcher, *The Transcendental Masque: An Essay on Milton's Comus* (Ithaca: Cornell University Press, 1970), pp. 8–68.

26. "Quell'altro che ne' fianchi è così poco, / Michele Scotto fu, che veramente / de le magiche frode seppe 'l gioco" (*Inferno* xx, 115–117).

27. Iacopo della Lana's commentary reads: " . . . usando con gentili uomini e cavalieri, e mangiando come si usa tra essi in brigata a casa l'un dell'altro, quando venia la volta di lui d'apparecchiare" (Guido Biagi, *La Divina Commedia nella figurazione artistica e. nel secolare commento: Inferno* [Turin: UTET, 1924], p. 507). Cf. Branca's note, *Decameron*, p. 1447.

28. Tertullian, *De spectaculis, CSEL*, xx (pars. I), pp. 1–29; Cyprian, *De spectaculis, PL* 4, cols. 799–788. Boccaccio, *Genealogia deorum gentilium libri*, ed. Vincenzo Romano, 2 vols. (Bari: Laterza, 1951), xiv, 14, p. 724.

29. This seductive hypothesis, by no means to be entirely discarded, was eloquently put forward by Luigi Pirandello, "Il canto XXI dell'Inferno," in *Letture Dantesche: Inferno*, ed. Giovanni Getto (Florence: Sansoni, 1955). pp. 395–414.

30. There is in Dante's *Paradiso* what I call a theology of play, which deploys motifs such as the music of the spheres, the new Jerusalem as both a garden and an amphitheater (*Paradiso* xxx, 108ff.), songs, actors' craft, dance of the stars (which John Freccero, in a different context, has studied, see his "*Paradiso* x: The Dance of the Stars," *Dante Studies*, 86 [1968], pp. 85–111). In *Paradiso* this *theologia ludens*, of Neoplatonic origin, is the point of convergence of theology and esthetics, a question which deserves an ample investigation.

31. Giovanni Pico della Mirandola, *De hominis dignitate, Heptaplus, De ente et uno e scritti vari*, ed. E. Garin (Florence: Vallecchi, 1942). Cf. E. Garin, *Medioevo e rinascimento* (Bari: Laterza, 1954), pp. 150–191. Particularly cogent is Frances A. Yates, *Giordano Bruno and the Hermetic Tradition* (Chicago: University of Chicago Press, 1964), pp. 44–168. See also D. P. Walker, *Spiritual and Demonic Magic from Ficino to Campanella* (London: Warburg Institute, 1958). The Christian attack on magic was formulated by St. Augustine, among others. Cf. *The City of God*, viii, 18, 19, 26; ix, 1.

32. "Egli è troppo gran segreto quello che voi volete sapere, e è cosa da disfarmi e da cacciarmi del mondo, anzi da farmi mettere in bocca del lucifero da San Gallo, se altri il risapesse . . ." (*Decameron*, p. 746).

33. Lynn Thorndike, *A History of Magic and Experimental Science*, 1 (New York: The Macmillan Co., 1923), pp. 566–615. Cf. also A. J. Festugiere, *Hermétisme et mystique païenne* (Paris: Aubier, 1967), pp. 141–180.

34. "Hypocrita Graeco sermone in Latino simulator interpretatur . . . Nomen autem hypocritae tractum est ab specie eorum qui in spectaculis contecta facie incedunt, distinguentes vultum caeruleo minioque colore distincta . . ." (Isidore of Seville, *Etym.*, x, H, 118–120.

35. See chapter 1 [of *The World at Play in Boccaccio's* Decameron] on this polemical view of medicine.

36. [. . .] See also *Inferno* vii, 61–69. Cf. Vincenzo Cioffari, *The Conception of Fortune and Fate in the Works of Dante* (Cambridge, Mass.: Dante Society, 1940). More generally, see Howard R. Patch, *The Goddess Fortuna in Medieval Literature* (Cambridge, Mass.: Harvard University Press, 1927).

37. "Valorose donne, quanto più si parla de' fatti della fortuna, tanto più, a chi vuole le sue cose ben riguardare, ne resta a poter dire: e di cio' niuno dee aver maraviglia, se discretamente pensa che tutte le cose, le quali noi scioccamente nostre chiamiamo, sieno nelle sue mani, . . ." (*Decameron*, ii, 3, p. 108).

38. "Andreas . . . sermone autem Graeco a viro virilis appellatur" (Isidore, *Etym.*, vii, ix, 11).

39. " . . . dove giunto una domenica sera in sul vespro, dall'oste suo informato la seguente mattina fu in sul Mercato, . . ." (*Decameron*, ii, 5, p. 126). Carlo Muscetta, *Giovanni Boccaccio* (Bari: Laterza, 1972), p. 196, mistakenly believes the story takes place on Sunday night.

40. "Ella appresso, . . . con lui nella sua camera se n'entro', la quale di rose, di fiori d'aranci e d'altri odori tutta oliva" (*Decameron*, p. 128).

41. The point is stressed by Giovanni Getto, *Vita di forme e forme di vita nel Decameron* (Turin: Petrini, 1958), pp. 78–94. See also Aldo Rossi, "La *combinatoria decameroniana*: Andreuccio," *Strumenti critici*, 7 (1973), pp. 1–51. For a view that emphasizes the symmetrical correspondences in the *Decameron*, see Tzvetan Todorov, *Grammaire du Decameron* (The Hague and Paris: Mouton, 1969). Of interest are also Gregory Lucente, "The Fortunate Fall of Andreuccio da Perugia," *Forum Italicum*, 10

(1976), pp. 323–344: Millicent J. Marcus, *An Allegory of Form: Literary Self-Consciousness in the Decameron* (Saratoga, Calif: Anma Libri, 1979), pp. 27–43; Karl-Ludwig Selig, "Boccaccio's *Decamerone* and The Subversion of Literary Reality (Dec. ii / 5)," *Italien und die Romania in Humanismus und Renaissance*, eds. K.W. Hemper and E. Straub (Weisbaden: Steiner, 1983), pp. 265–269. More generally on the motif of circularity, see Teodolinda Barolini, "The Wheel of the *Decameron*," *Romance Philology*, 36 (1983), pp. 521–538.

42. Pierre Courcelle, *Les Confessions de Saint Augustin dans la tradition littéraire* (Paris: Etudes Augustiniennes, 1963), especially pp. 278–288 and pp. 623–640, where Courcelle gives abundant evidence for the occurrence of the *topos*. See also F. Chatillon, "Regio dissimilitudinis," in *Mélanges E. Podechard* (Lyon: Facultés Catholiques, 1945), pp. 85–102. The notion that the fallen world governed by Fortune is a *regio dissimilitudinis* is implied by Boethius, *Consolation of Philosophy*, ii, m. 3, 13–18.

43. The classical text for these temptations is 1 John 2:16 which urges man to give up "concupiscentia carnis, concupiscentia oculi et superbia vitae." In patristic exegesis the three sins are variously interpreted as gluttony, sexual pleasures, pursuit of riches and vainglory. For a literary application of the motif to the medieval English literature see Donald R. Howard, *The Three Temptations: Medieval Man in Search of the World* (Princeton: Princeton University Press, 1966).

44. This is a standard definition of allegory as "alieniloqui. Aliud enim sonat, et aliud intelligitur" (Isidore, *Etym.*, I, xxxvii, 22).

45. Boethius' text reads: "Thus doth she play, to make her power more known, / Showing her slaves a marvel, when man's state / Is in one hour both downcast and fortunate" (*The Consolation of Philosophy*, trans. H.F. Steward [Cambridge, Mass.: Harvard University Press, 1968], ii, m. 1, p. 179.)

46. Giuseppe Mazzotta, "The *Canzoniere* and the Language of the Self," *Studies in Philology*, 75 (1978), pp. 271–296.

THE NOVELS OF WILLIAM GOLDING

"The Prometheus Myth in the Novels of William Golding"
by Sohana Manzoor, in
BRAC University Journal (2007)

INTRODUCTION

In his novels, William Golding often employs the image of suffering trickster Prometheus. Traditionally seen as a champion of mankind, Prometheus is the bringer of *techne* and fire. For the classical Greek writer Aeschylus, Prometheus was a rebel, one who defied the gods by befriending humanity. He has also been seen as a trickster figure who upset the order of the human and the divine. For his defiance, Prometheus is bound to a rock for eternity with a cruel punishment: Every day Zeus, in the form of an eagle, eats out his liver, which then regrows so that his torment is endless and excruciating. For Sohana Manzoor, the Prometheus figure in the novels of William Golding represents humanity in the form of a trickster.

In classical antiquity, the Prometheus myth was immortalized by the Greek dramatist Aeschylus (525–456 B.C.) in his trilogy of which

---

Manzoor, Sohana. "The Prometheus Myth in the Novels of William Golding." *BRAC University Journal* 4.2 (2007): 105–111.

only the first, *Prometheus Bound*, survives in complete form. Originally, Prometheus was a Titan, a pre-Hellenic fire god later replaced by Hephaestus. He stole fire from Zeus and presented it to mankind. As punishment for this crime along with other offences, Zeus, the supreme god had him tied on the highest peak of Caucasus. There Prometheus endured terrible sufferings as an eagle tore at his immortal liver during day time. During the night the liver got replenished only to be devoured the next day. Thus Prometheus is not just a symbol of aspiring humanity but suffering humanity as well. For poets and writers from the ancient times to the modern Prometheus has been a very attractive figure, and among other things he has been presented as the creator of mankind, a fire-bringer, a trickster and a skilled craftsman, a redeemer, a rebel against the gods, and a great humanitarian.

Aeschylus showed proper reverence to the immortal gods, and there are suggestions of a reconciliation between Prometheus and Zeus. At other times, other writers have imbued the influence and attitude of their times in his character. So in Shelley's *Prometheus Unbound* (1820), the chained and tormented Prometheus is a symbol of afflicted humanity. During the time span of over two thousand years between Aeschylus and Shelley, Prometheus grew into a hero of humanistic, liberal and suffering man. In his essay, "On Pincher Martin," Samuel Hynes defines Prometheus as "an indestructible life worshipping identity whose very existence gives meaning to his suffering and whose suffering gives meaning to his existence" (130). Commenting on the essential sufferings of human life, Hynes points out that a central theme of Golding's novels is that the sufferings of human beings arise from their lack of understanding of their own nature and the world around them. And these men are the Prometheuses of the confused, modern world.

Indeed the world of modern men is one of intense suffering and anxiety. The disbelief and lack of faith in religious dogma reflected in English literature that started at the end of the Victorian Age and deepened with the World Wars continued even after the Second World War. The literature of the early twentieth century thus reflects a profound sense of frustration. The later poems of Yeats, works by T.S. Eliot, Lawrence, Conrad, Green and Joyce acutely present this depression.

William Golding, one of the most religious novelists of this age, began to write in the middle of the twentieth century. His voice, however, was not that of a traditional or orthodox Christian. As a modern man, he could not afford to follow any established religion, though he made liberal use of Christian symbols, ideas and motifs in his work. In "The World of William Golding," Peter Green calls him "a spiritual cosmologist" (172) as he concerned himself with the philosophy of all religions of the world. He combined pagan and Christian myths. Golding is also referred to as a "Deist" in the same essay, because he seems to believe unquestioningly in an ultimate existence, although this belief is not based on one distinct religion but on a firm faith in God.

Golding's novels reflect a deep interest in mankind. He seems, however, not so much concerned about the redeeming features of human nature, but concentrates on its depraved side. In his work, the fallen or the debased aspects of man and his intense sufferings are inter-linked, since his fallen nature goads man to commit sin and sin leads to suffering. Yet Golding does not necessarily follow the traditional formula of sin–suffering–redemption. There is no perfect redemption in Golding's world, as he describes the complex world of modern men. These men suffer without knowing the reason for their suffering, and sometimes their whole lives are spent thus. Even if they know the reason, they cannot always help it. A faithless, God-defying utilitarian—that is how modern man is, as portrayed by Golding through characters like Pincher Martin in *Pincher Martin*, Sammy Mountjoy in *Free Fall*, or Wilfred Barclay in *The Paper Men*.

Golding's men deliberately choose a safe aesthetic creed that does not demand religious practices. But this belief can scarcely sustain them. Whenever they are dragged out of their puny shells to confront things beyond their comprehension, they collapse. Those that survive often turn into halfcrazy monomaniacs like Barclay or groveling creatures like Jocelyn in *The Spire*. A very few like Sammy can hope for a purgatorial existence. Nevertheless, Golding's world is a bleak one; one may spend one's entire life searching for a speck of light without ever finding it. And to enhance the significance of this purgatorial suffering, Golding has brought in the myth of Prometheus. He has shown how man the maker, the inventor, and the builder, must also suffer for his knowledge, which is to say that he must suffer for being what he is. The mythical Prometheus had fore and hindsight, but the sufferings he went through were imposed upon him. In contrast, ordinary men of our world lack self-knowledge, and therefore, often embark on ventures that bring disaster on themselves as well as their fellow human beings.

The myth of Prometheus is thus used as a central theme in Golding's novels. In *Lord of the Flies* one comes across Piggy, the fat, asthmatic, myopic friend of the protagonist Ralph. Although outwardly a most unheroic figure, Piggy is Golding's version of Prometheus as it is with the thick lens of his spectacles that fire is lighted on the lonesome island. He is the voice of sanity and reason that Ralph slowly comes to recognize. It is always Piggy who talks about returning home, civilization, rules and regulations. In spite of being harassed and ridiculed by his friends, he always tries to help them. In the end, like Prometheus, he too embraces a terrible fate while trying to introduce reason to his 'savage' companions.

A modern Prometheus, however, cannot be flawless. Piggy too has his faults. He is hated by Ralph's rival Jack and his hunters. Unfortunately, he is unable to oppose them strongly. On the contrary, he asks for his share in the pig he did not hunt. He is wise, but his wisdom is tainted with fear, greed and irresponsibility. He adamantly refuses to acknowledge his or Ralph's share of responsibility in the death of Simon:

> "It was an accident," said Piggy suddenly, "that's what it was. An accident." His voice was shrill again. "Coming in the dark—he hadn't no business crawling like that out of the dark. He was batty. He asked for it." (193)

Piggy is afraid of the hunters. And he never fully realizes that they hate him in return for his sanity, and for his logical turn of mind. In a world of darkness and confusion, where man is deliberately committed to evil, a Prometheus like Piggy cannot survive. His dependence on logic makes him emotionally sterile. And intellect and logic alone cannot solve the problems he is faced with. He wants to return to a civilization that is incapable of protecting itself. So at first he is blinded and reduced to futility when the hunters steal his glasses, and in the end he is brutally killed by Jack and his hunters.

In his second book, *The Inheritors*, Golding does not introduce any distinct Promethean figure, but he makes deliberate references to the link between knowledge and evil, and indicates in the novel how they came upon man and led to his sufferings. Actually, he makes a fusion of the Biblical myth of Fall and Prometheus as in both knowledge and sufferings are interlinked. One of the two groups of men depicted in the novel, the Neanderthalers, lived in absolute peace and harmony until the arrival of the other group. These new men with their superior knowledge and craftsmanship, however, sought to destroy the older race. In this intricately woven story Golding shows how man with greater knowledge and ability has a tendency to destroy things and not to create.

In the course of the story Golding makes us note how the two innocent Neanderthalers called Lok and Fa come to taste the rotten honey procured by the new men. In the process they partake in the vision of a world seen through the eyes of the new race. In the earlier novel, Piggy had stolen fire from heaven; and in this one Lok and Fa eat the forbidden fruit. Naturally, as punishment they are expelled from their respective Edens. Of all the boys in *Lord of the Flies*, Piggy with his rational approach was possibly the most grown up person in the island world, always dwelling in a world beyond childhood ignorance. In *The Inheritors,* after his weird experience with the rotten honey, Lok loses his innocence. With a guilty feeling he realizes that the world that lies beyond him is not as simple as he had considered it to be. For Golding, however, this casting away from heaven is only a beginning. As Peter Green suggests, this expulsion "leads by slow degrees to the purgatorial Caucasian rocks, the eagle tearing endlessly at his vitals. So the scene is set for the third Aeschylean novel: *Pincher Martin*" (89).

Indeed the extraordinary setting of *Pincher Martin* is Aeschylean, since from the very beginning one can sense an inevitable fate maneuvering the life of the protagonist. In the beginning it seems like a typical adventure story set in the tradition of sagas about men against the sea. But soon one begins to notice the strange half-mythic, nightmare-like qualities of the struggle of the man called Christopher Martin. Ultimately, one realizes that none of the happenings associated with him had taken place in reality. They had been visualized in Martin's sub-conscious mind and had registered there in the space of a few moments. Pincher Martin is actually the story of a man who died twice. Golding's American publishers had published the book under the title *The Two Deaths of Christopher Martin.* Indeed, Martin is the man who has always desperately clung to life, and therefore, refuses to die when the moment comes, and goes through tremendous metaphysical suffering.

Through a series of flashbacks Martin's character is shown to be opposite to the heroic and mythic Prometheus. Martin is an unscrupulous egotist who stops at no depravity, no betrayal of love and friendship to fulfill his own ego. One of his victims portrays his depraved character with precision thus:

> He takes the best part, the best seat, the most money, the best notice, the best woman. He was born with his mouth and his flies wide open and both hands out to grab. He's a cosmic case of the bugger who gets his penny and someone else's bun. (120)

From the memory of an aching tooth Pincher fabricates his survival on a rock shaped like his own teeth (30). Like the seaweed, mussels, and shells cleaving to a rock, he lives and breathes. He sustains himself on these lowest forms of life and boasts that he can defeat nature. Samuel Hynes suggests that the qualities that keep Martin alive in the hostile atmosphere of the rock are also the qualities that make him repulsive:

> By seeing *this* character developed parallel to the Promethean survivor, we are forced to acknowledge that the same qualities that have kept him alive against such odds are the qualities that make him morally repulsive. And so in the middle of the eleventh chapter we face a moral dilemma: on what grounds can we condemn those qualities by which man survives? (127)

In his agony, Pincher begins to identify himself with mythical characters such as Prometheus, Atlas and Ajax. As Prometheus made men out of clay, Pincher makes a 'dwarf' in the shape of an old woman with rocks, and hopes to be spotted by some ship. He has led a godless life in the past, and continues to do so on the rock. He even refuses to die and grunts, "I'm damned if I die!" (72) This assertion is ironic, because by refusing to die, and by declining to commit himself to a selfless act, he chooses damnation. He visualizes himself as a mythic hero tormented alone on a rock, exposed to sun, rain, and all sorts of natural calamities. Like Odysseus, he is thrown on a rock by the sea; like Ajax he is deprived of his ship; like Atlas he is made to stand with the weight of the sky overhead; and like Prometheus he is tormented on a barren rock. He becomes a symbol of suffering humanity defying fate, crying out: "I am Atlas. I am Prometheus" (164).

But then, the figure of Pincher lacks the heroic stature of Prometheus and of the other mythical heroes he compares himself to. He does not, for example, fight the gods as Atlas did for the continued existence of his own race, the Titans. Not being a hero like Ajax, Pincher joined the navy only when driven to do so, and his intelligence was not used in heroic causes as Odysseus' was. And whereas Prometheus was conniving for the welfare of mankind in general, Pincher is selfish for his own personal gains. Though critics like Peter Green see Pincher Martin as a Promethean figure, as one who "sums up every quality that distinguishes man from the beasts" (90), he reminds one more of Loki—the mischievous giantgod of the Nordic myths. Loki was originally a giant allowed by the gods to live with them. He was later tied down to a rock for contriving the death of another god, Balder, and for his other misdeeds. There he continues to suffer under drops of venom which keep falling from a serpent's mouth, until Ragnarok, the final battle between the gods and the monsters. As a professional actor, Pincher may play the role of Prometheus or any other hero, but his 'Dwarf' fails to save him whereas Prometheus's man ultimately set him free from his purgatorial existence.

Nevertheless, in Pincher one can identify Campbell's version of a Modern Prometheus, portrayed in *The Hero with a Thousand Faces* (1949) as the self-centred hero who "instead of submitting to all of the initiatory tests, has like Prometheus, simply darted to his goal (by violence, quick device, or luck) and plucked the boon for the world . . . then the powers that he has unbalanced may react so sharply that he will be blasted from within or without—crucified, like Prometheus, on the rock of his own violated unconscious" (37). Pincher has always taken anything that caught his fancy, done everything a man would to pacify his own ego, and has been an epitome of selfishness throughout his life. And so at the end of it he has to suffer, though he refuses to accept or understand any of it.

Modern men are puny creatures absorbed in the triviality of everyday life. Golding himself once commented on the mythical aspect of Pincher, that he was "a fallen man . . . Very much fallen—he's fallen more than most" (Hynes 132). The author also said that he had tried to make Pincher as unpleasant and nasty as he could, and was interested in seeing how the critics identified their own selves in him. Thus it becomes very clear that modern men would not accept a great heroic Prometheus as their spokesman, but a dwarfed one who would be very like themselves, or someone like Eliot's Phlebas the Phoenician in the *The Waste Land*, whom Pincher sees in himself:

> I was young and handsome with an eagle profile and wavy hair;
> I was brilliantly clever and I went out to fight your enemies. I
> endured in water, I fought the whole sea . . . Now I am thin and
> weak . . . my hair is white with salt and suffering. My eyes are
> dull stones—(188)

At the end, however, Pincher is denied even of a purgatorial stay. As Golding himself commented in an interview:

> He is not fighting for bodily survival but for his continuing
> identity in the face of what will smash it and sweep it away—
> the black lightning, the compassion of God. For Christopher,
> the Christ-bearer has become Pincher Martin who is little but
> greed. Just to be Pincher is purgatory; to be Pincher for eternity
> is hell. (Kermode 60)

The mythic Prometheus was redeemed for his human qualities. Though he flouted the gods, he was compassionate toward humanity. He created and nursed something that was able to relieve him of his sufferings. On the other hand, Pincher nurses and nourishes his own arrogantly proud self. The only heaven or freedom it can provide him with is that rock. Appropriately enough, the last portion of Pincher's body that is destroyed are his claw-like hands. To escape his insignificant existence, Eliot's protagonist in "The Love Song of J. Alfred Prufrock" wanted to become "a pair of ragged claws / Scuttling across the floors of the silent seas." Pincher, as if to justify his borrowed name truly becomes so. After all, he has been a 'pincher' throughout his life, and with his claw-like hands he never built anything fruitful, but always tried to grab what belonged to others.

Through the figure of Pincher Martin, Golding commits himself to criticizing man's capacity to reason. Pincher thinks that with his intellect, reason, and sanity he can survive. But the author notes pointedly that in man's battle for salvation much more is needed than these qualities. Love, faith and selfless actions, for instance, seem more effective to Golding in this case. And these are precisely the qualities absent in Pincher's character. It seems that he willfully blocks his way to salvation. In their book, *The World of William Golding* (1965), Oldsey and Weintraub comment that there are no redeemers in Golding's theology. That the modern Prometheus must continue suffering without redemption appears to be the ultimate message of *Pincher Martin*.

Golding was less successful in using the Prometheus myth in the novels he wrote after *Pincher Martin*. Yet the single play Golding wrote, *The Brass Butterfly*, later published as a novella under the title "Envoy Extraordinary," in his collection called *The Scorpion God*, presents a very fascinating Promethian figure in the character of Phanocles. Phanocles is a scientist and inventor who brings several astonishing gifts for the Emperor of Rome. He claims that through these epoch-making inventions, which consist of a pressure cooker, a steam engine, explosives, and the technique of printing, he can make man advanced in technology and change the world. The Caesar accepts the pressure cooker enthusiastically, calling it the most Promethean invention of all. The inventions of steam engine and explosives prove to be disastrous as foretold by the Emperor when he first set his eyes upon them. He also refuses to do anything with the method of printing. The farsighted Emperor explains that people were ready to accept a small change, like cooking in a pressure cooker, but they were not yet prepared for a revolution.

The mythic Prometheus gave men fire and that brought a revolutionary change in the life of prehistoric man. But as a realist Golding knows that the receiver of the gift must also be ready and willing to accept it. Phanocles, say Oldsey and Weintraub, "sees no limits to what man can do with his universe, but cannot comprehend the danger of playing Prometheus" (153). He is able to see only the good side of technological advancement, but is completely blind to the baser instincts of human nature. Phanocles is a reminder of Mary Shelley's Frankenstein, whom its author herself called "the modern Prometheus," in his attempt to unlock the secret of creation. Frankenstein thought that by bringing the dead back to life he would change human history. But what he created turned into a monster. Somewhat like him, Phanocles wants to play the part of Prometheus by bestowing his notable gifts on common men who shrink away from them. The Roman soldiers, whom he wants to present with the gift of gunpowder, prefer hand to hand combat. Even the galley slaves do not like steam engines, as they fear that for the new mechanism they will cease to have any meaning for their masters. Now at least they have a life, however miserable it might be. If engines take away their work, they will simply be eliminated. So the wonderful gifts of Promethean Phanocles are refused on the ground that they are dangerous and self-destructive.

Perhaps what Golding wants to suggest is that human beings have never been quite ready to accept all that modern technology has offered them. And the situation has not much altered since Caesar's time, although that was some two thousand years back. Far from utilizing the power put into his hands, man is using it wildly to destroy his own world. Thus Golding makes us ponder whether man can get anywhere despite the Promethean gifts bestowed upon him.

The last of Golding's Promethean figures is Ionides Peisistratides in *The Double Tongue* (1994), the incomplete novel that was published after the author's death. Ionides is possibly one of the most truthful representations of modern characters portrayed by Golding. He is shown to be an Athenian and an interpreter in the Oracle of Delphi during a time of the Roman rule in Greece. His friends call him Ion, and this is significant since according to Greek myths, Ion was a son and priest of the god Apollo. Although he appears to be a devotee of Apollo, Golding's Ion is virtually an atheist. He does not believe in the existence of divinities, but accepts their necessity. For him gods are the creation of a class of people who intend to use them to rule the mob. He himself uses the oracle chiefly for espionage.

Ion resembles Golding's earlier creation Pincher Martin. Like Martin he believes too fervently in his own identity. But he is not a greedy "pinch-all" like the protagonist of the earlier novel. Ion is a learned person and considers himself to be a wise man. He firmly believes in and dreams of an independent Greece. He chooses Arieka, a simple rural girl, to be a seeress in the temple of Delphi and uses her partly to conceal his own spying activities.

Golding gives to Ion the rhetoric of a modern Prometheus—one who would use gods for the profit of man:

> (Arieka): "Surely the god doesn't need to be told what is happening?"
> (Ionides): "Reminded, shall we say. It's a good theological point. What does the god need to know? After all he needs

to know what the question is. Therefore he needs to know
something. Therefore there is no reason why he should not need
to know what is happening in Asia, or Africa, or Achaia. . . . Or
Rome." (63)

Ionides cannot bring himself to believe in gods or a supreme existence. He is also shown to be a homosexual. For Golding, this is a
person cultivating unnatural practices. He is someone who has never
faced dishonour until almost the very end. Reminiscent of Piggy and
Pincher, Ionides is a flawed Prometheus in his search for something
his reason and intellect cannot provide him.

The close and compassionate relationship between Ion and Arieka,
and Ion's fondness for his slave Perseus apparently make him a more
likable and redeemable character than Pincher Martin. Nevertheless,
like Golding's other Promethean characters, Ion too leans too much
on his own beliefs. He considers himself a steady and sturdy freedom
fighter although his country Greece seems quite content under the
Roman Empire. When the Romans let him go free as a harmless
conspirator, he feels robbed of his identity, honour, and lifelong
beliefs. That is something he cannot accept, and as a result, loses his
sanity. Although the novel is an unfinished one, Golding does enough
to suggest the pitiful ending of Ionides fully and superbly by relating
it from the standpoint of Arieka:

> He did become silly, not in the way he always had been at
> times, but a silliness without any wisdom in it. There was
> oblivion and presently his body died. I did not suffer with him
> as so often in these cases of extreme age, he had really died a
> long time before. (164)

Somewhat like Pincher, he too has to face death twice. Whereas
Pincher's subconscious mind continued to struggle even after death,
Ion's body continued to live after his mind had succumbed to death.
The nature of problem in these two men is the same. When they fully
realize the loss of their identity, they have to accept death. Although
Pincher appears to be the more egotistical of the two men, to a
modern reader Pincher also seems more appealing and acceptable as
a modern Prometheus. He grabs whatever he can lay his hands on. He
cheats, he lies and does all sorts of unspeakable things a man can do.

He also suffers terribly, but unlike Prometheus, and like the suffering millions of the modern world, he does not know why he suffers. Yet, he is accepted by the readers as a modern Prometheus because he is a creation of the world they themselves belong to. And like Pincher, too, they do not know the reason behind their sufferings that the modern life-style has inflicted them with.

On December 10, 1950, in his acceptance speech to the Nobel Academy, referring to the impending Cold War and constant fear, William Faulkner said, "the young man or woman writing today has forgotten the problems of the human heart in conflict with itself which alone can make good writing because only that is worth writing about, worth the agony and the sweat."[1] Indeed, the theme lying at the center of Modern literature is the suffering of the human mind, and the soul struggling with itself. This idea explains why the figure of Prometheus—the archetypal symbol of suffering humanity, has always been so attractive to writers and critics of all ages. Twentieth century men and women often pride themselves on their sense of privacy, and of the progress they have made in the field of communication. But what they have achieved amount only to screens that have shut off their thoughts and feelings. They have managed to lock themselves up in their purgatories, with only occasional social calls made at each other's drawing rooms. They are, as writers such as Eliot, Conrad, and Greene have suggested, afraid of one another and of human relationships, and thus they identify themselves with Prometheus in their sufferings, paying the price of knowledge and aspiration.

Golding was a theologist with an aversion to the theories practiced by Darwin, Marx and Freud. In the last chapter of their book, Oldsey and Weintraub note that Golding did not consider it proper to look for a pattern in every field of life. In particular, he disliked Freud's various theories of psychological conflicts and interpretations. But myth critics like Frye and Campbell have suggested that "the myth critic sees the work holistically, as the manifestation of vitalizing, integrative forces arising from the depths of humankind's collective psyche" (Guerin et al 167). Consciously or unconsciously, Golding himself set patterns while drawing and sketching his characters. For example, his Promethean characters usually have borrowed identities. We never come to know the real name of Piggy. Christopher Martin becomes Pincher Martin when he joins the navy. Golding's last hero Ionides is mostly known by the name of

Ion, the mythical son of Apollo. Fools and simpletons in his novels come closest to identify or discover meaning of the universe. Similarly, through his Promethean figures, he attempts to throw light on man's suffering from different perspectives.

A critic of the lack of morality in modern men, Golding nevertheless follows the footsteps of his subjects closely and sympathetically. Understanding the intensity of man's suffering and pain, he shows that in a world such as ours, no redeemer can be perfect. In view of all these ideas, Golding's visions have been often termed pessimistic. The figure of Prometheus, however, stands as a saviour of mankind. By bringing back this redeeming symbol from time to time, Golding perhaps wanted to indicate that even though the world is corrupt and vile, there is always a possibility of redemption. True that his Promethean characters are not always strong or faultless, or even effective enough to enlighten the dark, chaotic world, yet they symbolize the undying human spirit that refuses to surrender in the most oppressive and overwhelming situation.

NOTE

1. *Nobel Lectures, Literature 1901–1967.* 27 Jan. 2006. 20 June 2006. <http://nobelprize.org/cgibin/literature/laureates/1949/Faulkner-speech.html>

WORKS CITED

Bayley, John. "The Impersonality of William Golding: Some Implications and Comparisons." *William Golding: the Man and his Books.* London: Faber and Faber Ltd., 1986.

Campbell, Joseph. *The Hero with a Thousand Faces.* Princeton University Press, 1949. Rpt. London: Fontana Press, 1993.

Eliot, T.S. "The Love Song of J. Alfred Prufrock." *Selected Poems.* London: Faber and Faber Ltd., 1978.

Golding, William G. *Lord of the Flies.* London: Faber and Faber Ltd., 1954. Rpt. Delhi: The Oxford University Press, 1980.

———. *The Inheritors.* London: Faber and Faber Ltd., 1955. Rpt.1988.

———. *Pincher Martin.* London: Faber and Faber Ltd., 1956. Rpt.1990.

———. *The Scorpion God.* London: Faber and Faber Ltd., 1971. Rpt.1973.

———. *The Double Tongue.* London: Faber and Faber Ltd., 1994. Rpt.1996.

Green, Peter. "The World of William Golding." *Transactions and Proceedings of the Royal Society of Literature* 32 (1963). Rpt. *William Golding's* Lord of the Flies: *A Sourcebook.* Ed. W. Nelson. New York: 1963.

Guerin, Wilfred L., Earle Labor, Lee Morgan, Jeanne C. Reesman and John R. Willingham. *A Handbook of Critical Approaches to Literature.* Rev. ed. New York: Oxford UP, 2004.

Hynes, Samuel. "On Pincher Martin" (1976). *William Golding: Novels, 1954–67.* London: The Macmillan Press Ltd., 1985.

Kermode, Frank. "Golding's Intellectual Economy" (1962). *William Golding: Novels, 1954–67.* London: The Macmillan Press Ltd., 1985.

Oldsey, Bernard S. and Stanley Weintraub. *The Art of William Golding.* Harcourt, New York, Inc., 1965.

HAMLET
(WILLIAM SHAKESPEARE)

"The Grave Diggers in 'Hamlet'"
by Frederick Warde, in *The Fools of Shakespeare:*
An Interpretation of their Wit and Wisdom (1915)

INTRODUCTION

In this selection from *The Fools of Shakespeare: An Inter-pretation of Their Wit, Wisdom and Personalities*, Frederick Warde explicates one of the comic scenes in this famous tragedy—the passage in which the two men, who, in digging Ophelia's grave, engage in playful conversation, bantering with each other and Hamlet. For Warde, the two are the sort of tricksters one might find in everyday life, artful representa-tions fashioned by Shakespeare, the ultimate artisan, who captures the most poignant sentiment, infuses it with wit, and gives performers endless possibilities for play. Thus, Warde concludes by regaling us with antecdotes about actors as tricksters who elicit laughter from audiences and one another.

"Has this fellow no feeling of his business, that he sings at grave-making?"

Warde, Frederick. "The Grave Diggers in 'Hamlet.'" *The Fools of Shakespeare: An Interpretation of their Wit and Wisdom.* 1915. Los Angeles, Calif: Times-Mirror Press, 1923. 153–173.

It would scarcely seem possible that a graveyard attached to a church, with a half-dug grave in the foreground, for the scene; midnight or near thereto, for the time; a pickax, a spade, a heap of fresh earth, some human skulls and bones for the properties; and two grave-diggers for the *dramatis personae* would furnish a location and material for comedy and humor, yet in the first scene of the fifth act of the tragedy of "Hamlet," Shakespeare has taken these materials and conditions, and given us a series of incidents, a variety of character, and a dialogue replete with the most delightful comedy, brilliant repartee, ready wit and subtle humor.

The circumstances are these: A young lady attached to the court of the King of Denmark has been drowned, the general opinion being that she committed suicide. In the time of Shakespeare, and prior thereto, such unfortunates were denied Christian burial. Their remains were interred outside of consecrated ground without service or any of the rites of the church. In fact, it was not unusual to bury them at the intersection of the highways, very deeply, and to drive a strong stake through the body. The object of this barbarous proceeding being, to impale and destroy the evil spirit, which the prevailing superstition supposed to be in possession of the suicide. In the present instance, the King has commanded that the remains of the unfortunate lady should be buried in the consecrated ground of the church-yard.

The King's command, violating all the ancient and accepted traditions of the church, arouses the indignation of the old sexton, who combines the office of grave-digger. To this personage Shakespeare has given such a strong individuality, such a pungency of wit and wealth of humor, together with such delightful touches of nature, making it so true to life, that I cannot but think the poet must have had a prototype in his own observation and experience.

In the list of characters in the play this personage and his assistant are set down as "Two Clowns as Grave-diggers," but modern editors have separated them in the cast, and called them "First and Second Grave-diggers." This method has been adopted in all the acting editions, and in the following observations I shall so designate them.

The First Grave-digger is of a type that may be found in many of our country villages today,—a quaint sententious old fellow "dressed in a little brief authority," and full of his own importance. He has a little knowledge of law, quotes one or two legal phrases in Latin incorrectly, and preaches a crude idea of socialism to his younger assistant, much to the awe and admiration of that simple individual, who addresses his acknowledged superior as "Goodman delver."

I picture the old fellow in my mind as robust of figure, ruddy of feature, with distinct evidences of bibulous taste on his nose and cheeks, a humorous twinkle in his eyes, in spite of an assumed severity, dressed in the homely smock of the peasant of that place and period, and about fifty years of age. He has the courage of his convictions for he has seldom found any one to combat them, so he advances his arguments with the authority of one whose dictum is not to be questioned. Should these fail him, however, he can command the respect of his fellows by a ready tongue and homely wit, as exampled in his dialogue with his subordinate, and later with Prince Hamlet.

He is no respecter of persons: his replies to the questions of Hamlet being as straightforward and blunt as those to his peasant companion, while his replications in the exchange of wit with the former indicate so much irreverence and independence, that it draws from the Prince the significant observation "By the Lord, Horatio. . . . the age is grown so picked that the toe of the peasant comes so near the heel of the courtier, he galls his kibe."

The character of the old sexton bears in some small degree a resemblance to that of "Dogberry" in "Much Ado About Nothing," in its self-importance, but it is more consistent, less bombastic, and never servile.

Our first acquaintance with the old fellow is made at the beginning of the first scene of the fifth act of the play, when he enters the churchyard followed by his assistant, who carries a spade and a mattock. That his mind is disturbed by the violation of ancient traditions is evidenced in his first speech given in the form of a question to his follower: "Is she to be buried in Christian burial that willfully seeks her own salvation?" To which his assistant, evidently a younger man, with the assurance of accurate information, replies: "I tell thee she is; and therefore make her grave straight: the crowner hath sat on her and finds it Christian burial."

Now comes the inherent love of argument in the old man: "How can that be, unless she drowned herself in her own defense?"

The younger man has no reply to this proposition, but contents himself with reiteration "Why, 'tis found so." To the ordinary peasant of the time this would have concluded the matter, but the sexton, who has small respect for the verdict of the crowner's quest, and perceiving an opportunity to expound his wisdom, proceeds with his argument.

It requires little imagination to realize the pomposity of the sturdy old stickler for tradition, as he emphasizes his points; or to note the syllabic orotundity with which he utters the Latin phrase that he has probably heard in some legal proceedings, and memorized for use at a future time, to awe his adversary with his learning; and to observe the originality of his logic in the conclusion that the lady's death was not accidental. "It must be 'se offendendo'; it cannot be else. For here lies the point: if I drown myself wittingly, it argues an act: and an act hath three branches; it is, to act, to do, and to perform: argal, she drowned herself wittingly."

His assistant is not without some self-assertion in spite of Latin and logic, and makes a valiant attempt to enter a protest against the old man's prejudiced conclusions. "Nay, but hear you, goodman delver." But the goodman will not be silenced with flattery nor does he propose to honor his youthful disputant with more controversy, but proceeds to demonstrate his theory in a practical fashion.

Taking his spade he lays it down on the smooth turf of the church-yard, explaining: "Here lies the water! good." Then at some little distance from the spade he stands the pick or mattock on end: "Here stands the man, good," and taking a position between the two implements, with judicial gravity, he delivers himself as follows: "If the man go to this water and drown himself, it is will he, nill he, he goes; mark you that; but if the water come to him and drown him, he drowns not himself: argal, he that is not guilty of his own death shortens not his own life."

This demonstration almost convinces the rustic skeptic, but he is still in doubt as to the legal aspect of the case, and inquires: "But is this law?" "Ay, marry, is't; crowner's quest law," concludes the old man.

Finding no argument to combat this conclusion, the young fellow falls back on the elemental socialistic question of human inequality. "Will you ha' the truth on't? If this had not been a gentlewoman she should have been buried out o' Christian burial." The old fellow fully indorses this proposition, and emphasizes it with a still more forcible example, though, perhaps some may not recognize the advantages of the special privileges quoted. "Why, there thou sayest: and the more pity that great folks should have countenance in this world to drown or hang themselves, more than their even-Christian. Come, my spade." The old man takes his spade, but before proceeding to work, asserts the natural dignity of his trade, and bemoans the degeneracy of the age; which provokes the following bit of delightful equivoque:

> 1ST GRA. There is no ancient gentlemen but gardeners, ditchers and grave-makers: they hold up Adam's profession.
> 2ND GRA. Was he a gentleman?
> 1ST GRA. A' the first that ever bore arms.
> 2ND GRA. Why, he had none.
> 1ST GRA. What; art a heathen? How dost thou understand the Scripture? The Scripture says Adam digged: Could he dig without arms?

After a hearty laugh at the jest, the old fellow propounds a conundrum, a very popular form of entertainment among simple country wits. However, to realize the significance of the riddle and the preceding dialogue, it is essential to have the full picture in one's mind: the solemn background of the church, the grim environment of the old headstones and tombs, ghostlike in the midnight shadows, the newly made grave waiting for its tenant, the odor of the fresh earth, and the homely figures of the two sextons with the dismal tools of their trade, form a combination in strong contrast with the humor of the dialogue, and yet in complete harmony with the spirit of the occasion. The old grave-digger standing with one foot on his spade, his eyes sparkling with humor, emphasizes with his index finger the question that is to confuse the wits of his younger assistant; the other leaning on the mattock listens with parted lips, eager to catch every word, and match his wit against that of the veteran humorist.

"What is he that builds stronger than either the mason, the ship-wright, or the carpenter?" The young man is puzzled for a moment, scratches his head, then with a look of triumph, answers quickly: "The gallows-maker; for that frame outlives a thousand tenants."

It is a good answer and the old fellow is not slow to acknowledge it, but it is not the correct one, so the momentary satisfaction of the young man is turned to chagrin, and his wits spurred to another effort. How the old fellow chuckles as the young one wrestles with the knotty problem, and how deliciously is the patronage of the old egotist's superior wisdom expressed in the passage that follows: "I like thy wit well, in good faith: The gallows does well: but how does it well? It does well to those that do ill: now thou dost ill to say the gallows is built stronger than the church: argal: the gallows may do well to thee. To't again, come."

The young man repeats the proposition: "Who builds stronger than a mason, a shipwright, or a carpenter?" and ruefully struggles to find another fitting reply. But his mental faculties are dull; it is beyond him; he has to confess it, and the old fellow does not spare him, but accentuates his triumph, and completes the poor fellow's humiliation by giving the answer, and then dismissing him to fetch a stoop of liquor.

"Cudgel thy brains no more about it, for your dull ass will not mend his pace with beating, and when you are asked this question next, say 'a grave-maker': the houses that he makes last till doomsday. Go, get thee to Yaughan, fetch me a stoop of liquor."

The traditional business at this point was for the old grave-digger to remove with great deliberation a number of vests or waist-coats of various colors and patterns, carefully fold and lay them at one side, and then roll up his sleeves before descending into the uncompleted grave to proceed with his work. This absurd piece of business has, however, long since been discarded, and the actor of today plays the part with more appropriate action, consistent with the character, and within scope of human possibility. Laying his spade and pick by the side of the grave he gradually lowers himself into it with the natural effort of a man of his age, then in a workman-like manner proceeds first to loosen the earth with his pick, then to throw it out, together with the skulls and bones as the dialogue calls for them, chanting the words of the old ballad at the proper cues, emphasizing the effort, and punctuating his singing with the strokes of his mattock, and the work of the spade.

It is at this point that Prince Hamlet and his friend Horatio appear outside of the low wall that encloses the graveyard. Seeing the old man's grim occupation, and hearing his humorous song, the incongruity of the proceeding surprises the Prince, who inquires of his friend: "Has this fellow no feeling of his business that he sings at grave-making?" To which Horatio sagely replies: "Custom hath made it in him a property of easiness."

Unconscious of observation, the sexton continues his work and his song, throwing out the earth, some human bones, and two chapless skulls; while the Prince and his friend look on and philosophize on the gruesome relics that are so irreverently handled by the old man. The second skull thrown from the grave is about to roll away, when the sexton strikes it sharply with his spade to imbed it in the soft, fresh earth. This apparent brutal indifference to the grim remains of poor mortality is the subject of further speculative philosophy on the part of the Prince, who finally steps over the wall, advances to the side of the grave, and addresses the grave-digger, asking: "Who's grave's this, sirrah?"

I imagine the old man has been asked this question so frequently, and by all manner of people, that he has grown impatient at the query, and with scarcely a glance at his questioner he answers abruptly, "Mine, sir," and continues his work and his song.

I recall when I was a very small boy, living in an English country village, an old cobbler, whose shop, or rather stall, was on the side of the street by which I went to school. He was a quaint, good-natured old fellow, and I would frequently stop, watch him at work and talk to him. All of his work was done by hand. He used to sit at the end of a low bench on which were all of his materials and tools, in little square compartments. He wore a large pair of spectacles with horn frames, and would bend over a wooden last, held fast to his knee by a circular leathern strap from his foot, make holes with an awl, insert and draw the wax end tightly, as he attached the upper to the sole of the shoe he was making. I used to regard him with great interest, and wonder at his dexterity and rapidity. I knew practically everybody in the village, and with boyish curiosity would ask the old cobbler who the shoes were for. He would invariably reply: "Mr. Wearem." This puzzled me for some time, as I knew no one of that name; but ultimately I comprehended: it was a reproof to my curiosity, the old man's standing jest, and a whimsical evasion of the question he was asked so frequently. I find a parallel in my old cobbler's jest and the grave-digger's reply to Hamlet.

The Prince, however, is not disposed to be silenced by this discourtesy, but makes a rejoinder that bluntly charges the old man with a lie. Against this accusation the grave-digger stoutly defends himself, and makes countercharge with a shrewd wit in a dialogue replete with ingenious punning, and a crude logic that carries his point, and compels recognition from the Prince, who diplomatically changes the subject.

To facilitate the reader's appreciation, I quote the dialogue that follows the grave-digger's reply:

> HAM. I think it be thine indeed, for thou liest in't.
>
> GRA. You lie out on't, sir, and therefore 'tis not yours: for my part, I do not lie in't and yet, it is mine.
>
> HAM. Thou dost lie in't, to be in't and to say it is thine: 'tis for the dead, not for the quick: therefore thou liest.
>
> GRA. 'Tis a quick lie, sir, 'twill away again from me to you.
>
> HAM. What man dost thou dig it for?
>
> GRA. For no man, sir.
>
> HAM. What woman then?
>
> GRA. For none neither.
>
> HAM. Who is to be buried in't ?
>
> GRA. One that was a woman sir, but, rest her soul, she's dead.
>
> . . . .
>
> HAM. How long hast thou been a grave-maker?

The answer is given with characteristic loquacity, by the old man, who still maintains his reputation as a wit-snapper.

The most casual reader of Shakespeare cannot but observe how much is connoted as well as expressed in many of the brief passages of the poet. In answer to the above simple question, the valor of the late King, and the martial character of the Danes is suggested; we are told the day of Hamlet's birth; we learn of the gossip of the people and the general impression of the Prince's mental condition, the supposed reason of his despatch to England, together with some satirical allusions to the people of that country; and, while the old man ingeniously reveals the age of Hamlet, he incidentally suggests his own. "I have been sexton here, man and boy, thirty years."

This, granting he was about twenty years old when he began his work as a grave-maker, and it is improbable to suppose that he would be entrusted with such serious work at an earlier age, would make him fifty at this time, as I have before suggested.

Hamlet's next question: "How long will a man lie in the earth ere he rot?" provokes more punning by the old man and some very plain and original reasoning as to the time and process of the decay of mortal remains; those of a tanner in particular.

The dialogue is terminated by the selection of one of the skulls by the grave-digger to illustrate his arguments, which the old man asserts is the skull of Yorick, the late King's jester.

The "property of easiness," suggested by Horatio, is again exampled by the irreverence and familiarity with which the grave-maker handles this skull. As he recalls the pranks of the dead jester, he laughingly slaps the hollow temples of the unconscious remnant, as if he were boxing the ears of the living jester, and gleefully chuckles as memory revives the "mad rogue's" wit and humor, before handing it to the Prince.

This incident diverts the mind of Hamlet from his catechism of the grave-digger to tender memories of his childhood's friend and playmate, so that the sentiment of the scene is changed, but to this I have referred at some length elsewhere.

The funeral procession enters the churchyard, the sexton assists in lowering the body of the unfortunate lady to its last resting place, and with that duty done, the character of the grave-digger in the play is concluded. But if we permit our imagination a little scope, we might see, after the funeral party has left the scene, the old fellow shoveling the earth back into the newly-tenanted grave, and hear the refrain of his quaint song borne upon the stillness of the early morning air:

> A pick-axe, and a spade, a spade,
> For and a shrouding sheet
> O a pit of clay for to be made
> For such a guest is meet.

The most conspicuous figure that I can recall as a representative of the First Grave-digger, was the late J.H. McVicker, founder and proprietor of McVicker's Theater, Chicago. He played the part when en tour with Edwin Booth, his son-in-law, who was then under his management. I had the honor of being Mr. Booth's principal support, and played the part of Laertes. Mr. McVicker was of Irish and Scotch descent, and combined the general characteristics of those two nationalities. He was strong in his own opinions, somewhat harsh and dictatorial in his manner, but with a vein of quaint humor that was much in evidence when not obsessed with business. Hardly the temperament for an artist, you would say? True! but in the case of the old sexton these very qualities fitted the character. Mr. McVicker used little if any make-up. In fact he did not need any; he was at this time, I should judge, about sixty years of age, rotund of figure, full in the face, which was clean-shaven, and with sparse gray hair, that was always disheveled. He dressed the part in a dark brown tunic or smock; his arms were bare, but his legs and feet were encased in rough buskins and sandals. He looked the part to perfection; he did not have to act, only to speak the lines, and he was the old grave-digger. The self-importance, the grave assumption of knowledge, and the air of "brief authority" over his fellow-worker were finely given; while his surprised expression at the audacity of the younger man in questioning his judgment was a splendid illustration of the assurance of ignorance and self-conceit.

At the time of which I speak (1876), very little, if any, scenery and few properties were carried by touring dramatic companies. We carried none, but depended on the stock of the theaters we visited for the scenery, and borrowed the properties and furniture from local stores, giving in return complimentary tickets to the performance. The two human skulls were especially difficult to obtain in the smaller towns. Our property-man, however, was of considerable experience and full of resource in an emergency and when unable to obtain the real article invariably found a substitute that served the purpose. For the skulls he used two large turnips, shaping them like the human head, excavating the eye sockets, hollowing the jaws and mouth, and then coloring them with brown paint. Indeed, they looked remarkably well and few of the audience could detect the imposition from the front of the theater. One night, however, when Mr. McVicker, as the grave-digger, handed the supposed skull to Mr. Booth, as Hamlet, the latter gentleman failed to grasp it securely and it fell with a heavy thud to the stage. The deception was then obvious, and the audience roared with laughter. But worse consequences followed. The confounded turnip rolled down to the footlights, knocked off one of the tips of the gas jets (electricity was not then in use), a big flame rose from the broken jet, a cry of fire was raised, and a panic in the audience was only averted by the prompt action of the leader of the orchestra, who reached over and smothered the flaming gas-jet with his pocket handkerchief.

On another occasion, during our Southern tour, Mr. McVicker called me to one side prior to the beginning of the last act of Hamlet, and whispered in my ear, "Watch me when I hand Edwin the skull, tonight." I watched.

It appeared that our property-man had been unable to obtain even turnips with which to fashion skulls for the graveyard scene, so he had procured a couple of very large Bermuda onions, cut and perforated them as he had done the turnips, colored, and placed them in the grave, Mr. McVicker alone being cognizant of the character of the remains. The grave-digger threw them out at the proper cue, and the deception passed unnoticed, but when the old sexton handed the supposed skull of poor dead Yorick to Mr. Booth, who had a particular aversion to onions in any form, the aroma of that mutilated sphere, mingled with the odor of the paint, became so offensive to him that he was seized with nausea, and with difficulty completed the delivery of the tender apostrophe to the remains of his dead friend. However, his final questions to Horatio, as he handed, with unusual alacrity, the repulsive vegetable to that gentleman: "Dost thou think Alexander looked o' this fashion i' the earth? And smelt so? pah!" had a significance that heretofore had not been in evidence. Subsequently, Mr. Booth joined in a hearty laugh at the incident, and shortly afterwards two human skulls were purchased for the performance.

HOUSE MADE OF DAWN
(N. SCOTT MOMADAY)

"The Trickster Discourse of *House Made of Dawn*"
by Susan R. Bowers, Susquehanna University

N. Scott Momaday's *House Made of Dawn,* the novel that inaugurated the Native American literary renaissance and helped force scholars and other readers to take Native American literature seriously, turned 40 in 2008. The novel's use of "trickster energy" allowed Momaday both to draw attention to the boundaries between cultures and to show how individuals caught in the no-man's-land can find their way.

Abel, the protagonist of *House Made of Dawn,* is a member of a tiny pueblo modeled on Jemez, New Mexico, the village where Momaday grew up. We first meet him returning home from World War II so inebriated that he staggers off the bus and cannot recognize the grandfather who raised him. Abel is so far removed from his tribal upbringing that he misreads a man's ritual behavior toward him and murders him. After serving his prison term, he is relocated to Los Angeles, where he finds a community of displaced Native Americans, but nonetheless is profoundly alienated. When he returns home again after a deadly beating, he discovers that his grandfather is dying.

Abel cannot re-enter tribal society because his experiences outside the tribe—in the war and later in prison and Los Angeles—have so estranged him from its relationships and practices. But his tribal upbringing also renders him incapable of joining the majority culture, so that he becomes the quintessential outsider, wandering in the liminal space of the in-between.

The in-between, the space between boundaries of all kinds, is the realm of the trickster, an ancient figure who is sometime messenger and sometime thief, mediator between heaven and earth, the living and the dead. Tricksters are characteristic of many cultures, but as Alan R. Velie declares, "The trickster is an archetype universal among Indians, and in most tribes the most important mythic figure" (324). Tricksters are multidimensional. Michael Carroll contends that Trickster's two most important roles, usually held at the same time, are as selfish buffoon and the culture hero "who makes human society possible" (301). The Native American trickster possesses the traits of such creatures as coyotes and ravens. Velie points out that Momaday has been most influenced by the Kiowa and Blackfeet tricksters (Sendeh and Napi, respectively). Both are benefactors of their tribes—Sendeh provides the Kiowa with the buffalo and the sun, and Napi is the creator of the Blackfeet. But he notes that these "tricksters are amoral figures" with huge appetites who are "usually irresponsible and often cruel and bloody" (324).

Multiple, often conflicting interpretations have been offered of who or what is the trickster in *House Made of Dawn:* the narrative itself; Santiago, the legendary hero of the pueblo's founding; the "priest of the sun" whom Abel meets in Los Angeles; or Abel himself. All of these interpretations afford understanding into the dynamics of Momaday's text.

The leading candidate in much recent criticism of *House Made of Dawn* is the narrative itself: Momaday's multiple narrative voices, seemingly random insertion of flashbacks, ambiguous time references, and frame (the beginning taken from the ending) often make for a confusing read. The trickster-like narrative of *House Made of Dawn* doesn't allow us to use the usual codes with which we read texts. However, as Frederic Jameson tells us, those codes actually support a political agenda (9), which Elizabeth Ammons identifies as "the preservation of elite white male power in the United States" (viii). However, Dee Horne points out that Native American writers can avoid and confront these codes "by creating a multi-voiced discourse that illustrates the 'complex relationalities' of power" (15). Thus the form alone of *House Made of Dawn* can be seen as undermining the hegemonic white culture with which tribal peoples must negotiate. Paul Tidwell seems to agree. He sees the fragmentary narrative, the complexity of the visions, and the "oddly juxtaposed images" as producing a subversive critique (626). Similarly, Guillermo Bartelt points to the heteroglossia (the conflicting world views revealed by different kinds of discourse) in Momaday's text, which he sees as the product of "the clash of antagonistic ideologies—Native and Anglo-American ... marked by sudden defamiliarizing shifts in register" (469). He traces how the disruptions to the hegemonic registers (the uses of language by the dominant culture) reflect Abel's psychological and spiritual fragmentation.

The novelist and critic Gerald Vizenor characterizes narratives such as Momaday's as "trickster discourse" and points out that Native American stories are imagined from "wisps of narratives":

> Tribal tricksters are comic *holotropes* ...
> an invitation to a reader and listener to deconstruct the
> wisps in a language game. (Vizenor 5)

Vizenor seems to be saying that these narratives are not so much a stable whole as a fragile construction made of pieces of stories, a construction that, like a trickster, can change shape at any time. In this way, *House Made of Dawn* mimics the temporality of oral narrative, so that for any given reader, it is a particular momentary whole constantly on the verge of collapse. In a similar vein, Amy J. Elias identifies what she calls a "coyote aesthetics" that features the fragmentation of trickster tales and the constant flux of the trickster world (193). Most significantly, she points out that this aesthetics can "allow Native American writers to counter Gayatri Spivak's claim that 'There is no space from where the subaltern ... subject can speak [122]'" (195).[1] The instability of trickster discourse, its fragility and invitation to deconstruction, allows both author and reader to enter the liminal, interactive world of oral storytelling, which, in turn, places both writer and reader in the world of the trickster.

The idea that the narrative is a site of trickster energy is augmented by the presence of characters who exhibit trickster characteristics. A seemingly minor one, Santiago, patron saint of Walatowa, is significant because of his role in the Pueblo myth of origin. Alan R. Velie explains that the story of Santiago is both the legend of a saint and a trickster tale (325). Santiago saved all of the Pueblo people by dismembering a rooster whose "blood and feathers ... became cultivated plants and domestic animals, enough for all the Pueblo people"

(Momaday, HMD, 40). As Velie points out, "The Jemez have taken the saint's life, with its obligatory miracle, and transformed it to conform with the chief genre of their own sacred literature, the myth of origin with wondrous deeds by a trickster acting as culture hero" (325). The relevance of Santiago as trickster is huge for the culture of Wala-towa—the myth enabled the tribe to integrate their own beliefs with the Catholicism imposed upon them by Spanish conquerors, so that their principal religious festival, the Festival of Santiago, celebrates their own heritage even more than the conqueror's religion because Santiago is remembered more as trickster than saint.

Even the protagonist is a candidate for trickster. For example, as Velie notes, Abel plays the role of the trickster as buffoon during the Santiago festival (325). When the killing and dismemberment of the rooster is re-enacted by an albino, Abel is the one he chooses to strike with the dead rooster. Although that action is part of the ritual, Abel mistakes it for a personal assault and kills the albino for the affront. Though Abel possesses many trickster behaviors, such as his drunken-ness, fighting, and outsider status, he does not qualify as a trickster because Trickster tends to be an agent of change, an active manipu-lator of events, while Abel is almost always a victim.

The most prominent candidate for trickster in *House Made of Dawn* is John Big Bluff Tosamah because of his appearance, manner, words, and, most importantly, his role in Abel's healing. This priest of the Los Angeles Holiness Pan-Indian Rescue Mission exhibits his trickster qualities from the moment of his first appearance:

> There was a ripple in the dark screen; the drapes parted and the Priest of the Sun appeared, moving shadow-like to the lectern. He was shaggy and awful-looking in the thin, naked light: big, lithe as a cat, narrow-eyed, suggesting in the whole of his look and manner both arrogance and agony. He wore black like a cleric; he had the voice of a great dog. (HMD 90–91)

To begin with, Tosamah joins other Native American tricksters typi-cally identified with animals. Moreover, as Lewis Hyde points out, "Trickster is the mythic embodiment of ambiguity and ambivalence, doubleness and duplicity, contradiction and paradox" (7). Tomasah is both catlike *and* doglike. His manner juxtaposes both arrogance *and* agony. Although he is the priest of the sun, he moves "shadow-like."

Even the performance of his sermon reflects trickster paradox: "Conviction, caricature, callousness: the remainder of his sermon was a going back and forth among these" (92). However, particularly significant is the borderline he occupies between Anglo religion and Native American spirituality. He may be clothed like a cleric, but his sermon critiques and mocks Christian belief. Yet, although he reverently tells the story of how the Kiowa tribe[2] emerged into the world, he dismisses his congregation with the flippant "Good night . . . and get yours" (98). Finally, tricksters tend to be in touch with the powers of the universe—as is Tosamah: "In his mind the earth was spinning and the stars rattled around in the heavens. The sun shone, and the moon" (98).

Tosamah's trickster role, however, is demonstrated most powerfully through how he epitomizes the power of words, since words carry such enormous power in American Indian culture, as Gary Witherspoon found when he studied the Navajo: "By speaking properly and appropriately one can control and compel the behavior and power of the gods" (60). Momaday has written, "A word has power in and of itself. It comes from nothing into sound and meaning; it gives origin to all things. By means of words can a man deal with the world on equal terms. The word is sacred" (*The Way* . . . 42). Tosamah not only conveys the significance of words, but he also understands how they function differently in Anglo and Native American cultures. Here is his version of the Genesis creation story:

> There was nothing. But there was darkness all around, and in the darkness something happened. *Something happened!* There was a single sound. . . . Nothing made it, but it was there; and there was no one to hear it, but it was there. It was there, and there was nothing else. It rose up in the darkness, little and still, almost nothing in itself—like a single soft breath, like the wind arising; yes, like the whisper of the wind rising slowly and going out into the early morning. But there was no wind. There was only the sound, little and soft. . . . It scarcely was; but it *was*, and everything began. (91)

Tosamah claims that Christians have diminished the power of the word and diluted it by overuse, that they have made it "soft and big with fat" (93). He contrasts how "the white man deals in words . . .

with grace and sleight of hand" (94) with the story of his grandmother, a storyteller who "had learned that in words and in language, and there only, she could have whole and consummate being" (94).

Tosamah's association with the power of words makes him the most important source of trickster energy in *House Made of Dawn*. Rosemary King believes that one of the most important lessons that he teaches Abel is why words are important: "Language is important because they originally created life; therefore, words—perhaps the original ones—must be preserved from generation to generation" (3). Indeed, Tosamah's sermon is a powerful reminder of the Kiowa belief in language,[3] and a crucial lesson for Abel, but it is not enough by itself to effect a cure for his sickness.

Abel's inarticulateness has been cited as the cause of his illness; however, it is not cause but symptom of his deep alienation from all things. The extent of his sickness is symbolized at the beginning of the "Priest of the Sun" chapter by the spawning fish that "writhe in the light of the moon" on the beach—not unlike Abel himself, who lies on the beach writhing in pain and near death after a terrible beating. The fish are described as "the most helpless creatures on the face of the earth" (*HMD* 89), and Abel "had the sense that his whole body was shaking violently, tossing and whipping, flopping like a fish" (*HMD* 115). All the while Abel lies on the beach, his thoughts keep coming back to the fishes.

> Why should Abel think of the fishes? He could not understand the sea; it was not of his world. It was an enchanted thing, too, for it lay under the spell of the moon . . . 'Beautyway,' 'Bright Path,' 'Path of Pollen'—his friend Benally talked of these things. . . . The sea . . . and small silversided fishes spawned mindlessly in correlation to the phase of the moon and the rise and fall of the tides. The thought of it made him sad, filled him with sad, unnamable longing and wonder. (98)

Abel's ability to be filled with "sad, unnamable longing and wonder" about the helpless fish and to think of them in terms of such mythic and ritual concepts as "Beautyway" and "Path of Pollen" indicates that he has reached some clarity of vision in his path toward healing. He is emerging from his solipsism enough to have compassion for other beings and is on the verge of understanding his own helplessness through his empathy. Abel has been able to achieve this clarity because of Tosamah's actions as a trickster/shaman, not an uncommon combination according to Karl W. Luckert, who indicates that the trickster-shaman was characteristic of the archaic Navajo traditions, which were absorbed into Pueblo ceremonial practices (148). Later, we will see how Tosamah also facilitates Abel's healing through his other trickster qualities as rogue or bully.

The clearest example of Tosamah's use of ceremony to heal Abel is the all-night peyote ritual over which he presides. He is identified at the beginning of the ceremony as "orator, physician, Priest of the Sun, son of Hummingbird." The "physician" designation is appropriate, for the peyote ceremony is a highly structured ritual designed to heal both mental and physical illness. It is intended to reunite its participants with the Great Mystery of Being. "To live according to its inspiration is to follow the peyote road of personal dignity and respect for nature and other people" (Kiyaani 48). It works to clear the mind (Jones 411) and expand access to parts of consciousness (Jones 412). The participants in Tosamah's ceremony pray to the Great Spirit to "be with us. We gone crazy for you to be with us poor Indi'ns" and "Come to us now in bright colors and sweet smoke. Help us to make our way" (113). They experience waves of both ecstasy and of sadness and grief. "Everyone thought of death, and the thought was overwhelming in itself" (112). Tosamah performs a blast of an eagle-whistle in each of the four sacred directions at midnight to "serve notice that something holy was going on in the universe" and Abel's friend, Benally, declares at one point, "Look! Look! There are blue and purple horses . . . a house made of dawn" (114).

Although the peyote ceremony is the most obvious example of Abel's ceremonial healing by Tosamah, it is crucial that we recognize the larger ceremonial dimensions of the entire novel in order to appreciate fully Tosamah's role. Momaday's narrative incorporates the powerful centuries-old Navajo healing ceremony known as the Nightway or Night Chant. This ceremony contains 324 separate songs and typically takes nine days to complete, concluding near dawn when the final song is sung. Its purpose is to restore the person for whom the Nightway is being conducted to "mental and physical health, to a sense of balance and harmony and completeness" (Overstreet 58). The first paragraph of *House Made of Dawn* is actually a paraphrase of the first song of the Night Chant, of which the first stanza is as follows:

> House made of dawn,
> House made of evening light,
> House made of the dark cloud.
> House made of male rain.
> House made of dark mist.
> House made of female rain.
> House made of pollen.
> House made of grasshoppers.
>   (Evers and Pavich 17)

The rest of this song seeks restoration of the person's body, mind and voice and asks, "May it be beautiful before me [and behind me, below me, above me, and all around me]." Of course, the novel both begins and ends at dawn with Abel's running in the ceremonial winter dawn race. Momaday begins *House Made of Dawn* with the invocation *Dypaloh* and ends it with the benediction *Qtsedaba* in the tradition of oral storytelling as a means of establishing the novel's ceremonial character.

Navajo healing ceremonies contain two main parts: a retelling of the tribe's origin or emergence story and a tracing of how the patient became ill (Selinger 65). Thus Lawrence J. Evers explains how the first part puts the patient through this "ritual re-emergence journey paralleling that of the People" (116). The second part is necessary because of the Navajo belief that the impacts of any event can reverberate at any future moment, so that no matter how far away the past is, it still can affect the present.

Tosamah plays a significant role in both parts of Momaday's refashioning of this ceremony. Evers emphasizes the importance of the singer's role in the first part—putting the individual through the ritual origin journey: "Through the power of the chanter's words the patient's life is brought under ritual control, and he is cured" (116). Tosamah's sermon and the Peyote ceremony constitute this part of Abel's ceremony. However, he also plays a critical role in the second part—walking the person back through the beginning of his illness. Thus Abel's flashbacks to the war and other painful events in his life occur in the same chapter after he hears the sermon and participates in the peyote ceremony. However, the fact that Abel is near death as he experiences these flashbacks is also relevant. Why is he near death? Because he has been horribly injured from a terrible beating while drunk and is unable to defend himself. We can infer from what his friend Benally tells us that Tosamah's taunts probably goaded Abel into the drunken state that resulted in his beating by the Los Angeles cop Martinez. Actually, some critics dismiss Tosamah as a trickster because of his arrogant and cruel words about Abel: a "poor degenerate Indian" (149) and "too damn dumb to be civilized" (148). Benally recalls Tosamah's attitude toward Abel:

> He was going to get us all in trouble, Tosamah said. Tosamah sized him up right away, and he warned me about him. But, you know, Tosamah doesn't understand either. He talks pretty big all the time, and he's educated, but he doesn't understand. (148)

What Benally and others do not understand is that Tosamah *does* understand: He knows that Abel not only must reach rock bottom before he can return to health and harmony, but he also must revisit his pain. Bernard Selinger points out that the Navajo "recognize that the path to psychic health and well-being winds through the forest of insanity" (65). Indeed, as we have seen, as Abel painfully recollects the experiences that stole his health and sanity and sense of connectedness to his tribe and the whole of creation, he achieves new vision. He comes to realize what had driven him into the fog of alcoholism—that "he had always been afraid. Forever at the margin of his mind there was something to be afraid of, something to fear" (116). Indeed, many of his memories have featured fear: after the death of his mother (he could not go near her grave for a long time after she died), of the woman who had screamed some unintelligible curse at him, of the hole in the rock and the moaning wind that "for the rest of his life . . . would be for him the particular sound of anguish" (12), of his brother's death, of the machine that bears down upon him in the battlefield, and of the albino, so that "in his terror he knew only to wield the knife" (83). Abel's fear is of death. In order for him to love life again, he must confront that fear. Thus he is brought so near death that he finally understands that "He had to get up. He would die of exposure unless he got up" (125). Once he has struggled up and is finally walking back, "in his pain and weariness," he has a vision of being with his friends running on the beach "and the moon was high and bright and the fishes were far away in the depths" (126). After Abel has moved psychologically through the fearsome experiences of his life—when Death had been near—he can remember pleasure and beauty.

Claude Levi-Strauss identifies the "underlying conceptual opposition in the trickster myths [as] that between the abstract concepts Life and Death" (302). Tosamah can lead Abel back into life through ritual stories and ceremonies because he has helped to propel him through his remembered encounters with Death.

The penultimate aspect of the entire narrative of *House Made of Dawn* as healing ceremony—not only for Abel, but also for other Native Americans—is Abel's experience of being present at his grandfather Francisco's death bed. Listening to Francisco tell stories of his own rites of passage at the end of life, Abel demonstrates that he has conquered his terror of death, both by being able to stay with his grandfather during the dying process and by executing the appropriate rituals for his grandfather's body. The process of dying is perhaps the most profoundly liminal period in any life. Thus, his grandfather's stories are especially salient because Abel hears them during this liminal time. The stories are his final instruction in how to relate to the Great Mystery of Being. Not surprisingly, Abel's experience of hearing his grandfather's stories echoes Tosamah's stories of his grandmother.

Momaday is able to reveal language in Abel's world as the profoundly moral and spiritual practice that it is in the hands of Trickster. Yet, Momaday is very careful to indicate at the end that although Abel is on a healing path, he is not yet finished with his journey because he does not yet completely possess language: "He was running, and under his breath he began to sing. There was no sound, and he had no voice; he had only the words of the song. And he went running on the rise of the song. *House made of pollen, house made of dawn. Qtsedaba*" (212). Both dawn and pollen speak of beginnings; both are liminal elements. As Victor Turner reveals, "Liminality is pure potency, where anything can happen" (577). Abel is running and singing because, thanks to his trickster, he now knows that anything can happen. Because Momaday concludes his story with this liminal moment, we have faith that Abel will find his voice.

House Made of Dawn is a visionary novel that appeared at a time when both Native Americans and the Anglo culture were in desperate need of vision. Momaday declared later that Abel represents "a great many people of his generation" and is "an important figure in the whole history of the American experience in this country" (Coltelli

94). What we must not forget is that the source of this vision is the creative power of the trickster.

NOTES

1. The subaltern is a member of an oppressed, typically colonized group, such as Native Americans.
2. Momaday integrates Kiowa and Navajo references throughout the novel.
3. Roemer points out that Tosamah's sermon "links Abel's disease and potential forcuring to the absence and the development of a voice" (7).

WORKS CITED

Ammons, Elizabeth and Annette White-Parks, Ed. *Tricksterism in Turn-of-the-Century American Literature: A Multicultural Perspective.* Hanover: UP of New England, 1994.

Bartelt, Guillermo. "Hegemonic Registers in Momaday's *House Made of Dawn." Style* 39:4 (Winter 2005): 469–478.

Carroll, Michael P. "Levi-Strauss, Freud, and the Trickster: A New Perspective upon an Old Problem." *American Ethnologist* 8:2 (May 1981): 301–313.

Coltelli, Laura. *Winged Words: American Indian Writers Speak.* Lincoln: U of Nebraska P, 1990.

Elias, Amy J. "Fragments that Rune Up the Shores: Pushing the Bear, Coyote Aesthetics, and Recovered History." *Modern Fiction Studies* 45:1 (1999): 185–211.

Evers, Lawrence J. "Words and Place: A Reading of *House Made of Dawn." Critical Perspectives on Native American Fiction.* Ed. Richard F. Fleck. Washington, D.C.: Three Continents Press, 1993. 114–133.

Evers, Lawrence J. and Paul Pavich. "Native Oral Traditions." *A Literary History of the American West.* Ed. Thomas J. Lyon. Fort Worth, Texas: Texas Christian University Press, 1987. 11–28.

Horne, Dee. *Contemporary American Indian Writing; Unsettling Literature.* New York: Peter Lang, 1999.

Hyde, Lewis. *Trickster Makes This World: Mischief, Myth and Art.* New York: Farrar, Straus and Giroux, 1998.

Jameson, Frederic. *The Politically Unconscious: Narrative as a Socially Symbolic Act.* Ithaca: Cornell UP, 1981.

Jones, Peter N. "The Native American Church, Peyote, and Health: Expanding Consciousness for Healing Purposes." *Contemporary Justice Review* 10:4 (December 2007): 411–425.

King, Rosemary. "Betwixt and Between: Liminality and Language in *House Made of Dawn.*" February 2001. 09 January 2009. http://limen.mi2.hr/limen2.2001/king.html.

Kiyaani, Mike. "On the Peyote Road." As told to Thomas J. Csordas. *Natural History* 106 (March 1997): 48–49.

Levi-Strauss, Claude. *From Honey to Ashes.* Chicago: University of Chicago Press, 1983.

Luckert, Karl W. *The Navajo Hunter Tradition.* Tucson: U of Arizona P, 1975.

Lyotard, Jean-Francois, *Instructions painnes* quoted by David Carroll, "Narrative, Heterogeneity, and the Question of the Political: Bakhtin and Lyotard." New York: Columbia UP, 1987.

Momaday, N. Scott. *House Made of Dawn.* New York: Harper & Row, 1968.

Momaday, N. Scott. *The Way to Rainy Mountain.* New York: Ballantine, 1969.

Overstreet, William. "The Navajo Nightway and the Western Gaze." *boundary 2*: 19:3 (1992): 57–76.

Roemer, Kenneth M. "Introduction." *The Cambridge Companion to Native American Literature.* Ed. Joy Porter and Kenneth M. Roemer. New York: Cambridge University Press, 1995.

Selinger, Bernard. "The Navajo, Psychosis, Lacan, and Derrida." *Texas Studies in Literature and Language*: 49:1 (2007): 64–100.

Tidwell, Paul L. "Imagination, Conversation, and Trickster Discourse: Negotiating an Approach to Native American Literary Culture." *American Indian Quarterly* 21:4 (Autumn 1997): 621–631.

Turner, Victor. *The Forest of Symbols; Aspects of Ndombu Ritual.* Ithaca: Cornell UP, 1981.

Velie, Alan R. "Indians in Indian Fiction: The Shadow of the Trickster." *American Indian Quarterly* 8:4 (Autumn 1984): 315–329.

Vizenor, Gerald. "Trickster Discourse." *Wicazo Sa Review* 5:1 *Native American Literatures* (Spring 1989): 2–7.

Witherspoon, Gary. *Language and Art in the Navajo Universe.* Ann Arbor: U of Michigan P, 1977.

"A Hunger Artist"
(Franz Kafka)

"Making the Incomprehensible Incomprehensible: The Trickery of Kafka's 'A Hunger Artist'"
by John Becker, Independent Scholar

Much like his hunger artist, we starve in Kafka's world. The ambiguities and contradictions we encounter in his stories are carefully constructed to starve readers of plausible answers. In so far as we can think of Kafka as a writer of oblique tales that defy expectation, "common sense," and easily digestible glosses, he resembles the figure of the trickster. Found in the mythology of many different cultures, the half-divine trickster is a liminal figure poised on the threshold between life and death, the profane and the sacred, mortal and divine. Like the mysterious doorkeeper in "Before the Law," a parable Kafka placed in his novel *The Trial*, who taunts "a man from the country" with the possibility and impossibility of gaining admittance to the Law, the trickster often frustrates the desires of men for an ordered, just universe (*The Trial* 215). Mircea Eliade asserts that the trickster figure's presence in sacred literature ". . . reflects what can be called a *mythology of the human condition*. He opposes God's decision to make man immortal and to assure him an existence somehow paradisiacal, in a pure and rich world free of all contraries" (157). Thus, the trickster, a deceiving and fallible being who actively frustrates the orderliness of creation, is for Eliade a mythic personification of the ambivalences and mystery we encounter in an imperfect world. As William Hynes notes in his deft and nuanced discussion of the trickster across cultures, "all semblances of truth and falsity are subject to his rapid alchemy" (Hynes 35). Such "rapid alchemy" is, for many critics, characteristic of Kafka's style of writing and of "A Hunger Artist" in particular. After attempting to paraphrase the story, R.W. Stallman observes that "it is impossible to reduce Kafka's facts to a single self-consistent system of meaning. The trouble is that his meanings emerge at several planes at once, and the planes are interconnected. No complete paraphrase is possible" (151).

"A Hunger Artist" is, like most of Kafka's tales, both cryptic and seductive. Upon finishing this brief story written during the twilight of Kafka's life, readers are tempted to ask a number of questions that not only bear upon the strange particulars of the story itself but also upon the nature of art. How can the hunger artist's performance be considered an aesthetic achievement if he has no choice but to fast? Did Kafka intend his emaciated protagonist to be a representative of the artist (himself included) in modern commercial society? If so, is he a sincere example of the "misunderstood artist" at odds with his inferiors or a satirical creation meant to ridicule the self-importance of pursuing "art for its own sake," irrespective of his audience or his life? Is the hunger artist's asceticism—his denial of life and its sustenance for a higher purpose—meant to conjure the image of Christ (whose fast in the desert, like the hunger artist's early performances, lasted for forty days)? What exactly does the caged panther that takes the hunger artist's place symbolize: a gross, materialistic being at odds with the spiritual purity of the hunger artist (as Robert Stallman argues) or, in the words of critic Meno Spann, a beautiful animal possessing in "abundance everything the hunger artist missed" ("Franz Kafka's Leopard" 92)? Or perhaps the panther is a culmination of the hunger artist's life, a "higher, more 'joyous' artistic attraction" that he gives birth to through his strivings (Cesaretti 304). "A Hunger Artist" seems able to sustain all of these possibilities without ever satisfying the sense of wholeness and closure we crave.

Many of Kafka's stories resemble parables, a genre of writing that employs allegory to demonstrate a moral truth. The characters, images, and events in parables have significance in a realm that is commensurate with but set apart from the world of the story itself, a realm that determines its shape and significance. For the responsible reader of Kafka's fiction, such tidiness is nearly impossible to find (or create) without ignoring other plausible alternatives. Kafka's refashioned parables seem to deliberately obscure the allegorical "truths" a reader might expect them to demonstrate. Kafka achieves this effect in "A Hunger Artist" by presenting readers with images that defy their commonplace associations and changing the significance of his protagonist's fast. In his short parable "On Parables," Kafka traces a paradoxical argument:

> [...] All these parables really set out to say merely that the incomprehensible is incomprehensible, and we know that already. But the cares we have to struggle with every day; that is a different matter.
>
> Concerning this a man once said: Why such reluctance? If you only followed the parables you yourselves would become parables and with that rid of all your daily cares.
>
> Another said: I bet that is also a parable.
>
> The first said: You have won.
>
> The second said: But unfortunately only in parable.
>
> The first said: No, in reality: in parable you have lost. (*Basic Kafka* 158)

Here the rationale for following parables is itself defined as a parable, one that makes life more bearable. But such a realization, though perhaps comforting, does not make parables themselves intelligible: The condition that enables the first speaker to relate parables to his daily life destroys the possibility of successfully unraveling them. Kafka's stories are refashioned parables that refuse to point to their allegorical significance. As Heinz Politzer states, in his aptly titled study *Franz Kafka: Parable and Paradox*, "[Kafka's] parables are as multilayered as their Biblical models. But, unlike them, they are also multifaceted, ambiguous, and capable of so many interpretations that, in the final analysis, they defy any and all" (21). This is the source of profundity modern readers find in Kafka's works: We recognize in Kafka's difficult fictions the difficulty of understanding our lives.

As the narrative of "A Hunger Artist" progresses, we are introduced to many contradictions. "Strangely enough," the narrator comments, those given the task of watching the hunger artist starve himself in his cage are "usually butchers" who enjoy a hearty breakfast at his expense every morning (244–245). Here, the respective roles of the hunger artist and the butchers seem absurdly confused: The starving man feeds men who normally provide food. He performs songs and tells stories to these watchmen to prove that he is not eating. Here the hunger artist uses aesthetic performances to validate his fast which, predicated as it is on self-denial, is fraudulent. Despite the hunger artist's strong aversion to food, we are told that these watchmen are unnecessary because of his devotion to the rules of his craft ("the honor of his profession forbade it" [244]). After just a brief survey of the first half of the story, suggestive contradictions and juxtapositions abound: The hunger artist takes the greatest pride in his aesthetic labors while openly admitting that his work is "the easiest thing in the world" (246). The reader discovers that the source of the hunger artist's unhappiness is ambiguous: First presented as a consequence of his acts of self-denial, we learn that the premature ending of his performances by the impresario (and, by extension, the limited attention span of his audiences) is the cause of his displeasure ("What was a consequence of the premature ending of his fast was here presented as the cause of it!" [250]). The hunger artist's strict adherence to the rules of his fast, which he will not break "even under forcible compulsion," is allegedly motivated by his sense of honor and artistic integrity, despite the fact that he has no desire for any food whatsoever (244).

During the celebratory culmination of one of his fasts, the impresario implores ". . . Heaven to look down upon its creature here in the straw, this suffering martyr" who, it turns out, is about to suffer a martyr's hardship when he is forced to eat (248). The ritualistic spectacle of eating "a carefully chosen invalid repast" presents the greatest challenge to the hunger artist, who becomes nauseated at the mere thought of it. It is interesting to note that the strongest emotional response the hunger artist elicits from his audience directly precedes this meal: "to the great delight of the spectators," one of his young female attendants bursts into tears, unable to keep her face from touching his emaciated frame (248). So recently fascinated by this cathartic moment, the audience is kept preoccupied during the artist's meal with "cheerful patter designed to distract [their] attention from the artist's condition" (248). Thus, the nature of the hunger artist's "martyrdom" is complicated by the narrator's description of this spectacle: We are told that the hunger artist does not want to get out of his cage, that he becomes sick at the mere idea of eating, that he is only a "suffering martyr" in "quite another sense" than the impresario implies, and, finally, that his performance evokes the strongest emotions when he is moments away from eating (248). Though this last element of the narrator's description makes perfect sense if we accept the impresario's definition of the hunger artist's martyrdom (he is, after all, at his most grotesquely malnourished), it also suggests that the spectacle itself is the hunger artist's greatest sacrificial act. When the "nauseated" hunger artist sits at the table and submits to the impresario's feeding, he eats what he cannot stand, a bitter reminder of the food he can never find. Consumption, rather than self-deprivation, becomes the defining characteristic of the hunger artist's martyrdom. At the end of "A Hunger Artist," Kafka robs his protagonist's feat of its meaning by having him reveal that he was not denying himself of a desired sustenance but found himself incapable of enjoying what others eat. Thus, the ascetic, Christlike posture of the protagonist is satirically undercut: Rather than forgoing life to effect some moral or aesthetic response in his audience, the hunger artist is revealed to be averse to food. His art is an attempt to negate it; his art depends on its absence.

The inversion of the hunger artist's martyrdom and its relationship to life and death is typical of trickster tales. In such tales, tricksters are mediators capable of crossing and redefining the divide between life and death. As William Hynes notes, "As situation-invertor, the trickster is often a psychopomp, a mediator who crosses and resets the lines between life and death. . . . More often associated with conducting individuals to restored life, he can also be the messenger of death" (40). Transgressing our notions of sacrifice, the narrator forces us to revise our understanding of the hunger artist's fast: Instead of forgoing life and its sustenance, the impresario's "martyr" must endure being let out of his cage; he must submit to life. This trope inverts our notions of martyrdom and its relation to mortality: Rather than giving up his life, the hunger artist must postpone his pursuit of self-destruction. This contradiction between what the impresario tells his audience and what the narrator implies might help explain the ambiguous reaction of the hunger artist's weeping attendant. Does she cry because she feels empathy for her pitiful charge? Is it because she cannot bear the intimate and grotesque physical presence of the artist, a ghastly reminder of human frailty, a "messenger of death"? Or, perhaps, she is ecstatically moved by the presence of a martyred saint. All of these—empathy, disgust, fear, and transfiguration—seem to be evoked by the narrator's words, which are made all the more poignant by the impresario's insistence that his suffering has passed and the pervasive suggestion that his suffering has just begun. Just as mythic trickster figures challenge cultural taboos by urinating, defecating, farting, thieving, and copulating in inappropriate ways, the hunger artist performs a sacred ascetic form of self-sacrifice for the sake of aesthetic self-expression—a posture that makes the artist and the performance itself both sacred and profane. The artist destroys himself to express himself; the ascetic penitently honors himself and the godlike importance of his task. As the hunger artist himself concludes, such a life does and does not deserve our admiration.

When the hunger artist becomes irate with audience members who console his "troubled" spirit by suggesting that his fasts might be the cause of his unhappiness, the impresario punishes him by lauding his "high ambition," "good will," and inspiring capacity for "self-denial" (249). The impresario rationalizes his outburst to the onlookers by brandishing a photograph of his emaciated body after forty days of fasting. Ironically, we learn that the hunger artist thinks this is a "perversion of the truth," factually accurate though it may be (250). When the popularity of fasting fades, the narrator informs us that the hunger artist is "not only too old for [a different career,] but too devoted to fasting," which, upon reading the story again, becomes absurd: Can one be "too devoted" to a compulsion? As the hunger artist's audience diminishes, his freedom to pursue his art increases accordingly. Time itself ceases to witness his performances: The clock that was in his cage during his glory days is gone; the circus attendants no longer update the calendar affixed to his new cage. The more the hunger artist achieves in the art of fasting, the more familiar he becomes. Kafka's story tricks readers in much the same way that the hunger artist misleads his audiences. The protagonist of Kafka's short story is a paradoxical figure, an artist who has literally devoted his life to his art: the art of dying. But, we find out, the hunger artist performs these feats with no effort, as he finds no earthly food satisfying. Thus, the hunger artist occupies an intermediate position among art, life, and death. When his audience stares at him through the bars of his cage, they are witnessing a spectacle in which the artist's life is yoked to his aesthetic creations, which are in turn pointed inexorably toward death. Art, in effect, calls for its own destruction within the confines of "A Hunger Artist."

By allowing different allegorical possibilities to coexist in this parable-like narrative, Kafka performs a similar act. Traditionally, a parable is written to exemplify or demonstrate a moral truth that precedes its telling. Kafka's parable, much like the hunger artist's admission that he expends no special effort during his fasts, obscures the possibility of exegesis and consequently seems to destroy the ground upon which it was built. Like trickster characters throughout world mythology, Kafka and his hunger artist are boundary figures, functioning as intermediaries between life and death, text and meaning, art and artist, parable and intelligible allegory. Like Hermes, the archtrickster and messenger of Greek mythology, Kafka stands between our experience of reading his tales and the rarified significance we (often) presume they possess. For Kafka, parables that point unequivocally to the sacred wisdom they are meant to demonstrate do so untruthfully; only through indeterminate, playful language can we begin to confront what is beyond our experience.

WORKS CITED AND CONSULTED

Cesaretti, Enrico. "Consuming Texts: Creation and Self-effacement in Kafka and Palazzeschi." *Comparative Literature* 56.4 (Fall 2004): 300–316.

Doty, William G. "A Lifetime of Trouble-Making: Hermes as Trickster." Hynes and Doty 46–65.

Doueihi, Anne. "Inhabiting the Space Between Discourse and Story in Trickster Narratives." Hynes and Doty 193–201.

Eliade, Mircea. *The Quest: History and Meaning in Religion*. Chicago: University of Chicago Press, 1969.

Heller, Erich. "Introduction." *The Basic Kafka*. New York: Washington Square Press, 1979.

Hyde, Lewis. *Trickster Makes This World: Mischief, Myth, and Art*. New York: North Point Press, 1998.

Hynes, William J. "Mapping the Characteristics of Mythic Tricksters: A Heuristic Guide." Hynes and Doty 33–45.

Hynes, William J. and William G. Doty, eds. *Mythical Trickster Figures: Contours, Contexts, and Criticism*. Tuscaloosa, Ala.: University of Alabama Press, 1993.

Janouch, Gustav. *Conversations with Kafka*. 1968. Trans. Goronwy Rees. New York: New Directions, 1971.

Kafka, Franz. *The Blue Octavo Notebooks*. 1954. Ed. Max Brod. Trans. Ernst
Kaiser and Eithne Wilkins. Cambridge: Exact Change, 1991.

———. "A Hunger Artist." 1922. *The Metamorphosis, In the Penal Colony, and
Other Stories*. Tran. Willa and Edwin Muir. New York: Schocken Books,
1948, 1995.

———. "On Parables." *The Basic Kafka*. Trans. Willa and Edwin Muir. New
York: Washington Square Press, 1979.

———. *The Trial*. 1925. Trans. Breon Mitchell. New York: Schocken Books,
1998.

Kermode, Frank. *The Genesis of Secrecy: On the Interpretation of Narrative*.
Cambridge, Mass.: Harvard University Press, 1979.

Politzer, Heinz. *Franz Kafka: Parable and Paradox*. Ithaca, N.Y.: Cornell
University Press, 1962.

Ricoeur, Paul. *Time and Narrative, Volume One*. 1983. Trans. Kathleen
McLaughlin and David Pellauer. Chicago: University of Chicago Press,
1984.

Sheppard, Richard W. "Kafka's *Ein Hungerkünstler*: A Reconsideration." *The
German Quarterly* 46.2 (March 1973): 219–233.

Spann, Meno. "Don't Hurt the Jackdaw." *The Germanic Review* 37.1 (January
1962): 68–78.

———. *Franz Kafka*. Boston, Mass.: Twayne Publishers, 1976.

———. "Franz Kafka's Leopard." *The Germanic Review* 34.2 (April 1959):
85–104.

Stallman, R.W. "'A Hunger Artist.'" *Explain to Me Some Stories of Kafka*. Ed.
Angel Flores. New York: Gordian Press, 1983.

Steinhauer, Harry. "Hunger Artist or Artist in Hungering: Kafka's 'A Hunger
Artist.'" *Criticism* 4.1 (Winter 1962): 28–43.

Thiher, Allen. *Franz Kafka: A Study of the Short Fiction*. Boston, Mass.: Twayne
Publishers, 1990.

A Midsummer Night's Dream
(William Shakespeare)

"'This Sport Well Carried Shall Be Chronicled': Puck as Trickster in Shakespeare's *A Midsummer Night's Dream*"
by Robert C. Evans, Auburn
University at Montgomery

Although it is quite common to consider Puck a "trickster" in Shakespeare's *A Midsummer Night's Dream*, extended discussion of that idea appears to be relatively rare. Jan Kott, in a much-cited essay, does mention Puck as trickster, but only briefly and in passing (49–50). Richard Hillman, who seems to offer the most extended discussion of the topic of tricksters and tricksterism in Shakespeare's drama, cites only the two pages from Kott and one page from a 1975 book by Kirby Farrell (*Shakespeare's Creation*) as precedents for his own reference to Puck (256). Hillman calls Puck "the most obvious trickster-figure of all" of Shakespeare's characters (7), yet his most detailed discussion of *A Midsummer Night's Dream* (65–70) barely mentions Puck, either as a trickster or in any other respect. There seems some justification, then, for reopening a topic that one might have assumed had been too frequently or too extensively discussed to merit any further examination.

Part of the problem of dealing with any figure (Puck or otherwise) as a trickster is the problem of defining that crucial term. William J. Hynes and William G. Doty, in one of the best available anthologies and overviews dealing with the topic (*Mythical Trickster Figures:*

Contours, Contexts, and Criticisms) note the many disagreements and debates that occur among scholars who have long studied the issue. They report, for instance, that some writers "see the trickster as so universal a figure that all tricksters speak with essentially the same voice," while other scholars "counsel that the tricksters belonging to individual societies are so culture-specific that no two of them articulate the same messages" ("Introducing" 2). Hynes and Doty note that

> at one extreme one finds colleagues trained in Jungian psychology talking about *the* trickster as a universal archetype to be encountered within each of us and in most belief systems. At the other extreme, some anthropologists have called for the elimination of the term "trickster" altogether because it implies that a global approach to such a figure is possible whereas they find it appropriate to focus only upon one tribal or national group at a time.... ("Introducing" 4–5)

Further complications also present themselves. Although tricksters are often "comical if not marginal figures" in many traditions, "they represent sacred beings in some cultures, but not in others" (Hynes and Doty, "Introducing" 7). Moreover, some scholars have argued that the trickster "figure progresses developmentally within cultures as within an individual's psychological growth, learning over time to deal with its bodily and sexual appetites. Hence the figure represents a sort of primitive developmental level common to humanity" (Doty and Hynes, "Historical" 15). On the other hand, many other scholars (including Doty and Hynes) have disputed this evolutionary approach ("Historical" 22). Indeed, so many various and often conflicting traits have been associated with the term *trickster* that by the time Hynes and Doty have concluded their overview of scholarship on the topic it is easy to sympathize with Hynes, who suggests that the "sheer richness of trickster phenomena can easily lead one to conclude that the trickster is indefinable" ("Mapping" 33). One scholar has listed as many as sixteen different traits that allegedly characterize the typical trickster figure, while other students of the phenomenon have listed as few as six (Doty and Hynes, "Historical" 23).

There seems some value, then, in simply exploring the ways in which Puck, in Shakespeare's play, fits the various criteria that scholars have proposed as the common characteristics of tricksters. When he first appears in Act 2, scene 1 of the play, for instance, he behaves (and is described) in ways that recall many of the claims discussed in the collection of essays edited by Doty and Hynes. Thus, an unnamed "Fairy," almost immediately after recognizing Puck, describes him as "shrewd" (2.1.34)—an adjective that fits with one scholar's description of an African trickster who combines foolishness with "cunning, intelligence, and knowledge" (Makarius 84). Likewise, the fairy next describes Puck as "knavish" (2.1.34)—an assertion that matches Hynes' claim that one of the six most basic characteristics of any trickster is his (or her) function as "a consummate and continuous trick-player and deceiver" ("Mapping" 35). In the same way, the fairy's description of Puck as "knavish" also matches one particular item from Doty's similar list of six fundamental traits associated with Hermes, the classical messenger, as a trickster: his typical "deceitful thievery" ("A Lifetime" 46). Puck, then, is no sooner identified in the play than he begins to be associated with some of the most common features of an archetypal trickster.

His tendency to "Mislead night-wanderers" (2.1.39), for instance, once more associates him with the trickster as deceiver, while his habit of "laughing at their [the night-wanderers'] harm" (2.1.39) links him with Hermes's (and other tricksters') traits of "comedy and wit" (Doty, "A Lifetime" 46), as well as the related traits of the trickster as a "malicious practical joker" who is an "inventor of ingenious stratagems" (Makarius 67). At the same time, Puck's role as a frequent bringer of "good luck" (2.1.41) helps link him to the common idea that the "trickster quite regularly brings gifts essential to human culture" (Hynes, "Mapping" 40) and that he can be both "a creator and restorer" (Doty, "A Lifetime" 46). By the end of his first full description, therefore, Puck has already been associated with several of the complex and "paradoxical qualities" that Doty sees as the main traits of most trickster figures ("A Lifetime" 46). The anonymous fairy's first description of Puck foreshadows many of the traits and much of the behavior that Puck will demonstrate throughout the rest of the play.

Puck himself, in responding to the fairy, describes himself as a "merry wanderer of the night" (2.1.43), thus linking himself to a restlessness that has often been seen as a common trait of many tricksters, especially in North American Indian lore (Doty and Hynes, "Historical" 15). Puck also boasts, "I jest to Oberon, and make him smile / When I a fat and bean-fed horse beguile, / Neighing in

likeness of a filly foal" (2.1.44–46)—thereby displaying the relationship between the trickster and (in the words of Robert Abrahams) the
"clown, fool, [and] jokester" (qtd. in Doty and Hynes, "Historical" 17)
as well as exhibiting another highly important feature of the archetypal trickster: his talent as a shape-shifter (Hynes, "Mapping" 36–37).
In addition, like the classical trickster Hermes, Puck can often seem "a
ridiculous character" who appears "especially close to ordinary human
lives" (Doty, "A Lifetime"), as when he brags that "sometimes lurk
I in a gossip's bowl / In very likeness of a roasted crab, / And when
she drinks, against her lips I bob, / And on her wither'd dewlap pour
the ale" (2.1.47–50). Puck here makes literal physical contact with
a woman near the very bottom of the Elizabethan social structure,
playing his typical tricks in a way that can almost be seen as "erotic
and relational" (Doty, "A Lifetime" 46) and that is certainly "playful"
and "clownlike" (Doty, "A Lifetime" 64). Indeed, Puck sounds very
much like a clown when he describes his entertaining deception of
"The wisest Aunt, telling the saddest tale," who

> Sometime for a three-foot stool mistaketh me;
> Then slip I from her bum, down topples she,
> And 'tailor' cries, and falls into a cough;
> And then the whole quire hold their hips and loffe
> And waxen in their mirth, and neeze, and swear
> A merrier hour was never wasted there. (2.1.51–57)

Such behavior exhibits, almost literally, the trickster's skill as a "situation-invertor," able to "overturn" almost anything (Hynes, "Mapping"
37), as well as the trickster's common associations with "symbolic
inversion" and his "close relationship to the feminine" (Doty, "A
Lifetime" 64). In view of that last trait, it hardly seems surprising
that Puck not only helps women with their housework (2.1.41) but
also deceives both a "gossip" (2.1.47) and an "aunt" (2.1.51) and even
turns himself into "a filly foal" (2.1.46). Indeed, his transformation of
himself into a female horse also links him with the "gender multi-
plicity" that Doty sees as a highly common trait of many trickster
figures ("A Lifetime" 64).

   In spite of Puck's skill in (and enjoyment of) deceptive trickery,
and despite his predilection for the kind of playful mischief that causes
women to spill ale on themselves and fall on their bums, Oberon

nevertheless first addresses him as "My gentle Puck" (2.1.148). Such phrasing suggests that Puck, like other tricksters, is a more complex character than we might at first assume. Thus, Doty and Hynes report that the anthropologist Claude Lévi-Strauss saw the trickster as "the embodiment of all complementary opposites" ("Historical" 20), and Hynes himself argues that tricksters tend to be "fundamentally ambiguous, anomalous, and polyvalent" ("Mapping" 34). To the extent that Puck is "gentle" as well as devious and mischievous, then, he displays the kinds of complications that help make tricksters such intriguing figures. He not only deceives women but helps them with their housework, and he is not only playfully malicious but also positively "gentle." Yet Puck is also (like many tricksters) complex in other ways as well. Thus he is clearly more powerful than the mortals he famously mocks, yet he is also less powerful than the supernatural figures—especially Oberon—whom he serves and sometimes fears. Oberon, indeed, soon after affectionately calling Puck "gentle," nevertheless explicitly reminds him of his limitations (by recalling "That very time I saw [but thou couldst not] / . . . / Cupid all arm'd" [2.1.155–57]). Puck thus exemplifies the trickster's typical "position midway between the gods and humans" (Hynes, "Mapping" 40; see also Vecsey 106), and in fact in no time at all Oberon makes Puck's subsidiary position emphatically clear by dispatching him on the first of various missions he performs in the play (2.1.169). Puck, meanwhile, responds to this command with a statement that clearly links him to another of the prime traits of many tricksters. When he says, "I'll put a girdle round about the earth / In forty minutes" (2.1.175–76), Puck implies the trickster's common ability to move "swiftly and impulsively back and forth across all borders with virtual impunity. Visitor everywhere, especially to those places that are off limits, the trickster seems to dwell in no single place but to be in continual transit through all realms marginal and liminal" (Hynes, "Mapping" 34–35). Like many other tricksters (Hermes in particular), Puck wastes no time (Doty, "A Lifetime" 60). His speed, nimbleness, and agility are traits often emphasized in stage and film productions of the play and are just a few of the characteristics that make him seem a typical trickster. When Puck returns from his mission, Oberon's two-word greeting—"Welcome, wanderer" (2.1.247)—helps remind us of this prime characteristic of numerous tricksters, who are constantly in motion (Doty and Hynes, "Historical" 15).

Throughout his later scenes in the comedy, Puck displays again and again many of the standard traits of the typical trickster. Thus he delights in the opportunity to take a mischievously active role in the play being rehearsed by Peter Quince and his troupe ("What, a play toward? I'll be an auditor; / An actor too perhaps, if I see cause"; [3.1.75–76]), thereby illustrating the trickster's typical behavior as a "trick-player and deceiver" (Hynes, "Mapping" 35) as well as the usual trickster's literally "playful" nature (Doty, "A Lifetime" 64). Meanwhile, his decision to put an ass's head on Bottom reminds us not only of the trickster's ability to trick and deceive but also of his talent for acting as a kind of "bricoleur" or "tinker" who is "noted for his ingenuity in transforming anything at hand" (Hynes, "Mapping" 42). By turning Bottom into an ass with whom Titania falls comically in love, Puck delights both the vengeful Oberon and Shakespeare's audience, who take pleasure in the trickster's tricks. In particular, by arranging things so that the queen of the fairies falls in love with a common workman transformed into an ass, Puck fulfills another standard function of the trickster: the function of turning social distinctions upside down and "dispelling" (at least temporarily) "the belief that any given social order is absolute and objective" (Doty and Hynes, "Historical" 21). By helping to make a fool of Titania in much the same way that he earlier deceived lower-class gossips and aunts, Puck briefly undermines Titania's power even as he thereby reinforces the power of Oberon. In this way, then, as in so many other respects, Puck (like many other tricksters) is a paradoxical figure who is associated both with social disruptions and with the ultimate reaffirmation of a culture's most fundamental values (Hynes, "Inconclusive" 207).

Few speeches by Puck reveal more compactly so many traits of the typical trickster as his gleeful threats to the terrified mechanicals, who flee at their first glimpse of the transformed Bottom:

> *Puck.* I'll follow you: I'll lead you about a round!
> Through bog, through bush, through brake, through briar;
> Sometime a horse I'll be, sometime a hound,
> A hog, a headless bear, sometime a fire;
> And neigh, and bark, and grunt, and roar, and burn,
> Like horse, hound, hog, bear, fire, at every turn. (3.1.101–06)

These lines emphasize the trickster's powers as a shape-shifter (Hynes, "Mapping" 36–37) and as a deceiver, as well as his ability to appear "*unexpectedly* and in an unforeseen manner" (Doty, "A Lifetime" 60; italics in original). The lines also exemplify the typical trickster's common associations with animals (indeed, many tricksters *are* animals or *appear as* animals) and with athleticism (see Doty, "A Lifetime" 64). And, of course, these lines also display the trickster's frequent delight in mischief, magic, and even a certain comic malice (Makarius 67). In moments such as this, Puck displays enormous independent inventiveness, even though he also—like many tricksters—functions as "both a messenger and imitator of the gods" (Hynes, "Mapping" 39). Oberon, indeed, at their very next meeting, explicitly calls Puck "my messenger," but he also calls him a "mad spirit" (3.2.4)—a phrase that nicely epitomizes the trickster's associations with "anarchic social behavior" (Doty and Hynes, "Historical" 23) and with the breaking of divine taboos (Hynes, "Mapping" 40). In this case the taboo that is broken is the one that dictates that a goddess should not fall in love with an ass.

Yet it is not only Bottom, in this drama, who plays the ass. In certain respects, Puck does as well, especially when he accidentally places the love-juice that Oberon had intended for Demetrius's eyes into the eyes of Lysander (3.2.88). By making this mistake, Puck not only frustrates Oberon, confounds Oberon's good intentions toward Helena, and produces comic romantic mayhem; he also illustrates yet another common trait of many a trickster—the trickster's tendency to bumble, make mistakes (Doty and Hynes, "Historical" 33), fall "into his own traps," become "the victim of his own ruses" (Makarius 84), and be deceived by his own practical jokes, so that "the inventor of ingenious stratagems is presented as an idiot" and "the master of magical power is sometimes powerless to extricate himself from quandaries" (Makarius 67). With Oberon's guidance and direction, Puck, of course, soon attempts to fix his mistake, and when he dashes off to do so ("I go, I go, look how I go! / Swifter than arrow from the Tartar's bow" [3.2.100–01]) he once again exemplifies the standard speed of the typical trickster. And when he quickly returns, ten lines later, and soon pronounces perhaps his most famous line of the whole play—"Lord, what fools these mortals be!" (3.2.115)—it should be borne in mind that Puck, only a few lines earlier, had himself seemed a bit of a fool. Perhaps his eagerness to mock "these mortals" in the presence of the Fairy King is thus driven, in part, by his desire to obfuscate his own recent foolishness. In any case, the joy he takes in the comic complications of the lovers' behavior is entirely typical of the standard trickster: "those things do best please me / That befall prepost'rously" (3.2.120–21).

Oberon, needless to say, does not entirely share Puck's anarchic sense of humor, and when the king of the fairies sees the chaos that Puck has helped produce, he berates his servant in a tone that shows that he is not amused: "This is thy negligence: still thou mistak'st / Or else committ'st thy knaveries wilfully" (3.2.345–46). Once more, then, it is Puck who seems a fool, and the play seems even funnier than it would otherwise appear since Puck so often proves a trickster (like many other tricksters) who is never entirely in control of the anarchy he unleashes. Ironically, however, Oberon begins to suspect that precisely the opposite may be true. Thus, when Oberon asks whether Puck has committed his "knaveries wilfully," Oberon begins to worry that he, too—even though he is king of the fairies—has now fallen victim to the trickster's pranks. Puck is such a force of potential disorder and comic turmoil that even Oberon begins to fear that his "gentle" servant and subservient messenger may be out of control. And Puck is, in fact, out of control—just not in the sense that Oberon suspects. Puck has merely lost his control (temporarily) of the people and events he attempts to manipulate.

In this respect (it goes without saying), Puck differs from Shakespeare himself in the latter's role as a writer of convoluted romantic comedies. Shakespeare, indeed, is the ultimate trickster in this play—the ultimate player of jokes, who manipulates his audience as wittily as he manipulates his characters. In this sense, in fact, Shakespeare most resembles Oberon, the powerful figure who unleashes the comic and anarchic energy of Puck without ever letting that energy get out of control, become immoral, or cause real harm. Like Oberon, Shakespeare enjoys Puck's energy and trickery and uses both for his own (ultimately benign) purposes.

Both qualities of Oberon—his enjoyment of Puck's trickery, but also his essential goodness—can be seen in the instructions he issues to Puck for dealing with the combative Athenians:

> . . . lead these testy rivals so astray
> As one come not within another's way.
> Like to Lysander sometime frame thy tongue,
> Then stir Demetrius up with bitter wrong;

And sometime rail thou like Demetrius:
And from each other look thou lead them thus,
Till o'er their brows death-counterfeiting sleep
With leaden legs and batty wings doth creep. (3.2.358–65)

In this passage, the first and final couplets frame four lines in which Oberon seems not only to permit but actually to encourage Puck's "knavery," but those first and final couplets make it clear that Oberon's intentions are ultimately well intentioned. He encourages Puck to unleash a certain anarchy between Demetrius and Lysander, but he keeps that anarchy clearly and purposefully under control. No one will be hurt; no one will really suffer; nothing will be damaged except (temporarily) the dignity of the young and comic feuders. Like Shakespeare himself, Oberon harnesses and controls Puck's trickery in ways that prevent it from ever seeming truly dangerous or destructive.

In the episode that follows—in which Puck, while carrying out Oberon's instructions, manages to thoroughly confuse and exhaust Demetrius and Lysander while also causing all four lovers to fall asleep (3.2.396–463)—Puck exhibits for one last time practically all the standard traits of the typical trickster, including deception, swift movement, shape-shifting (or at least voice alteration), cleverness, humor, wit, athletic ability, and the ingenuity needed to transform anything and anyone for his own purposes. Acting at the behest of Oberon, he turns chaos into order, conflict into love, and bitterness into the very sort of gentleness with which Oberon had initially linked him (2.1.148). Indeed, when Puck, in almost his last lines of Act 3, calls the sleeping (and thus highly vulnerable) Hermia a "Gentle lover" and offers her "Remedy" (3.2.452), he inadvertently manifests a very real and very attractive aspect of his own ethical character. No wonder, then, that Oberon is soon calling him "good Robin" (4.1.45) and "gentle Puck" (4.1.63). Puck is a trickster, but his trickery is never really cruel or malevolent, and by the end of the play he has begun to embody many of the most positive aspects of the trickster archetype, including creativity (Doty and Hynes, "Historical" 19), contributions to "the birth and evolution of culture" (Doty and Hynes, "Historical" 23), gift-giving (Hynes, "Mapping" 40), cultural transformation (Hynes, "Mapping" 40), and the setting of useful limits and boundaries (Doty, "A Lifetime" 64). By helping untangle the romantic confusions of the middle part of the play (entanglements he had, ironically, also helped create), and particularly by helping to promote the eventual marriage of the young Athenians, Puck as trickster not only helps produce "deeply satisfying entertainment" (Hynes, "Inconclusive" 202) but also helps reaffirm some of the most basic values of Renaissance Christian culture (Hynes, "Inconclusive" 205–06). In particular, by playing his crucial role in helping to lead the young lovers to marriage, Puck helps resolve one very crucial set of "complementary opposites" that exists in almost any human culture: "that between immediate sexual gratification and the demands of civilization" (Doty and Hynes, "Historical" 20).

It is with little wonder, then, that in his last lines in the play (which are also the last lines of the play as a whole), Puck the trickster calls himself "honest Puck" (5.1.417) and emphasizes his desire to "be friends" and to "restore amends" (i.e., give satisfaction; 5.1.423–24). In these lines, Puck is no longer playing the trickster as mischievous, deceitful thief or potentially malevolent practical joker; by this point he has become the trickster as comrade and kindly benefactor, the trickster as a well-intentioned messenger sent, if not from the gods, then at least from a supremely creative and benevolent mind.

WORKS CITED AND CONSULTED

Doty, William G. "A Lifetime of Trouble-Making: Hermes as Trickster." In Doty and Hynes, eds., *Mythical Trickster Figures*, 46–65.

Doty, William G. and William J. Hynes. "Historical Overview of Theoretical Issues: The Problem of the Trickster." In Doty and Hynes, eds., *Mythical Trickster Figures*, 13–32.

Farrell, Kirby. *Shakespeare's Creations: The Language of Magic and Play*. Amherst, Mass.: University of Massachusetts Press, 1975.

Hillman, Richard. *Shakespearean Subversions: The Trickster and the Play-text*. London: Routledge, 1992.

Hynes, William J. "Inconclusive Conclusions: Tricksters—Metaplayers and Revealers." In Doty and Hynes, eds., *Mythical Trickster Figures*, 202–217.

———— "Mapping the Characteristics of Mythic Tricksters: A Heuristic Guide." In Doty and Hynes, eds., *Mythical Trickster Figures*, 33–45.

Hynes, William J. and William G. Doty. "Introducing the Fascinating and Perplexing Trickster Figure." In Doty and Hynes, eds., *Mythical Trickster Figures*, 1–12.

————, eds. *Mythical Trickster Figures: Contours, Contexts, and Criticisms.* Tuscaloosa: University of Alabama Press, 1993.

Kott, Jan. *The Bottom Translation: Marlowe and Shakespeare and the Carnival Tradition.* Transl. Daniela Miedzyrzecka and Lillian Vallee. Evanston, Ill.: Northwestern University Press, 1987.

Makarius, Laura. "The Myth of the Trickster: The Necessary Breaker of Taboos." In Doty and Hynes, eds., *Mythical Trickster Figures*, 66–86.

Shakespeare, William. *A Midsummer Night's Dream.* Ed. Harold F. Brooks. The Arden Shakespeare. 1979. Walton-on-Thames, Surrey: Thomas Nelson, 1997.

Vecsey, Christopher. "The Exception Who Proves the Rules: Anese the Akan Trickster." In Doty and Hynes, eds., *Mythical Trickster Figures*, 106–121.

ODYSSEY
(HOMER)

"A General View of the Epic Poem, and of the *Iliad* and *Odyssey*"
by René Le Bossu, in *The Odyssey of Homer, A New Edition* (1675)

INTRODUCTION

A storyteller who is aided and disguised by the goddess Athena, Ulysses (Odysseus) survives as a kind of trickster, who foils his adversaries by artful deception. In the following excerpt, René Le Bossu uses Aristotle's criteria in *Poetics* to evaluate both the *Odyssey* and the qualities and characteristics of Ulysses. Although criticized by both Samuel Johnson and also by Voltaire, Bossu's *Treatise of the Epick Poem* (1675) is important for what it says and also for what others have said about it. Bossu's analysis is invaluable in coming to understand Ulysses's wily authorial ways. In the end, Bossu concludes that Ulysses' tricks demonstrate his wisdom, that the "dissimulation of Ulysses is a part of his prudence."

Le Bossu, René. "A General View of the Epic Poem, and of the *Iliad* and *Odyssey*, Extracted from Bossu." *The Odyssey of Homer, A New Edition.* Vol. 1. Trans. Alexander Pope. London: printed for F.J. Du Roveray by T. Bensley, Bolt Court, 1806. 5–39.

SECT. III

The *Odyssey*[1] was not designed, like the *Iliad*, for the instruction of all the states of Greece joined in one body, but for each state in particular. As a state is composed of two parts, the head which commands and the members which obey, there are instructions requisite for both, to teach the one to govern and the others to submit to government.

There are two virtues necessary to one in authority: prudence to order, and care to see his orders put in execution. The prudence of a politician is not acquired but by a long experience in all sorts of business, and by an acquaintance with all the different forms of governments and states. The care of the administration suffers not him that has the government to rely upon others, but requires his own presence, and kings who are absent from their states are in danger of losing them, and give occasion to great disorders and confusion.

These two points may be easily united in one and the same man. 'A king forsakes his kingdom to visit the courts of several princes, where he learns the manners and customs of different nations. From hence there naturally arises a vast number of incidents, of dangers, and of adventures, very useful for a political institution. On the other side, this absence gives way to the disorders which happen in his own kingdom, and which end not till his return, whose presence only can reestablish all things.' Thus the absence of a king has the same effects in this fable as the division of the princes had in the former.

The subjects have scarce any need but of one general maxim, which is to suffer themselves to be governed and to obey faithfully, whatever reason they may imagine against the orders they receive. It is easy to join this instruction with the other by bestowing on this wise and industrious prince such subjects as in his absence would rather follow their own judgment than his commands, and by demonstrating the misfortunes which this disobedience draws upon them, the evil consequences which almost infallibly attend these particular notions, which are entirely different from the general idea of him who ought to govern.

But as it was necessary that the princes in the *Iliad* should be choleric and quarrelsome, so it is necessary in the fable of the *Odyssey* that the chief person should be sage and prudent. This raises a difficulty in the fiction, because this person ought to be absent for the two reasons aforementioned, which are essential to the fable and which constitute the principal aim of it; but he cannot absent himself without offending against another maxim of equal importance, viz., that a king should upon no account leave his country.

It is true there are sometimes such necessities as sufficiently excuse the prudence of a politician in this point. But such a necessity is a thing important enough of itself to supply matter for another poem, and this multiplication of the action would be vicious. To prevent which, in the first place, this necessity and the departure of the hero must be disjoined from the poem; and in the second place, the hero having been obliged to absent himself for a reason antecedent to the action and placed distinct from the fable, he ought not so far to embrace this opportunity of instructing himself as to absent himself voluntarily from his own government. For at this rate, his absence would be merely voluntary, and one might with reason lay to his charge all the disorders which might arise.

Thus in the constitution of the fable he ought not to take for his action and for the foundation of his poem the departure of a prince from his own country nor his voluntary stay in any other place, but his return, and this return retarded against his will. This is the first idea Homer gives us of it. His hero[2] appears at first in a desolate island, sitting upon the side of the sea, which, with tears in his eyes, he looks upon as the obstacle which had so long opposed his return and detained him from revisiting his own dear country.

And lastly, since this forced delay might more naturally and usually happen to such as make voyages by sea, Homer has judiciously made choice of a prince whose kingdom was in an island.

Let us see then how he has feigned all this action, making his hero a person in years, because years are requisite to instruct a man in prudence and policy.

> A prince had been obliged to forsake his native country and to head an army of his subjects in a foreign expedition. Having gloriously performed this enterprise, he was marching home again, and conducting his subjects to his own state. But spite of all the attempts with which his eagerness to return had inspired him, he was stopped by the way by tempests for several years, and cast upon several countries differing from each other in manners and government. In these dangers his companions, not always following his orders, perished through their own fault. The grandees of his country strangely abuse his absence, and raise

no small disorders at home. They consume his estate, conspire to destroy his son, would constrain his queen to accept of one of them for her husband, and indulge themselves in all violence, so much the more because they were persuaded he would never return. But at last he returns, and discovering himself only to his son and some others who had continued firm to him, he is an eyewitness of the insolence of his enemies, punishes them according to their deserts, and restores to his island that tranquillity and repose to which they had been strangers during his absence.

As the truth which serves for foundation to this fiction is that the absence of a person from his own home or his neglect of his own affairs is the cause of great disorders, so the principal point of the action, and the most essential one, is the absence of the hero. This fills almost all the poem. For not only this real absence lasted several years, but even when the hero returned he does not discover himself; and this prudent disguise, from whence he reaped so much advantage, has the same effect upon the authors of the disorders, and all others who knew him not, as his real absence had before, so that he is absent as to them till the very moment of their punishment.

After the poet had thus composed his fable and joined the fiction to the truth, he then makes choice of Ulysses, the king of the isle of Ithaca, to maintain the character of his chief personage, and bestowed the rest upon Telemachus, Penelope, Antinous, and others, whom he calls by what names he pleases.

I shall not here insist upon the many excellent advices which are so many parts and natural consequences of the fundamental truth, and which the poet very dexterously lays down in those fictions which are the episodes and members of the entire action. Such for instance are these advices:—Not to intrude oneself into the mysteries of government which the prince keeps secret: this is represented to us by the winds shut up in a bull's hide, which the miserable companions of Ulysses would needs be so foolish as to pry into. Not to suffer oneself to be led away by the seeming charms of an idle and inactive life, to which the Sirens' song[3] invited; not to suffer oneself to be sensualized by pleasures, like those who were changed into brutes by Circe; and a great many other points of morality necessary for all sorts of people.

This poem is more useful to the people than the *Iliad*, where the subjects suffer rather by the ill conduct of their princes than through their own miscarriages. But in the *Odyssey* it is not the fault of Ulysses that is the ruin of his subjects. This wise prince leaves untried no method to make them partakers of the benefit of his return. Thus the poet in the *Iliad* says, 'He sings the anger of Achilles, which had caused the death of so many Grecians;' and on the contrary, in the *Odyssey*[4] he tells his readers, 'That the subjects perished through their own fault.'

SECT. IV

Aristotle[5] bestows great encomiums upon Homer for the simplicity of his design, because he has included in one single part all that happened at the siege of Troy. And to this he opposes the ignorance of some poets, who imagined that the unity of the fable or action was sufficiently preserved by the unity of the hero; and who composed their Theseids, Heracleids, and the like, wherein they only heaped up in one poem every thing that happened to one personage.

He finds fault with those poets who were for reducing the unity of the fable into the unity of the hero, because one man may have performed several adventures which it is impossible to reduce under any one general and simple head. This reducing of all things to unity and simplicity is what Horace likewise makes his first rule:

'Denique sit quodvis simplex duntaxat, et unum.'

According to these rules, it will be allowable to make use of several fables, or, to speak more correctly, of several incidents which may be divided into several fables; provided they are so ordered that the unity of the fable be not spoiled. This liberty is still greater in the epic poem, because it is of a larger extent, and ought to be entire and complete. I will explain myself more distinctly by the practice of Homer.

No doubt but one might make four distinct fables out of these four following instructions:

1. 'Division between those of the same party exposes them entirely to their enemies.'
2. 'Conceal your weakness, and you will be dreaded as much as if you had none of those imperfections of which they are ignorant.'

3. 'When your strength is only feigned, and founded only in the opinion of others, never venture so far as if your strength was real.'
4. 'The more you agree together, the less hurt can your enemies do you.'

It is plain, I say, that each of these particular maxims might serve for the ground-work of a fiction, and one might make four distinct fables out of them. May not one then put all these into one single epopea? Not unless one single fable can be made out of all. The poet indeed may have so much skill as to unite all into one body as members and parts, each of which taken asunder would be imperfect; and if he joins them so, this conjunction shall be no hinderance at all to the unity and the regular simplicity of the fable. This is what Homer has done with such success in the composition of the *Iliad*.

1. 'The division between Achilles and his allies tended to the ruin of their designs.' 2. 'Patroclus comes to their relief in the armour of this hero, and Hector retreats.' 3. 'But this young man, pushing the advantage which his disguise gave him too far, ventures to engage with Hector himself; but not being master of Achilles's strength (whom he only represented in outward appearance) he is killed, and by this means leaves the Grecian affairs in the same disorder, from which in that disguise he came to free them.' 4. 'Achilles, provoked at the death of his friend, is reconciled, and revenges his loss by the death of Hector.' These various incidents being thus united, do not make different actions and fables, but are only the incomplete and unfinished parts of one and the same action and fable, which alone, when taken thus complexly, can be said to be complete and entire: and all these maxims of the moral are easily reduced into these two parts, which in my opinion cannot be separated without enervating the force of both. The two parts are these,[6] That a right understanding is the preservation, and discord the destruction of states.

Though then the poet has made use of two parts in his poems, each of which might have served for a fable, as we have observed, yet this multiplication cannot be called a vicious and irregular polymythia, contrary to the necessary unity and simplicity of the fable; but it gives the fable another qualification, altogether necessary and regular, namely, its perfection and finishing stroke.

SECT. V

The action[7] of a poem is the subject which the poet undertakes, proposes, and builds upon. So that the moral and the instructions which are the end of the epic poem are not the matter of it. Those the poets leave in their allegorical and figurative obscurity. They only give notice at the exordium, that they sing some action; the revenge of Achilles, the return of Ulysses, &c.

Since then the action is the matter of a fable, it is evident that whatever incidents are essential to the fable, or constitute a part of it, are necessary also to the action, and are parts of the epic matter, none of which ought to be omitted. Such, for instance, are the contention of Agamemnon and Achilles, the slaughter Hector makes in the Grecian army, the reunion of the Greek princes; and lastly, the resettlement and victory which was the consequence of that reunion.

There are four qualifications in the epic action; the first is its unity, the second its integrity, the third its importance, the fourth its duration.

The unity of the epic action, as well as the unity of the fable, does not consist either in the unity of the hero, or in the unity of time: three things I suppose are necessary to it. The first is, to make use of no episode but what arises from the very platform and foundation of the action, and is as it were a natural member of the body. The second is, exactly to unite these episodes and these members with one another. And the third is, never to finish any episode so as it may seem to be an entire action; but to let each episode still appear, in its own particular nature, as the member of a body, and as a part of itself not complete.

Aristotle[8] not only says that the epic action should be one, but adds, that it should be entire, perfect, and complete; and for this purpose ought to have a beginning, a middle, and an end. These three parts of a whole are too generally and universally denoted by the words, beginning, middle, and end; we may interpret them more precisely, and say, that the causes and designs of an action are the beginning; that the effects of these causes, and the difficulties that are met with in the execution of these designs, are the middle; and that the unravelling and resolution of these difficulties are the end.

Homer's[9] design in the *Iliad* is to relate the anger and revenge of Achilles. The beginning of this action is the change of Achilles from a calm to a passionate temper. The middle is the effects of his passion, and all the illustrious deaths it is the cause of. The end of this same action is the return of Achilles to his calmness of temper again. All was quiet in the Grecian camp, when Agamemnon their general provokes Apollo against them, whom he was willing to appease afterwards at the cost and prejudice of Achilles, who had no part in his fault. This then is an exact beginning; it supposes nothing before, and requires after it the effects of this anger. Achilles revenges himself, and that is an exact middle; it supposes before it the anger of Achilles, this revenge is the effect of it. Then this middle requires after it the effects of this revenge, which is the satisfaction of Achilles: for the revenge had not been complete, unless Achilles had been satisfied. By this means the poet makes his hero, after he was glutted by the mischief he had done to Agamemnon, by the death of Hector, and the honour he did his friend, by insulting over his murderer; he makes him, I say, to be moved by the tears and misfortunes of king Priam. We see him as calm at the end of the poem, during the funeral of Hector, as he was at the beginning of the poem, whilst the plague raged among the Grecians. This end is just, since the calmness of temper Achilles re-enjoyed, is only an effect of the revenge which ought to have preceded: and after this nobody expects any more of his anger. Thus has Homer been very exact in the beginning, middle, and end of the action he made choice of for the subject of his *Iliad*.

His design[10] in the *Odyssey* was to describe the return of Ulysses from the siege of Troy, and his arrival at Ithaca. He opens this poem with the complaints of Minerva against Neptune, who opposed the return of this hero, and against Calypso, who detained him in an island from Ithaca. Is this a beginning? No; doubtless, the reader would know why Neptune is displeased with Ulysses, and how this prince came to be with Calypso? He would know how he came from Troy thither? The poet answers his demands out of the mouth of Ulysses himself, who relates these things, and begins the action by the recital of his travels from the city of Troy. It signifies little whether the beginning of the action be the beginning of the poem. The beginning of this action is that which happens to Ulysses, when upon his leaving Troy he bends his course for Ithaca. The middle comprehends all the misfortunes he endured, and all the disorders of his own government. The end is the reinstating of the hero in the peaceable possession of his kingdom, where he was acknowledged by his son, his wife, his father, and several others. The poet was sensible he should have ended ill, had he gone no farther than the death of these princes, who were the rivals and enemies of Ulysses, because the reader might have looked for some revenge which the subjects of these princes might have taken on him who had killed their sovereigns: but this danger over, and the people vanquished and quieted, there was nothing more to be expected. The poem and the action have all their parts, and no more.

But the order of the *Odyssey* differs from that of the *Iliad*, in that the poem does not begin with the beginning of the action.

The causes[11] of the action are also what the poet is obliged to give an account of. There are three sorts of causes, the humours, the interests, and the designs of men; and these different causes of an action are likewise often the causes of one another, every man taking up those interests in which his humour engages him, and forming those designs to which his humour and interest incline him. Of all these the poet ought to inform his readers, and render them conspicuous in his principal personages.

Homer has ingeniously begun his *Odyssey* with the transactions at Ithaca, during the absence of Ulysses. If he had begun with the travels of his hero, he would scarce have spoken of any one else; and a man might have read a great deal of the poem, without conceiving the least idea of Telemachus, Penelope, or her suitors, who had so great a share in the action; but in the beginning he has pitched upon, besides these personages whom he discovers, he represents Ulysses in his full length; and from the very first opening one sees the interest which the gods take in the action.

The skill and care of the same poet may be seen likewise in inducing his personages in the first book of his *Iliad*, where he discovers the humours, the interests, and the designs of Agamemnon, Achilles, Hector, Ulysses, and several others, and even of the deities. And in his second he makes a review of the Grecian and Trojan armies, which is full evidence, that all we have here said is very necessary.

As these causes[12] are the beginning of the action, the opposite designs against that of the hero are the middle of it, and form that difficulty, or intrigue, which makes up the greatest part of the poem; the solution or unravelling commences when the reader begins to see that difficulty removed, and the doubts cleared up. Homer has divided each of his poems into two parts, and has put a particular intrigue, and the solution of it, into each part.

The first part of the *Iliad* is the anger of Achilles, who is for revenging himself upon Agamemnon by the means of Hector and the Trojans. The intrigue comprehends the three days fight which happened in the absence of Achilles: and it consists on one side in the resistance of Agamemnon and the Grecians, and on the other in the revengeful and inexorable humour of Achilles, which would not suffer him to be reconciled. The loss of the Grecians, and the despair of Agamemnon, prepare for a solution by the satisfaction which the incensed hero received from it. The death of Patroclus, joined to the offers of Agamemnon, which of themselves had proved ineffectual, remove this difficulty, and make the unravelling of the first part.

This death is likewise the beginning of the second part; since it puts Achilles upon the design of revenging himself on Hector. But the design of Hector is opposite to that of Achilles: this Trojan is valiant, and resolved to stand on his own defence. This valour and resolution of Hector are on his part the cause of the intrigue. All the endeavours Achilles used to meet with Hector, and be the death of him; and the contrary endeavours of the Trojan to keep out of his reach, and defend himself, are the intrigue; which comprehends the battle of the last day. The unravelling begins at the death of Hector; and besides that, it contains the insulting of Achilles over his body, the honours he paid to Patroclus, and the intreaties of king Priam. The regrets of this king, and the other Trojans, in the sorrowful obsequies they paid to Hector's body, end the unravelling; they justify the satisfaction of Achilles, and demonstrate his tranquillity.

The first part of the *Odyssey* is the return of Ulysses into Ithaca. Neptune opposes it by raising tempests, and this makes the intrigue. The unravelling is the arrival of Ulysses upon his own island, where Neptune could offer him no further injury. The second part is the reinstating of this hero in his own government. The princes that are his rivals, oppose him, and this is a fresh intrigue: the solution of it begins at their deaths, and is completed as soon as the Ithacans were appeased.

These two parts in the *Odyssey* have not one common intrigue. The anger of Achilles forms both the intrigues in the *Iliad*; and it is so far the matter of this epopea, that the very beginning and end of this poem depend on the beginning and end of this anger. But let the desire Achilles had to revenge himself, and the desire Ulysses had to return to his own country, be never so near allied, yet we cannot place them under one and the same notion; for that desire of Ulysses is not a passion that begins and ends in the poem with the action; it is a natural habit: nor does the poet propose it for his subject, as he does the anger of Achilles.

We have already observed what is meant by the intrigue, and the unravelling thereof; let us now say something of the manner of forming both. These two should arise naturally out of the very essence and subject of the poem, and are to be deduced from thence. Their conduct is so exact and natural, that it seems as if their action had presented them with whatever they inserted, without putting themselves to the trouble of a farther inquiry.

What is more usual and natural to warriors, than anger, heat, passion, and impatience of bearing the least affront or disrespect? This is what forms the intrigue of the *Iliad*; and every thing we read there is nothing else but the effect of this humour and these passions.

What more natural and usual obstacle to those who take voyages, than the sea, the winds, and the storms? Homer makes this the intrigue of the first part of the *Odyssey*: and for the second, he makes use of almost the infallible effect of the long absence of a master, whose return is quite despaired of, viz. the insolence of his servants and neighbours, the danger of his son and wife, and the sequestration of his estate. Besides, an absence of almost twenty years, and the insupportable fatigues joined to the age of which Ulysses then was, might induce him to believe that he should not be owned by those who thought him dead, and whose interest it was to have him really so. Therefore if he had presently declared who he was, and had called himself Ulysses, they would easily have destroyed him as an impostor, before he had an opportunity to make himself known.

There could be nothing more natural nor more necessary than this ingenious disguise, to which the advantages his enemies had taken of his absence had reduced him, and to which his long misfortunes had inured him. This allowed him an opportunity, without hazarding any thing, of taking the best measures he could, against those persons who could not so much as mistrust any harm from him. This way was afforded him, by the very nature of his action, to execute his designs, and overcome the obstacles it cast before him. And it is this contest between the prudence and the dissimulation of a single man on one hand, and the ungovernable insolence of so many rivals on the other, which constitutes the intrigue of the second part of the *Odyssey*.

If the plot[13] or intrigue must be natural, and such as springs from the very subject, as has been already urged, then the winding-up of the plot, by a more sure claim, must have this qualification, and be a probable consequence of all that went before. As this is what the readers regard more than the rest, so should the poet be more exact in it. This is the end of the poem, and the last impression that is to be stamped upon them.

We shall find this in the *Odyssey*. Ulysses by a tempest is cast upon the island of the Phaeacians, to whom he discovers himself, and desires they would favour his return to his own country, which was not very far distant. One cannot see any reason why the king of this island should refuse such a reasonable request to a hero whom he seemed to have in great esteem. The Phaeacians indeed had heard him tell the story of his adventures; and in this fabulous recital consisted all the advantage that he could derive from his presence; for the art of war which they admired in him, his undauntedness under dangers, his indefatigable patience, and other virtues, were such as these islanders were not used to. All their talent lay in singing and dancing, and whatsoever was charming in a quiet life. And here we see how dexterously Homer prepares the incidents he makes use of. These people could do no less, for the account with which Ulysses had so much entertained them, than afford him a ship and a safe convoy, which was of little expence or trouble to them.

When he arrived, his long absence, and the travels which had disfigured him, made him altogether unknown; and the danger he would have incurred, had he discovered himself too soon, forced him to a disguise: lastly, this disguise gave him an opportunity of surprising those young suitors, who for several years together had been accustomed to nothing but to sleep well, and fare daintily.

It was from these examples that Aristotle drew this rule, that 'Whatever concludes the poem should so spring from the very constitution of the fable, as if it were a necessary, or at least a probable consequence.'

SECT. VI

The time[14] of the epic action is not fixed, like that of the dramatic poem: it is much longer; for an uninterrupted duration is much more necessary in an action which one sees and is present at, than in one which we only read or hear repeated. Besides tragedy is fuller of passion, and consequently of such a violence as cannot admit of so long a duration.

The *Iliad* containing an action of anger and violence, the poet allows it but a short time, about forty days. The design of the *Odyssey* required another conduct; the character of the hero is prudence and long-suffering; therefore the time of its duration is much longer, above eight years.

The passions[15] of tragedy are different from those of the epic poem. In the former, terror and pity have the chief place; the passion that seems most peculiar to epic poetry, is admiration.

Besides this admiration, which in general distinguishes the epic poem from the dramatic, each epic poem has likewise some peculiar passion, which distinguishes it in particular from other epic poems, and constitutes a kind of singular and individual difference between these poems of the same species. These singular passions correspond to the character of the hero. Anger and terror reign throughout the *Iliad*, because Achilles is angry, and the most terrible of all men. The Aeneid has all the soft and tender passions, because that is the character of Aeneas. The prudence, wisdom, and constancy of Ulysses do not allow him either of these extremes, therefore the poet does not permit one of them to be predominant in the *Odyssey*. He confines himself to admiration only, which he carries to an higher pitch than in the *Iliad*: and it is upon this account that he introduces a great many more machines in the *Odyssey*, into the body of the action, than are to be seen in the actions of the other two poems.

The manners[16] of the epic poem ought to be poetically good, but it is not necessary they be always morally so. They are poetically good, when one may discover the virtue or vice, the good or ill inclinations, of every one who speaks or acts: they are poetically bad, when persons are made to speak or act out of character, or inconsistently, or unequally. The manners of Aeneas and of Mezentius are equally good, considered poetically, because they equally demonstrate the piety of the one, and the impiety of the other.

It[17] is requisite to make the same distinction between a hero in morality, and a hero in poetry, as between moral and poetical goodness. Achilles had as much right to the latter as Aeneas. Aristotle says, that the hero of a poem should be neither good nor bad; neither advanced above the rest of mankind by his virtues, or sunk beneath them by his vices; that he may be the proper and fuller example to others, both what to imitate and what to decline.

The other qualifications of the manners are, that they be suitable to the causes which either raise or discover them in the persons; that they have an exact resemblance to what history, or fable, have delivered of those persons to whom they are ascribed; and that there be an equality in them, so that no man is made to act, or speak, out of his character.

But this equality is not sufficient for the unity[18] of the character; it is further necessary, that the same spirit appear in all sorts of encounters. Thus acting with great piety and mildness in the first part of the Aeneid, which requires no other character; and afterwards appearing illustrious in heroic valour, in the wars of the second part; but there, without any appearance either of a hard or a soft disposition; would, doubtless, be far from offending against the equality of the manners: but yet there would be no simplicity or unity in the character. So that, besides the qualities that claim their particular place upon different occasions, there must be one appearing throughout, which commands over all the rest; and without this, we may affirm, it is no character.

One may indeed make a hero as valiant as Achilles, as pious as Aeneas, and as prudent as Ulysses. But it is a mere chimaera to imagine a hero that has the valour of Achilles, the piety of Aeneas, and the prudence of Ulysses, at one and the same time. This vision might happen to an author, who would suit the character of a hero to whatever each part of the action might naturally require, without regarding the essence of the fable, or the unity of the character in the same person upon all sorts of occasions: this hero would be the mildest, best-natured, prince in the world, and also the most choleric, hard-hearted, and implacable creature imaginable; he would be extremely tender like Aeneas, extremely violent like Achilles, and yet have the indifference of Ulysses, that is incapable of the two extremes. Would it not be in vain for the poet to call this person by the same name throughout?

Let us reflect on the effects it would produce in several poems, whose authors were of opinion, that the chief character of a hero is that of an accomplished man. They would be all alike; all valiant in battle, prudent in council, pious in the acts of religion, courteous, civil, magnificent, and, lastly, endued with all the prodigious virtues any poet could invent. All this would be independent of the action and the subject of the poem; and, upon seeing each hero separated from the rest of the work, we should not easily guess, to what action, and to what poem, the hero belonged. So that we should see, that none of those would have a character, since the character is that which makes a person discernible, and which distinguishes him from all others.

This commanding quality in Achilles is his anger, in Ulysses the art of dissimulation, in Aeneas meekness. Each of these may be styled, by way of eminence, the character in these heroes.

But these characters cannot be alone. It is absolutely necessary that some other should give them a lustre, and embellish them as far as they are capable; either by hiding the defects that are in each, by some noble and shining qualities, as the poet has done the anger of Achilles, by shading it with extraordinary valour; or by making them entirely of the nature of a true and solid virtue, as is to be observed in the two others. The dissimulation of Ulysses is a part of his prudence; and the meekness of Aeneas is wholly employed in submitting his will to the gods. For the making up this union, our poets have joined together such qualities as are by nature the most compatible; valour with anger, meekness with piety, and prudence with dissimulation. This last union was necessary for the goodness of Ulysses; for without that, his dissimulation might have degenerated into wickedness and double-dealing.

NOTES

1. The fable of the *Odyssey*.
2. *Odyssey* v.
3. *Improba Siren desidia*. Horat.
4. *Odyssey* i.
5. Of the unity of the fable.
6. 'Concordia res parvae crescunt: discordia magnae dilabuntur.' Sallust. de Bello Jug.
7. Of the action of the epic poem.
8. Of the beginning, middle, and end of the action.
9. The action of the *Iliad*.
10. The action of the *Odyssey*.
11. Of the causes and beginning of the action.
12. Of the middle or intrigue of the action.
13. Of the end or unravelling of the action.
14. The time of the action.

15. The passions of the epic poem.
16. The manners.
17. Character of the hero.
18. Unity of the character. vol. I.

ON THE ROAD
(JACK KEROUAC)

"Faith on the Run"
by Gary Lindberg, in *The Confidence*
Man in American Literature (1982)

INTRODUCTION

In "Faith on the Run," Gary Lindberg examines Jack Kerouac's modern American trickster figure, *On the Road*'s Dean Moriarty, and his inspiration, Kerouac's friend Neal Cassady. Lindberg describes Moriarty as a kind of Walt Whitman on speed, a con man with an affable and transgressive attitude: "The world of particulars and appearances is a world of hassles and misleading entanglements, and much as Dean delights in complication, he leaves it behind on the road, rising above it, cruising past it, seeing beyond it, restoring his sense of control and order and personal authority." Lindberg argues that by presenting Moriarty as "an archaic trickster whose primal energy crashes through all cultural bounds," Kerouac creates a breaker of taboos, a universal figure who inspires others in his pursuit of "'the ragged and ecstatic joy of pure being.'"

We've all certainly got our money's worth every time he fleeced us, haven't we? . . . I feel *compelled* to defend my friend's honor

---

Lindberg, Gary. "Faith on the Run." *The Confidence Man in American Literature.* London: Oxford UP, 1982. 259–279.

as a good old red, white, and blue hundred-per-cent American con man.

—Ken Kesey

There he is on the midway, Grack the Frenchie, talking for his count-store or his zoo, while the loudspeaker clamored under his come-on with a *hee hee hee* and a *ho ho ho* . . . This was the big show, if they only knew it.

—Herbert Gold

Do you think we believe it.

—Gertrude Stein

Traveling light, like Yossarian, the Invisible Man, and Augie March, may be our central strategy of survival. It allows us to preserve our own reality in a fabricated world and yet to participate playfully in that world. We must be adaptive, resilient, and detached, like nineteenth-century shape-shifters. Traveling light is a way of facing the external world and keeping flexible. But in the American tradition of confidence men, flexibility was not the only central virtue, and dealing with the outside world was not the only art. Even more characteristic than the shape-shifter was the buoyant bringer of faith, who depended less on strategy than on charismatic force and who *was* less concerned with the surrounding world than with his own radiant energy.

The confidence men who carry on this tradition in the present differ markedly in style from Yossarian, the Invisible Man, and Augie March. In their brashness and frenetic gesturing they are more conspicuous, they take up more space. And they seem oddly out of date, as if they still believe things it is no longer fashionable to believe, or as if they were charlatans who didn't hear the show was over. They influence other people less by gambits and masquerade than by direct personal appeal. On the other hand, they are far less sensitive to the individual needs of other people. They make promises like the nineteenth-century booster, not as contracts but as creative gestures. The faith they appeal to is not directed toward something else—faith in God or faith that the railroad will run by one's land. It is reflexive. A person with "faith" in this sense is healthy, expansive, and energetic.

Although such a state of faith is a personal experience, it can also be shared. That is what the word confidence is all about. The person with extraordinary, buoyant, all-purpose faith and its accompanying energy can radiate this inner state to others. He is, in the purest sense of the term, a confidence man, a sharer of faith. In his presence something almost sacred takes place. But since there is no sacramental ground for him, no elevating official ritual, his touches of divinity are encased in more squalid circumstances, and he is as likely to appear in a carnival as in a church. He is often a cheat as well as a prophet. What is the appeal of the auctioneer's incantation, the carnie's fast talk, the medicine show's razzle-dazzle, the booster's verbal magic? We enjoy such performances even while we doubt the showman's specific promises, for they refresh the mind and renew the world. They excite and exhilarate us. Perhaps the tonic will not cure warts, and perhaps the tract of land is actually two feet under water, but the real promise is of another kind. If we share the con man's faith, allow ourselves to ride his words into his imagined world, we may literally be transported and thus tap a corresponding source of energy within ourselves.

Such free flowing of energy can only be temporary, but even when we fall back to our mundane reality and find his promises not literally fulfilled, we may still recollect the state to which the confidence man lifted us. This is why Nick Carraway maintains his loyalty to Gatsby, why Huck Finn doesn't give up on Tom Sawyer, why Arthur Mervyn's disillusionment does not end his ties to Welbeck, why Mark Twain couldn't simply laugh off Colonel Beriah Sellers. And it is in releasing such inward energy—by nature beyond good and evil, outside cultural bounds—that the modern confidence man most clearly approximates the archaic trickster. But the pressures toward doubt and diminishment are so great in the contemporary world that the shared moments of energy get abruptly cut off. The con man becomes in turn more desperate to recover his own faith and more extreme in his gestures of trying to share it. Even the most enthusiastic of his disciples find good reasons for discouragement. The fate of the contemporary booster shows what has happened to the old American promise-land spirit.

NEAL CASSADY

The personal energy that the confidence man can share has been particularly infectious for Americans in the closely related forms of fast movement and fast talk. Both were carried to new extremes in

post-war America by Neal Cassady (1926–68),[1] a figure who illuminates our world as P.T. Barnum illuminated his. As the model
for Dean Moriarty in *On the Road*, the "secret hero" of *Howl*, the
sledgehammer-flipping, speedrapping, manic driver of the Day-Glo
bus labeled "Further" on which Ken Kesey and the Merry Pranksters
helped spread a new culture in the sixties, Cassady occupied a position of considerable influence. What makes him important for an
understanding of a confidence culture is the nature of that influence,
the peculiar legends that grew up around him, the styles and images
that clung to him. Cassady became a culture hero of a special sort, one
who combines personal energy and speed, breathless talk and enthusiastic belief. In a diminished and skeptical world, he temporarily makes
credible again the old American faith in the future, but it is now a
madder faith tied up with a way of moving through the world, and it
requires constant recharging, as if the booster has become not only a
con man but an extension of the world of automobiles and electricity.

In every context Cassady is a figure of virtually boundless energy.
Images of his life in the forties and fifties repeatedly involve a nearly
nonstop "schedule" in which he splits his life between two women,
learns to write from Kerouac, talks with Ginsberg, nurses a broken
thumb and a broken nose cartilage, repairs tires faster than anyone
else in the business, and turns up in the lives of his friends with more
and more new plans and mad gestures. Then, as Houlihan in Kesey's
Over the Border, Cassady keeps appearing as the force to GO, the
zany driver and talker who can rig a tire change on a bus without a
jack, hotwire a car with paper clips, repair an accelerator with a coat
hanger, coast backwards down a hill without brakes when the gas runs
out, anything to keep the show moving. Descriptions of Neal Cassady
inevitably stress his feverish activity, as if his whole body were wired
to a high-power cell.

Speed was Cassady's obsession. Acquaintances spoke of him as
the fastest man alive. He ran instead of walking, honed his reflexes for
quickness, drove fast so as to keep on the very edge between control
and adventure. Tom Wolfe's description of his coasting the Further
bus down mountain roads without brakes is typical: "For all his wild
driving he always made it through the last clear oiled gap in the maze,
like he knew it would be there all the time, which it always was." Gary
Snyder theorized that Cassady's appeal was like that of the 1880s
cowboy, except that since the frontier had been closed in, the taste

for limitless space now expressed itself in faster and faster speed. But the outward motion was coupled with inner rapidity, and the nonstop driving was both literal and metaphoric. Tom Wolfe relates Ken Kesey's theory of the time lag between sensation and reaction, 1/30th of a second if you are the most alert person alive. Kesey's point is that only by artificially altering consciousness can one close that gap; but what is interesting is the place of Cassady here, for despite his use of miscellaneous drugs (speed especially), he personally represented the closest one can come on one's own power to joining sensation and reaction. Like Emerson, he would alter consciousness if he could without a little help from his friends, so that Wolfe describes him "fibrillating tight up against the 1/30th of a second movie-screen barrier of our senses, trying to get into . . . *Now*—"

"Now," however, was not exactly the state of consciousness Neal Cassady represented, nor was it the meaning of his obsession with speed. Wolfe comes closer to it in tracing the Merry Pranksters' "Superhero thing" to one of the primary feelings of being Super-kids in the Post-War, "with the motor running and the adrenaline flowing, cruising in the neon glories of the new American night." Such cruising keeps the world out there light, fleeting, insubstantial, and thus preserves its air of promise. Cassady, in his autobiography, re-creates the feeling: "Signs, signs, lights, lights, streets, streets; it is the dark between that attracts one—what's happening there at this moment? What hidden thing, glorious perhaps, is being passed and lost forever." But the effect is also inward, the sheer exhilaration of movement and thus of power. And where the two cross—where the promissory fleeting world fuses with the cruiser's inner ecstasy—was Cassady's domain: "my mind's gears were shifted by unknown mechanism to an increase of time's torrent that received in kaleidoscopic change searing images, clear as the hurry of thought could allow, rushing so quickly by that all I could do was barely catch one before another one crowded. . . ." That is the state of consciousness that Neal Cassady represented and that his driving, his letter writing, and his talking created for others.

[. . . Such] experiences of vertigo are related to Whitman's style of promise and movement. Cassady intensified the feelings by speeding up, because in the new technology the open road was neon-studded and he could travel it at rates Whitman couldn't dream of. He related to the world out there as to something going past. At its most exciting it consisted of experiences, things, people rushing by pell-mell so that each thing was briefly seized on before being lost forever. Kerouac describes the effect as "rushing through the world without a chance to see it," but Cassady puts the matter differently in his autobiography: "eyeball kicks are among the world's greatest." And the style applied to more than the world of objects and people. Kerouac's biographer, Ann Charters, says, "Neal, with his intensities and enthusiasms, burst in and out of ideas, coming to them, throwing them in the air, dropping them behind him and hurrying on to the next one. He made Kerouac feel thick and heavy. . . ."

If the contemporary world involves rapid changes, perpetual complications, overturnings of the familiar, or what Alvin Toffler calls "the kinetic image," Neal Cassady had a way of riding its changes for thrills. Instead of worrying about disruptions of the present scenario, he delighted in the making and revising of schedules and thrived on the breathless movement from one situation to another. This attitude Kerouac captures perfectly in *On the Road* when Dean and Sal learn that a hitchhiker who was going to give them gas money after arriving at his aunt's cannot keep his promise because his aunt shot her husband and went to jail. Dean revels in the entanglement: "Think of it! The things that happen; . . . the troubles on all sides, the complications of events—whee, damn!" Such embracing and such celebrating of things as they are recall the style of Augie March. Both Augie and Neal Cassady move through endlessly complicated, often squalid worlds with wide-eyed acceptance, too fluid to linger long enough for a situation to go really bad on them. Cassady's letters and autobiographical fragments veer from event to event with the erratic, plot-exploding approach of Augie March.

But there are critical differences between Augie March and Neal Cassady. Cassady emerges in his autobiography, his letters, the accounts of his friends, as a person more fascinated by the flowing through of situations than by each one in itself. In this sense he was more inwardly involved than Augie, less exhilarated by the world out there than by his own movement through it. His hyperactivity, his driving, his quick reactions, his fleeting enthusiasms all point to the same ideal conception of experience: the world is moving and so is the self. Each thing, person, idea, situation appears within the consciousness only to be rapidly displaced by the next one. William Burroughs describes Cassady as "the very soul of this voyage into pure abstract, meaningless motion." Whether the cause is running, driving, accelerating the sense of time, or falling into emotional and social complexities, the result is a thrilling mixture of personal ecstasy and a perpetually promising (because perpetually arriving) world.

That conception of a world in rapid motion can be generated in another way as well, and Neal Cassady was an expert at it. Cassady the driver was also Cassady the talker, and every reminiscence of him registers the excitement of his endless monologues with their staccato bursts of energy. The speed of his driving and of his reflexes was matched by the speed of his talk so that the compulsive words could be as infectious as the mountain rides without brakes. Tom Wolfe metaphorically suggests the fusion of Cassady's styles:

> Cassady is a monologuist, only he doesn't seem to care whether anyone is listening or not. He just goes off on the monologue, by himself if necessary, although anyone is welcome aboard. He will answer all questions, although not exactly in that order, because we can't stop here, next rest area 40 miles, you understand, spinning off memories, metaphors, literary, Oriental, hip allusions. . . .

The various re-creations of these monologues indicate that they were basically narratives of events and emotional entanglements, so rapid and disgressive, so full of mishaps and mad scramblings, as to suggest that Cassady in words was always trying to catch up with Cassady in action, or as he put it in his autobiography, "my mind was thinking such thoughts that soon I actually thought of how at last I could tell you on paper perhaps the knowledge of action—But later." Pointless as they may have been, however, Cassady's monologues did more than set the world spinning in a listener's head. Like the con man's fast talk, they promised something, too. Ken Kesey emphasizes this in his tribute to Cassady: "Only through the actual speedshifting grind and gasp and zoom of his high compression voice do you get the sense of the urgent sermon that Neal was driving madcap into every road-blocked head he came across."

Neal Cassady was a confidence man. He knew how to use his fast talk for his own ulterior purposes, as in the trial run of the "Further" bus when by prestidigitation and patient bewildering monologue he convinced a suspicious policeman that a nonexistent handbrake was perfectly functional. His letters and reminiscences dwell with adolescent pride on his ability to con girls, and his wife Carolyn remembers the art as more generally practiced: "He could talk and would talk with anybody and instantly they felt that he really cared about them. . . . Now part of that became conning, he learned how to use that to con. He was a master at getting you to think that he knew exactly where you were and what you needed and he could always supply it." John Tytell, in *Naked Angels*, sees Cassady's conning as a compulsion, a "habitual need to persuade people to act." But coupled with his fast driving, his urgent monologues, his sense of a world in promising motion, Cassady's direct conning takes on the ambivalence of a longer tradition of American confidence men. The people who remember his conning remember it as an attractive, well-nigh a spiritual, quality. His old Denver friend Jim Holmes describes him in terms that Nick Carraway could apply to Gatsby: "The man was very, very energetic and very personable and he would—I don't think intention-ally—but he would actually flatter you, your ego, in such a way that he would almost immediately be liked. . . . I don't think it was a put-on. It was a technique, however. But it wasn't a con." And that is where Cassady the man turns into Cassady the legend, the figure who would drive seventy-two hours straight across country because he had heard about a man with a vision; who would gravitate from Kerouac and Ginsberg to Kesey and become an exemplar to two generations of American experimenters.

What people saw in Neal Cassady's feverish activity was simply a modernized version of a very familiar American type, the protean, yea-saying bearer of confidence. He came into the lives of Jack Kerouac and Allen Ginsberg as a persuasive force to move out, to speed up, to experiment, to risk meeting life in a mad rush of frenzy. His driving and his talking made people experience a world in motion as a world full of promise, and his own restless energy seemed the ideal personal style with which to confront it. In contrast with the "absurd hero" of modern existentialism or the nihilistic spirit so often assumed as the appropriate response to the post-1945 world, the Neal Cassady legend draws on the affirmative, joyous, activist traditions of American values. Tom Wolfe contrasts this spirit, complicated by Merry-Prankster put-ons, with the spirit of Eastern mysticism:

> this 400-horsepower takeoff game, this American flag-flying game, this Day-Glo game, this yea-saying game, this dread neon game, this . . . *superhero* game, all wired-up and wound up and amplified in the electropastel chrome game gleam. It wasn't the

Buddha … satori is passive, just lying back and grooving and grokking on the Overmind and leave Teddy Roosevelt out of it.

And one of the last pictures in *The Electric Kool-Aid Acid Test* is Neal Cassady, wheeling into an Acid Test dominated by the Eastern-oriented Calliope Company which had replaced the Merry Pranksters, Neal's eyes jumping around, the others staring at him in passive tolerance, Neal saying, "Hey! Don't you want to *do* anything—get it started, you understand—slide it around—" and finally kicking and flailing out the door by himself.

He was, Kesey says, "one hell of a hero and the tales of his exploits will always be blowing around us." That is the other thing about the Cassady legend, the dimension of the heroic. Throughout *The Electric Kool-Aid Acid Test*, which traces Kesey's experience as it fuses with and becomes affected by a virtual group consciousness, Cassady is the one figure who remains distinctly himself, an individual whose qualities—alertness to the moment, instant flexibility, deadly competence—may be collective ideals, but who always practices them in a personal style. His endless seeking of something in the "new American night," his infectious energy, his dazzling drive talk merge in a figure who restores an older promise-land spirit to the strategies of survival in the Post-War world. And unlike the Invisible Man and Augie March, who told their own stories of play, evasion, shape shifting, and discovery, Neal Cassady in legend becomes someone *told about*, a figure who can bring buoyancy, energy, and daring to someone else. In his major legendary form, Neal Cassady becomes a full-scale, fully ambivalent confidence man as hero.

ON THE ROAD

Sal Paradise, the narrator of Jack Kerouac's *On the Road* (1957), sees the book's central character, Dean Moriarty, as a hero in a variety of American styles—the spirit of the West, the energetic mover and doer, the cowboy, the Whitman-like enthusiast, "that mad Ahab at the wheel" compelling others at hissing, incredible speeds across the country. But the subsuming model for the Cassady legend is of the American hero as a confidence man:

> He was simply a youth tremendously excited with life, and though he was a con-man, he was only conning because he wanted so much to live and to get involved with people who

would otherwise pay no attention to him. He was conning me and I knew it (for room and board and "how-to-write," etc.), and he knew I knew (this has been the basis of our relationship), but I didn't care and we got along fine. . . .

In Sal's usage, "con-man" is a phrase of admiration—"the holy con-man with the shining mind," "a great amorous soul such as only a con-man can have"—and the novel explores the meaning and value of a confidence man in modern American life.

Sal Paradise is essential to the creation of a con man as hero, for someone has to register that radiant energy, someone has to receive and interpret it, almost like a priest. A less prissy Nick Carraway discovering a more frantic Gatsby, Sal responds enthusiastically to Dean Moriarty: "I could hear a new call and see a new horizon." Something of Dean's mad faith is transmitted to Sal whenever they are together—"somewhere along the line the pearl would be handed to me." On his own Sal tends to brood and his imaginative energy runs down, but each time Dean appears or sends a summoning letter—even if in the guise of a frightful Angel or the Shrouded Traveler—Sal perks up and sets off, as if Dean were a tonic for a tired soul. He instills the energy to move, to do, to dare getting off dead center, and more important, he encourages Sal to believe. Once Dean enters his life, Sal becomes a devotee of Promise Land, alert to the hints of place names and prairie nights—Denver and San Francisco are jewels in the "Promised Land." "Beyond the glittering street was darkness, and beyond the darkness the West. I had to go." He and Dean share the vision of the country as an oyster for them to open, and Sal repeatedly re-enacts the promissory quest, as in calling Hollywood "the ragged promised land, the fantastic end of America."

The point is that Sal sees in Dean's frenzy and racing and hotwired talk what Nick Carraway sees in Gatsby's colossal pretense—the underlying faith: "the road must eventually lead to the whole world." All the frantic gestures and leavings behind of charred ruins, the zany risks and tangled pronouncements appear as merely the superficial forms through which Dean expresses his urgent vision, his effort to come to IT. Dean talks about IT as Emerson talks about the pure Poem in the Mind of the One:

> Here's a guy and everybody's there, right? Up to him to put down what's on everybody's mind. . . . All of a sudden somewhere in

the middle of the chorus he gets *it*—everybody looks up and knows; they listen; he picks it up and carries. Time stops . . . everybody knows it's not the tune that counts but IT.

Dean, in Sal's re-creation, is a visionary and an enthusiast. When he races compulsively about the city in the night, digging the streets, digging the jazz players, digging the intellectuals and the criminals, we are to believe that he is restlessly seeking IT in its many passing manifestations. The world pouring past the car window is merely the rush of appearances, and to perceive them in a rush is to come closer to what is beyond them. Thus as Dean and Sal race through experience they are doing a kind of high-voltage meditation, "our final excited joy in talking and living to the blank tranced end of all innumerable riotous angelic particulars that had been lurking in our souls all our lives."

It is this enabling faith that transfigures the outward gestures and style of Dean Moriarty. What could easily appear to others as restlessness, undependability, a mere compulsion at every moment to GO, turns out to have a metaphysical basis as Sal interprets it: "we all realized we were leaving confusion and nonsense behind and performing our one and noble function of the time, move." The world of particulars and appearances is a world of hassles and misleading entanglements, and much as Dean delights in complication, he leaves it behind on the road, rising above it, cruising past it, seeing beyond it, restoring his sense of control and order and personal authority. This is the inward content of Dean's obsession with speed, the promise behind his fast talk. He does not try to make people believe precisely what he says; they usually recognize that he is "making logics where there was nothing but inestimable sorrrowful sweats." Instead, he offers them a ride, no destination, you understand, but fleeting glimpses of IT through the rush of visions. "There's always more, a little further—it never ends." This is the sense in which Dean the con man has and shares "the tremendous energy of a new kind of American saint." And the American traditions, both popular and intellectual, that celebrated such bearers of faith and energy were precisely what gave Kerouac the perceptual framework to look beyond Neal Cassady and see Dean Moriarty and to look beyond both and see . . . IT.

Yet Dean Moriarty is, of course, a criminal. He is that kind of con man, too, a compulsive thief of cars who spent much of his youth in jail, a "change artist" of the first order who could wish a parking-lot customer Merry Christmas "so volubly a five-spot in change for twenty was never missed." Like Gatsby and Augie March, however, he can mingle with the criminal world and yet not become of it. Augie manages this by detachment. Dean Moriarty and Gatsby actually transfigure criminality itself. Dean has a "native strange saintliness to save him from the iron fate." In his first visit to Sal, Dean appears different from the down-putting, sometimes tedious intellectuals of the East and different from its criminals as well—"his 'criminality' was not something that sulked and sneered; it was a wild yea-saying overburst of American joy." By racing in society instead of putting it down, Dean somehow redeems crime. As long as he can be a bringer of faith and a celebrant of energy, he can without blame be the more exploitive kind of con man as well.

Or at least he can in Sal's eyes. Like so much American literature of the nineteenth century, *On the Road* divides the world into believers and doubters. There are people like Carlo Marx (modeled on Allen Ginsberg) who ask disturbing but finally wrong questions:

> Then Carlo asked Dean if he was honest and specifically if he was being honest with *him* in the bottom of his soul.
> "Why do you bring that up again?"

Carlo brings a demand for personal sincerity and for intellectual point that runs counter to Dean's whole mode of being. When he asks the book's central question—"Whither goest thou, America, in thy shiny car in the night?"—Sal and Dean have nothing to say: "The only thing to do was go." The other skeptics in the book are more practical in their demands. They look to Dean's outward behavior instead of his beliefs and lose patience with him. "Con-man Dean was antagonizing people away from him by degrees." His former friend Ed Wall "had lost faith in Dean." His cousin tells him, "Now look, Dean, I don't believe you any more or anything you're going to try to tell me." In San Francisco the old gang turns on him for his irresponsibility, his carelessness, "his enormous series of sins," and when Sal tries to argue that "he's got the secret that we're all busting to find," Roy Johnson replies that Dean is "just a very interesting and even amusing con-man." Even Sal has his days of doubt, losing faith when Dean leaves him moneyless on the streets of San Francisco to pursue his own pleasure, recognizing "what a rat he was" when Dean deserts him sick in Mexico at the end of the book. But underlying the vacillation of feeling, when Sal knows better than to *believe* Dean, is a constant belief *in* Dean. "I told Dean I was sorry he had nobody in the world to believe in him. 'Remember that I believe in you.'" From one perspective Dean cannot be trusted to keep his word or his loyalty. From another he can be counted on to turn up again and again with promise and exhilaration, to radiate his tremendous energy to others, to give them a good time just by being himself. On a deeper level Sal is responding to Dean not only as a modern American con man but as an archaic trickster whose primal energy crashes through all cultural bounds: "Bitterness, recriminations, advice, morality, sadness—everything was behind him, and ahead of him was the ragged and ecstatic joy of pure being."

NOTE

1. The literature that Neal Cassady haunts is extensive. He is Dean Moriarty in Jack Kerouac's *On the Road* and Cody in Kerouac's *Visions of Cody*. He is Houlihan in Ken Kesey's *Over the Border* (included in *Kesey's Garage Sale* [New York, 19731]). He appears often as himself in Tom Wolfe's *Electric Kool-Aid Acid Test* (New York, 1968). Biographical material is available in Ann Charters, *Kerouac: A Biography* (San Francisco, 1973); John Tytell, *Naked Angels: The Lives and Literature of the Beat Generation* (New York, 1976); Carolyn Cassady, *Heart Beat: My Life with Jack and Neal* (Berkeley, 1976); and Barry Gifford and Lawrence Lee, *Jack's Book: An Oral Biography of Jack Kerouac* (New York, 1978). "Appreciations" include an interview with Carolyn Cassady in *Rolling Stone* (October 12, 1972) and two pieces by Ken Kesey, "An Impolite Interview with Ken Kesey" (1971) and "Neal Cassady" (1971), both included in *Kesey's Garage Sale*. Finally, there is Cassady's own incomplete, posthumously published autobiography, *The First Third: A Partial Autobiography and Other Writings* (San Francisco, 1971), which develops extensively his experience in Denver and on the road from ages six to nine, an alternation between half-years

on Larimer Street with his wino father and half-years with his mother and half-brothers; it also contains some fragments on teenage and adult experiences and several letters to Kerouac and to Kesey.

ORLANDO
(VIRGINIA WOOLF)

"With Orlando in Wonderland"
by Rossitsa Artemis, University of Nicosia, Cyprus

Virginia Woolf has earned both notoriety and admiration among scholars and common readers for a number of "difficult" but beautiful works like *The Voyage Out* (1916), *Jacob's Room* (1922), *Mrs Dalloway* (1925), *To the Lighthouse* (1927), and *The Waves* (1931). Yet she is also well-known for the journalistic eloquence and essayistic power she demonstrates in other works, especially *A Room of One's Own* (1929) and *Three Guineas* (1938).

Considered by many literary critics a key text in feminism and, undoubtedly, a significant Modernist text, *Orlando: A Biography* (1928) especially challenges the readers' understanding of three key concepts in fiction: time, setting, and character. Although Woolf had already successfully questioned the function of these concepts in her novels *Mrs Dalloway* and *To the Lighthouse*, *Orlando* generated a few unexpected twists of its own: For a book conceived by Woolf as a "writer's holiday," the work poses some serious philosophical questions for the interpretation of "time" and "self" (*Diary*, III: 168). It also irreverently tackles the genre of biography. The difficulties in interpreting *Orlando*, then, are the result of the book's complexity as an unorthodox philosophic contemplation on time and self, all packed into a parodic biography of a (wo)man of protean quality, a trickster not in disguise but in full display of her unthinkable powers to reshape gender and sexual politics over a period of some five centuries.

The Biographer's "Tricks of the Trade"

Nigel Nicolson defines *Orlando* as "the longest and most charming love letter in literature" for its dedication to the life and persona of Vita Sackville-West, an extremely colourful figure in the Bloomsbury circle (qtd in Gilbert 1993: xv). Yet Woolf not simply dedicates the novel to her intimate friend Vita but uses the glorious ancestral history of the Sackville family and their family home, Knole, to produce a stunning combination of picaresque *Bildungsroman* and biography. To write a fictionalized "biography" of Orlando, a hero or a heroine who simultaneously embodies the "true" character of Vita so familiar to the author and, at the same time, a character who outgrows the realistic constraints imposed by the genre of biography, is what motivates Woolf to embark on a journey of creative enjoyment and exploration. Thus her impetus to "revolutionize biography in a night" and her desire to "toss this up in the air and see what happens" are married into the fantastic, parodic and polemic form of a fictional biography (*Diary*, III: 428). Then, indeed it will be reasonable for the lover of biographies to ask, "How can one be both faithful to facts and unfaithful and tell more of the truth without exactly telling it the same?"(Burns 1994: 342). In other words, if biography turns out to be more complicated than the standards of a reader expecting realism, what kind of "biography" is *Orlando* after all? Thus begins Woolf's foray into the sphere of authorial tricksterism, where the lines of expectation are blurred and the reader is forced to reconsider preconceived definitions of literature and reality.

Woolf had an impressive first-hand knowledge of the genre of biography through an extensive reading under the influence of her father, Sir Leslie Stephen. Among other duties, he was the editor of twenty-six volumes of the *Dictionary of National Biography* (1882–1890) and wrote many of the entries himself. The traditional belief of the Victorian biographer in an essential "self" that could be pinpointed and thus faithfully portrayed undoubtedly provoked Woolf to reconsider both the form and the claim. On the other hand, Woolf's *Orlando* is probably indebted to Bloomsbury friend (and one-time suitor) Lytton Strachey's *Eminent Victorians* (1918) and *Queen Victoria* (1921). While rejecting certain old-fashioned constraints inherent in the nineteenth-century biographies in favor of more psychologically based portraits, Strachey nonetheless espoused a rather masculine view of history and the individual in his biographies. Woolf, however, had been working for some time on the "tunnelling process" of representing the inner world of her fictional characters and seemed more interested in using the same method in *Orlando* to create a portrait of a living character rather than one "remembered," as if taken from the "archives" of the author (*Diary*, II: 272). Yet, without losing sight of the satirical aspect of the work of which she is so aware, as Woolf writes,

> No attempt is to be made to realize the character. Sapphism is to be suggested. Satire is to be the main note—satire & wildness . . . My own lyric vein is to be satirized. Everything mocked . . . I want to kick up my heels & be off. (*Diary*, III: 131)

With this motivation in mind, understanding *Orlando* turns into a picaresque exploration of the biography genre for the reader as well. Reading about the young man turning into a woman, masquerading as a man/woman on various occasions, challenges our expectations of traditional biography. *Orlando* also challenges the capability of the biographer to produce a "true to life" portrait by effecting a "parodic displacement of any essential and 'true' position" in *Orlando* (Burns 1994: 343). Thus, as Bowlby points out,

> Where even parody is parodied, footholds for the reader are in short supply; so, *a fortiriori*, are the points of reference that might ground a coherence relating to history and to human identity in a secure narrative style. (1997: 110)

Such a disruption of coherence, a quality so essential to the biographic account, is justified by Woolf's creative approach both to narration and to character. To make matters more confusing, Woolf's fictional biographer continually grasps for the right psychological depiction of Orlando, and very often falters on the way:

> The biographer is now faced with a difficulty which it is better perhaps to confess than to gloss over. [. . .] Our simple duty is to state the facts as far as they are known, and so let the reader make of them what he may. (47)

Such ambiguities will be quite confusing for readers expecting proper guidance and unequivocal judgment from a Victorian biographer. *Orlando* invites us to journey in search of the balance Woolf cherished in her work: Created "between truth & fantasy," the biography embraces both factual and fantastic aspects in the depiction of the self (*Diary*, III: 162).

SPACE-TIME WARPS, DOESN'T IT?

In *Orlando*, Woolf tackles the concepts of time and space, two key concepts in fiction. Woolf's unquestionable interest in the depiction of time's flow and the way it influences her characters is an inherent feature of her novels and short stories. The influential French philosopher Henri Bergson, a contemporary of Woolf's, distinguishes between the concepts of *temps* (clock time) and *durée* (psychological time) and argues that clock time produces a false idea of time, an idea pinned to clocks and calendars and their pseudo-precision in measuring human time. Psychological time, on the other hand, accounts for the individual consciousness and the way time becomes dissolved into "moments of being," coexistent and coextensive as Woolf liked to imagine them. Thus, as *Orlando*'s biographer contemplates,

> And indeed, it cannot be denied that the most successful practitioners of the art of life, often unknown people by the way, somehow contrive to synchronise the sixty or seventy different times which beat simultaneously in every normal human system so that when eleven strikes, all the rest chime in unison, and the present is neither a violent disruption nor completely forgotten in the past. [...] (210–211)

It becomes clear that Woolf's serious preoccupation with the idea of time and its representation in literature has found a way into this most straightforward of genres, the biography, where the writer simply cannot afford to deal with two kinds of time, least of all sixty or seventy. However parodic in its conception, *Orlando* still speaks about the difficulties in narrating human consciousness and the complex perceptions that inhabit it and form the self's relation to time and environment. In Woolf's hands, even the most categorical and undeniable matter for the biographer, the length of the subject's life, becomes relative and negotiable:

> The true length of a person's life, whatever the *Dictionary of National Biography* may say, is always a matter of dispute. For it is a difficult business—this time-keeping; nothing more quickly disorders it than contact with any of the arts. (211)

Still, the narrator in this particular biography, just like Orlando herself, does not mourn the stability that traditional clock time offers; quite the contrary: By acknowledging the potentials of psychological time, the biographer embraces the fantastic too. Thus Orlando manages to trick the calendar and gallop through some five centuries of English history, from the glorious times of Elizabeth I, through the Victorian era, to the "present time" of London in 1928. Such "time warps" in *Orlando* function not simply as fantastic gateways to historical periods but as gateways to the representation of historical consciousness that, according to Woolf, was so important to Vita Sackville-West. Never questioning how and why this is possible but simply accepting that it happens, Orlando embodies that human capacity to inhabit moments of being without reference to chronology, a creative mode of perception and remembering: "[...] she forgot the time. [...] She liked to think that she was riding the back of the world" (224). Just like Orlando, Knole too, the glorified ancestral home with 365 bedrooms and 52 staircases, symbolically stands for a year in the human life and easily weathers five centuries like its master. On the classic trickster border between the seriously philosophical and the tongue-in-cheek frivolous, *Orlando* is the account of moments we inhabit rather than the embodiment of one singular truth about human identity.

THE SELF DOESN'T WARP, OR DOES IT?

Woolf's gender-bending approach to the concept of self—and fictional character for that matter—strikes another blow to the traditional understanding of biography. Drawing upon the idea of androgyny she developed in her nonfiction work, Woolf treads again the grounds of the fantastic by endowing Orlando with the power to cross biological boundaries, an act that questions "the fluidity and artifice of gender" (Gilbert 1993: xvii). Again, the Victorian belief in one essential self is targeted by Woolf and by *Orlando*'s biographer in different but converging ways.

In her novels, Woolf plays with the notion of multiple selves inhabiting the traditionally unified, singular self. For example, in *Mrs Dalloway*, Clarissa contemplates her identity while looking in the mirror,

> That was her self—pointed; dart-like; definite. That was her self when some effort, some call on her to be her self, drew the parts together, she alone knew how different, how incompatible and composed so for the world only into one center, one diamond. (32)

Such a consideration of the existence of parts of a self refers once again to the Bergsonian concept of *durée*, the psychological time that the self inhabits. Yet in *Orlando*, a "miraculous" sex change is coupled with time travel to achieve the unquestionably fantastic nod toward androgyny. The biographer wryly narrates what could be conceived otherwise as a life-shattering finding for the protagonist,

> Orlando looked himself up and down in a looking-glass, without showing any signs of discomposure, and went, presumably, to his bath. [...] Orlando had become a woman—there is no denying it. But in every other respect, Orlando remained precisely as he had been. The change of sex, though it altered their future, did nothing whatever to alter their identity. (98)

The purposeful use of "their" in the last sentence substitutes the arbitrary use of the pronouns "he/his" and "she/her" in a society that endorses the "artifice" of gender. If, in Bergsonian terms, the coupling of intellect (as reason) and perceptive intuition of consciousness (as exercised in psychological time) account for the existence of different selves in one individual that "slide" into one another as time progresses, the sex change of the main character in *Orlando* could be interpreted as yet another kind of sliding. As the biographer observers, quite "inappropriately" for the genre,

> Different though the sexes are, they intermix. In every human being a vacillation from one sex to the other takes place and

> often it is only the clothes that keep the male or female
> likeness, while underneath the sex is the very opposite of what
> is above. (132–133)

The stability that sex offers for the delineation of the self is undermined to complicate and question the reader's understanding of
biography, even identity. However, the smoothness in the narration
that Woolf achieves through the accommodation of the truthful
(realistic) and the fantastic redirects the attention from the particu-
larity of the detail—as unbelievable as it might be—to the portrait
as a whole. Issues like compulsory heterosexuality and cross-dressing
are tackled on several occasions—most memorably, of course, in the
depiction of Orlando's life, but also in other characters like Arch-
duchess Harriet/Archduke Harry, for instance. The transformations
are hardly seen as "magical" but rather as a necessary acceptance of
the variable human identity.

As the biographer writes the story of Orlando's life and as Orlando
herself contemplates the world that engulfs her, an amazing narrative
that questions time and space, selves and gender identities, unfolds
for the reader. It portrays the picaresque life of the ultimate trickster:
one who outwits past, present, and future in her longevity and protean
identity. As Bowlby writes, "*Orlando* destroys illusions about history
and biography and not least about 'a man'—or it might be a woman—
'who can destroy illusions'" (1997: 110). By manipulating her readers'
expectations, Woolf creates a continually shifting and surprising text
that challenges her readers to reconsider the nature of human identity
and to resist the illusions that history fosters.

WORKS CITED

Bowlby, R. *Feminist Destinations and Further Essays on Virginia Woolf.*
    Edinburgh: Edinburgh University Press, 1997.

Burns, Christy. "Re-Dressing Feminist Identities: Tensions between Essential
    and Constructed Selves in Virginia Woolf's *Orlando*," *Twentieth Century
    Literature* 40 (Fall 1994): 342–364.

Gilbert, S. Introduction. *Orlando: A Biography*. V. Woolf. London: Penguin
    Books, 1993.

Goldman, J. *The Cambridge Introduction to Virginia Woolf*. Cambridge:
    Cambridge University Press, 2006.

Latham, J. (ed.) *Critics on Virginia Woolf*. London: George Allen and Unwin
      Ltd, 1970.
Sackville-West, V. "Virginia Woolf and *Orlando*." *Critics on Virginia Woolf*. Ed.
      J. Latham. London: George Allen and Unwin Ltd, 1970.
Whitworth, M. *Virginia Woolf*. Oxford: Oxford University Press, 2005.
Woolf, V. *Orlando: A Biography*. London: Penguin Books, 1993.
———. *The Diary of Virginia Woolf* (1915–1941), 5 vols. Ed. A. Bell and A.
      McNeillie. London: Hogarth Press, 1977–1984.
———. *To the Lighthouse*. London: Hogarth Press, 1927.
———. *Mrs Dalloway*. Oxford: Oxford University Press, 2000.

ROSENCRANTZ AND GUILDENSTERN ARE DEAD
(TOM STOPPARD)

"Tom Stoppard as Trickster in *Rosencrantz and Guildenstern are Dead*"
by Daniel K. Jernigan,
Nanyang Technological University

> There is only one world, the "real" world: Shakespeare's imagination is part of it, and the thoughts that he had in writing *Hamlet* are real. So are the thoughts that we have in reading the play. But it is of the very essence of fiction that only the thoughts, feelings, etc., in Shakespeare and his readers are real, and that there is not, in addition to them, an objective Hamlet.
> —Bertrand Russell, *Introduction to Mathematical Philosophy* (169)

There is much about Tom Stoppard's *Rosencrantz and Guildenstern are Dead* (*R & G*) that leaves the audience with the distinct impression of being had. The audience is likely, even, to find itself sympathizing with Guildenstern from the opening scene, as Guildenstern considers whether calling heads, spinning, and losing more than 90 coins in succession means that "We are now within un-, sub-, or supernatural forces" (17). Guildenstern considers the various possibilities:

GUIL: It must be indicative of something, besides the redistribution of wealth. (*He muses.*) List of possible explanations. One: I'm willing it. Inside where nothing shows. I'm the essence of a man spinning double-headed coins, and betting against himself in private atonement for an unremembered past . . . Two: time has stopped dead, and a single experience of one coin being spun once has been repeated ninety times . . . (*He flips a coin, looks at it, tosses it to* ROS.) On the whole, doubtful. Three: divine intervention, that is to say, a good turn from above concerning him, cf. children of Israel, or retribution from above concerning me, cf. Lot's wife. Four: a spectacular vindication of the principle that each individual coin spun individually (*he spins one*) is as likely to come down heads as tails and therefore should cause no surprise that each individual time it does. (16)

Here and throughout the play, we are left with the unmistakable impression that someone—or something—is making Rosencrantz and Guildenstern the butt of a grand cosmic and/or literary joke, that some trickster is causing the coins to fall so as not to comport with the laws of probability.

In the first few scenes that follow, we quickly discover that *R & G* is carefully constructed with Shakespeare's *Hamlet* as its template, but rather than making Prince Hamlet the focus of the play, Stoppard zeroes in on two minor characters instead, Rosencrantz (ROS) and Guildenstern (GUIL). The play tracks their travels to Castle Elsinore, where they have been summoned to assist Claudius and Gertrude in diagnosing Hamlet's despondency. Another key difference is that whenever *Hamlet* shifts away from ROS and GUIL, Stoppard maintains them as his focus; it is also worth noting that at these moments the two characters flounder and wander aimlessly, apparently not knowing what to do in the absence of a script.

In order to tease out the potential for reading a trickster motif at work in *R & G*, I turn to Paul Radin, who, after Jung himself, provides what is perhaps the most influential theorization of the trickster in literature.

Trickster is at one and the same time creator and destroyer, giver and negator, he who dupes others and who is always duped himself. He wills nothing consciously. At all times he is constrained to behave as he does from impulses over which he has no control. He knows neither good nor evil yet he is responsible for both. He possesses no values, moral or social,

line, but in the course of writing this book I realized that it needs to be modified in one important way, for there are also cases in which trickster creates a boundary, or brings to the surface a distinction previously hidden from sight. (7)

With Stoppard as our potential culprit, it quickly becomes apparent that all the "doubleness and duplicity" of *R & G* is in some respect part and parcel of its close examination of literary boundaries, especially for how the boundary crossing itself feels like the handiwork of a master literary trickster. For not only is nearly every scene from *Hamlet* that includes the two characters also found in *R & G*, but Stoppard also finds innovative ways to include references to scenes that make only the most minute references to the pair. And while the scenes that come directly from *Hamlet* are perhaps the most straightforward moments in Stoppard's play, there is often very surprising resonance between the characterizations that occur in those sections and what Stoppard adds in the other sections to flesh out the rest of the play.

The trickster element of this construction comes across in how this porousness between Shakespeare's text and Stoppard's own plays a substantial role in defining the character (or lack of it) of ROS and GUIL. This resonance between what Stoppard pilfers from Hamlet and what becomes perhaps the defining characteristics of ROS and GUIL is featured most prominently in the scene in which Claudius confuses the two:

> Claudius: Welcome, dear Rosencrantz ... (*he raises a hand at GUIL while ROS bows—GUIL bows late and hurriedly*) ... and Guildenstern. (35)

Claudius gets it right later, only to be "corrected" by Gertrude:

> Claudius: Thanks, Rosencrantz (*Turning to ROS who is caught unprepared, while GUIL bows.*) and gentle Guildenstern (*Turning to GUIL who is bent double*).
> Gertrude (*correcting*): Thanks, Guildenstern (*Turning to ROS, who bows as GUIL checks upward movements to bow too—both bent double, squinting at each other*) ... and gentle Rosencrantz. (*Turning to GUIL, both straightening up—GUIL checks again and bows again*) (37)

The only textual difference between what we see in this passage and the original from *Hamlet* comes in the stage directions, which indicates how clever Stoppard is at manipulating the text in order to highlight the fact that Claudius and Gertrude cannot distinguish between ROS and GUIL. And while it may simply be that Shakespeare is more subtle than Stoppard (and had intended this confusion all along), in any case, Stoppard takes the idea and runs with it such that the attitude of the scene is itself mirrored in the way ROS and GUIL are prone to confusing their names themselves, as they do when they role-play what they might say when they try to "glean what afflicts" (47) Hamlet:

> ROS: How should I begin?
> GUIL: Address me.
> *They stand and face each other, posing.*
> ROS: My honoured Lord!
> GUIL: My dear Rosencrantz!
> *Pause.*
> ROS: Am I pretending to be you?
> GUIL: Certainly not. If you like. Shall we continue? (48)

Notably, GUIL is embarrassed enough to try to cover for his mistake. But ultimately it is no use. Even as the play ends and first Rosencrantz and then he himself finally and simply "disappear," he calls out for his friend: "Rosen—?/Guil—?" (125). Clearly, Stoppard is transgressing well-defined literary boundaries, and doing so in such a way that his own characters suffer the consequences of his manipulations.

It is, moreover, this very indeterminacy of character that explains why ROS and GUIL don't quite know where they are going, let alone why. When asked about the first thing he remembers, ROS can only say: "Ah. No, it's no good, it's gone. It was a long time ago." (16) When pressed, ROS can barely even remember that very morning (notably, a scene that does not occur in *Hamlet*):

> GUIL (*tensed up by this rambling*): Do you remember the first thing that happened today?
> ROS (*promptly*): I woke up, I suppose. (*Triggered.*) Oh—I've got it now—that man, a foreigner, he woke us up—
> GUIL: A messenger. (*He relaxes, sits.*)

> ROS: That's it—pale sky before dawn, a man standing on
> his saddle to bang on the shutters—shouts—What's all the
> row about? Clear off—But then he called our names. You
> remember that—this man woke us up. (19)

That this is such poor recall of so recent an event, even for characters as dimwitted as ROS and GUIL, is the point, indicating that their very dimwittedness stems from the fact that they were "sent for" is only vaguely alluded to in the text: "The need we have to use you did provoke / Our hasty sending" (Act II Scene ii).

As it turns out, it is much more than ROS and GUIL's identity that is ill-defined in this play, as the very physical world that ROS and GUIL inhabit is perhaps equally ill-defined and ambiguous. Consider the following stage directions: "[Guildenstern] spins another coin over his shoulder without looking at it, his attention being directed at his environment or lack of it" (12). In effect, Stoppard asks that his audience question the indeterminacy that exists at the margins of all texts (including those of Shakespeare), not just at the margins of his own. And as Stoppard the trickster transgresses these traditional boundaries, ROS and GUIL find themselves continually trapped within the various quandaries that define (and confine) their existence.

However, if Stoppard plays off the way in which ROS and GUIL's physical environment is underdetermined by Shakespeare to play up the indeterminacy in both their character and their surroundings, he also plays off how their ending is overdetermined by Shakespeare to write a play in which the two are inevitably drawn toward certain death. And it is this characteristic of the play that returns us to Lewis Hyde's point that, for all his subversive elements, the trickster yet has the potential to "bring to the surface a distinction previously hidden from sight." In this case, what is previously hidden from sight is how, at least according to the logic of Stoppard's own play, it is Shakespeare himself who sends his characters to their deaths each time his play is performed for a new audience. What Stoppard is implying, then, is that Shakespeare, not himself, is the master trickster, as it is Shakespeare who has sentenced ROS and GUIL to an endless cycle of inevitable marches toward certain death, a perspective of Shakespeare that is wholly and uniquely Stoppard's.

NOTE

1. In *Jung as a Writer* Susan Rowland also makes this connection, noting: "Sent to England, Hamlet on voyage ceases to be torn apart by the psyche/Ghost and achieves temporary integration with his 'antic' personality by becoming a trickster. He succeeds in having his friends executed instead of himself, demonstrating both the amorality of the trickster and the instincts of a politician."

WORKS CITED

Burnett, Mark Thornton. "'For they are actions that a man might play': Hamlet as Trickster." *Hamlet.* Ed. Peter J. Smith and Nigel Wood. *Theory in Practice.* Buckingham: Open UP, 1996. 24–54.

Hyde, Lewis. *Trickster Makes This World: Mischief, Myth, and Art.* New York: Farrar, Strauss and Giroux, 1998.

Jung, Carl G. *The Archetypes and the Collective Unconscious.* Trans. R.F.C. Hull. Bollingen Series. Eds. Sir Herbert Read, et al. Second ed. Princeton, N.J.: Princeton University Press, 1959.

McHale, Brian. *Postmodernist Fiction.* London: Routledge, 1987

Radin, Paul. *The Trickster: A Study in American Indian Mythology.* 1956. New York: Schecken, 1971.

Rowland, Susan, *Jung as a Writer*, New York: Routledge, 2005.

Russell, Bertrand. *Introduction to Mathematical Philosophy,* George Allen and Unwin, London, U.K., 1919.

Stoppard, Tom. *Rosencrantz and Guildenstern Are Dead.* New York: Grove, 1967

TAR BABY
(TONI MORRISON)
PRAISESONG FOR THE WIDOW
(PAULE MARSHALL)

"The Journey as Crossing"
by Alma Jean Billingslea-Brown, in *Crossing Borders through Folklore: African American Women's Fiction and Art* (1999)

In this chapter Alma Jean Billingslea-Brown discusses the original Tar Baby trickster tale and then analyzes how protagonists with trickster-like qualities confront folk roots and values in Toni Morrison's *Tar Baby* and Paule Marshall's *Praisesong for the Widow*. For Billingslea-Brown, both *Tar Baby* and *Praisesong for the Widow* treat rural communities in the South, which "represent a return to folk roots, to folk values and traditions with which the protagonist must first reconnect, then accept or deny. Defining the character's development and marking identity, these places are vital links in the expression of the 'return to the source' as affirmation of cultural continuity." Billingslea-Brown contends that while the values and traditions that define the cultural identities are approached differently by their respective trickster-esque protagonists, they are ultimately salvaged and reclaimed by the conclusions.

Billingslea-Brown, Alma Jean. "The Journey as Crossing." *Crossing Borders through Folklore: African American Women's Fiction and Art*. University of Missouri Press, 1999. 67–83.

To advance their thematic definitions of continuity and inscribe the motif of return, Toni Morrison and Paule Marshall both effect literal and metaphorical crossings of spatial, temporal, and cultural borders. In Morrison's *Tar Baby* and Marshall's *Praisesong for the Widow*, the movement of characters across geopolitical and cultural borders, however, is for the purpose of reclamation and subversion. Reclaiming an African and diasporic folk heritage, these crossings subvert not only the distorted meanings imposed on that heritage but also the manifestations of Euramerican cultural dominance. Using the structural device of the journey as voluntary movement across space and time, these two novels reverse and revise the historical journey of forced migration of African people to the New World. Beginning typically in the first cities of Europe and the United States, this journey advances to the Caribbean and concludes symbolically at the African "source."

The literal crossings are mediated, however, with the configuration of the journey within a journey and a symbology of place that situates folk communities in the rural south as crucial stopping points in the preparation for the final return. For Avey Johnson in *Praisesong*, this place is Tatem, South Carolina. For Son Green and Jadine Childs in *Tar Baby*, it is Eloe, Florida. These rural communities in the South represent a return to folk roots, to folk values and traditions with which the protagonist must first reconnect, then accept or deny. Defining the character's development and marking identity, these places are vital links in the expression of the "return to the source" as affirmation of cultural continuity.

In creating a new dialogue with the "Tar Baby" tale and appropriating its meanings to the very contemporary situation of a black woman and a black man, Toni Morrison affirms this continuity on one level of meaning. "Tar Baby" itself is an example of cultural survival. With origins in Africa, where the principle character is the trickster figure, Anansi, the folktale has twenty-five documented variants in the English and French West Indies.[1] Joel Chandler Harris's "The Wonderful Tar Baby Story" is recognized as the first published version in the United States.

In the version Morrison uses, Harris's Brer Fox character becomes a farmer who attempts to outwit and trick Brer Rabbit by placing a doll covered with tar on the side of the road. Thinking the doll is human and wonderful, the rabbit attempts to make her acquaintance. When the doll does not respond to his overtures, the rabbit hits it, first with one hand, then the other, and becomes stuck. With the rabbit trapped, the gloating farmer makes him plead for his life. As the rabbit pleads, he tells the farmer that of all the things he might do to him, the worst would be to throw him in the briar patch. "Skin me . . . snatch out my eyeballs, tear out my ears . . . cut off my legs, but please . . . don't fling me in that briar patch."[2] Because he wants to inflict the worst possible harm on the rabbit, the farmer does just that: He flings him into the briar patch. Minutes later, the farmer hears laughter and finally Brer Rabbit's taunt: "Born and bred in a briar patch—born and bred in a briar patch." Morrison has explained the influence of this tale on the novel. In an early edition of *Tar Baby*, she wrote,

> I did not retell that story and needless to say, I did not improve it. . . . It was a rather complicated story with a funny happy ending. . . . Its innocence and reassurance notwithstanding, it worried me. Why did the extraordinary solution the farmer came up with to trap the rabbit involve tar? Of the two views of the Briar Patch, the farmer's and the rabbit's, which was right?[3]

The fruition of the writer's "worrying" is a complex narrative not easily summarized. Set in the 1970s and principally on the Caribbean "Isle des Chevaliers," *Tar Baby* chronicles human relationships: those of Valerian Street, who is a wealthy candy manufacturer from Philadelphia, with his wife, Margaret; with his son, who never appears in the novel; and with his servants, Sydney and Ondine, typical "Philadelphia Negroes." But essentially the novel is the story of Jadine Childs and Son Green. Jadine, niece to Sydney and Ondine, is a sophisticated art historian, high-fashion model, and part-time actress. Son Green is a fugitive musician on the run for killing his wife. Like the tar baby in the tale, Jadine lures and entraps Son. Realizing that her embrace is destructive, Son eventually releases himself from Jadine's grasp and at the end of the novel runs like Brer Rabbit, "lickety-lickety-lickety split" to the island's tribe of mythic horsemen, making a return to a primal, mythic "source."

Through the legend of the mythic horsemen and the characterization of Son and Jadine, Morrison presents her "two views" of the briar patch, of nature and culture, and of the tar baby archetype. These two views, referenced by one critic as "African values" and "Western chaos," are used to develop the writer's more compelling theme of continuity threatened and salvaged.[4] To develop this theme, Morrison structures the legend of the mythic horsemen as a recurring motif in the novel and presents it in two versions.

In one version, the sinking of a slave ship with French chevaliers aboard leaves one hundred French horsemen riding one hundred horses through the hills of the island. From this version, the island gets its name, "Isle des Chevaliers." And it is this version to which Valerian and the other wealthy Americans on the island subscribe. In Valerian's mind, ". . . one hundred French chevaliers were roaming the hills on horses. Their swords were in the scabbards and their epaulets glittered in the sun. Backs straight, shoulders high—alert but restful in the security of the Napoleonic Code."[5]

The other version, which is more central to the novel's expression of the idea of the "return to the source," is presented in more detail. The writer begins this version in the first chapter of the novel, when the narrator tells us that the slaves aboard the ship were "struck blind" the moment they saw the island. Unable to see how or where to swim after the ship sinks, these slaves floated, trod water, and ended up with the horses that swam ashore with them. Some, only partially blinded, were rescued by the French and returned to indenture. From these, a race of blind people descended. The others hid in the hills and were never caught. According to Gideon, an island native who relates the legend to Son, this tribe of blind horsemen rode "those horses all over the hills. They learned to ride through the rain forest, avoiding all sorts of trees and things. They race each other, and for sport they sleep with the swamp women in Sein de Veilles" (152–53). Later, when Son recollects the legend, he envisions this version: "somewhere in the back of Son's mind one hundred black men on one hundred unshod horses rode blind and naked through the hills and had done so for hundreds of years" (206).

The differences between the two versions are significant. In the first, the French chevaliers, representing the order and efficiency of Western civilization, roam the hills to guard and protect, under the Napoleonic Code, the fruits of their civilization. In the second, the blinded horsemen are a maroon community, a community of Africans never-enslaved.[6] Prizing fraternal bonds and mating with the swamp women, these blinded horsemen sustain primal, instinctual links with nature. And as the narrator tells us, "they knew all there was to know about the island and had not even seen it."

This second version is central to Morrison's expression of the idea of the "return to the source," because in characterizing this tribe as a maroon community, the writer suggests that they have had the opportunity to preserve their own values and links with nature, to sustain a different kind of order. The blind horsemen and the descendant race of blind people, the narrator tells us, had their "own ways of understanding that had nothing to do with the world's views" (151). In structuring this legend as motif, Morrison not only unifies narrative structure, but also develops one of the two views expressed in the novel: that of continuity salvaged, of culture preserved and sustained at a primal, mythic source.

It is through the characterization of Son and Jadine, however, that the writer gives this theme its most complete and concrete expression. Jadine, who represents the other "view," that of continuity threatened, is the product of European culture and training. Educated at the Sorbonne, she prefers the "Ave Maria" to gospel music and has learned that "Picasso *is* better than an Itumba mask." Featured on the covers of *Vogue* and *Elle*, she travels the "fast lane" from Paris to the Caribbean, to New York, to Florida. Her manipulation and mastery of the system have earned her money, prestige, and leisure. But on one of the happiest days of her life, the foundations of this American black woman's "benevolent circumstances" are shaken. An African woman with "skin like tar" and dressed in canary yellow strolls into a Parisian supermarket, removes three eggs from a carton, holds them aloft between her earlobe and shoulder and, before leaving, "shoots an arrow of saliva" at Jadine. Mesmerized like everyone else by the woman's presence and wanting this woman to "like and respect her," Jadine is shaken and derailed by the gesture.

As the insulting gesture "discredits her elements," the image of the "tar black fingers holding three white eggs" assails Jadine's dreams, both on Isle des Chevaliers and later in Eloe, Florida. Both the gesture and the lingering image are central to the novel's presentation of the other "view," that of continuity threatened. The African woman, the "tar lady," who had something in her eyes "so powerful it had burnt away the eyelashes," is a consummate representation of the sum total of African values, values that are intricately linked, by the three white eggs, to fecundity and procreation, racial and human continuity. As Jadine's color represents a threat to racial continuity, her values threaten human continuity. She sees babies as killers and hates

both. "'I hate killers,' she said. 'All killers. Babies. They don't understand anything but they want everybody to understand them. Lotta
nerve, don't you think?'" (175). This aspect of Morrison's characterization of Jadine imitates and parallels her characterization of Margaret, a
woman so overwhelmed by the role and responsibilities of mothering
and so distanced from the notion of human continuity that she abuses
her infant son. The intent is to show how far Jadine is removed from
African values and the degree to which she threatens the continuity
of the "ancient properties."

Son Green, as the name implies, is a "son" of earth-mother; he
sustains links with the ancient properties and with nature as well.
Morrison characterizes him as a man who flows instinctually with
the natural environment. When he attempts, in the first chapter, to
swim ashore, he is caught twice by a current. Though he initially fights
against this current, likened by the narrator to the "hand of an insis-
tent woman," he soon decides to let it "carry him." Because he flows
with the current and acquiesces to the "water-lady," Son does not
reach shore as he intends. He is propelled instead to a small boat, the
Seabird II, which carries Margaret and Jadine. Morrison's characterization of Son as the instinctual human in close connection with the sea,
trees, and currents may be said to embody what Wilfred Cartey calls
the "essential ontology of Africa." According to Cartey, this ontology,
in which the world of the spirit and nature is "alive and gives life
to the living," connects the generations: "The essential ontology of
Africa linking and curving through the ancestor and offspring, man
and nature, beast and trees, sea and fires. . . . An essential continuity is
preserved between earth-mother and child, earth-mother whose breast
provides sustenance to son, son who is son of all Africa."[7] Simultaneously "son" of earth-mother and "son" of Africa, Son Green is the
character who represents Morrison's view in the novel's dramatization
of the tension between African values and Western culture.

He forages the island for food for nearly two weeks undetected
by everyone but Marie Thereze of the "magical breasts." And Marie
Thereze detects his presence from his smell, "the smell of a fasting,
or starving as the case might be, human. It was the smell of human
afterbirth that only humans could produce. A smell they reproduced
when they were down to nothing for food" (105).

Belonging to the race of blind people and linked like mythic
horsemen and Son to nature, Marie Thereze recognizes the distinct

quality of a human smell because she understands the place of humans within the natural order, how they are linked yet distinct. Marie Thereze is also the only one who knows that this "son" of Africa sneaks by night into Jadine's room. There, with the sleeping Jadine, Son tries to insert into her dreams the dreams he wants her to have,

> about yellow houses with white doors which women opened and shouted Come on in, you honey you, and the fat black ladies in white dresses minding the pie table in the basement of the church and white wet sheets flapping on lines, and the sound of a six-string guitar plucked after supper while children scooped walnuts up off the ground. (119)

Images from Eloe, Florida, these dreams of a traditional folk community are the essence of Son's reality and values. These values, he intuits, are very different from those of Jadine who, he imagines, dreams of "gold and cloisonne and honey-colored silk" (120).

Although Morrison links Son to the distant past, to the "essential" African ontology, what she makes clear in this passage is that his American past is the most immediate and usable. And the immediate, usable past, the viable link in the African continuum, is the rural south, Eloe, Florida, with "black ladies in white dresses minding the pie table in the basement of the church." These dreams and images, drawn from the close familial and communal relationships Son has experienced in Eloe, are not at all a part of Jadine's experience.

Jadine is from Morgan Street in Baltimore, and from Philadelphia, New York, and Paris. Though raised by Sydney and Ondine, she has been educated in private schools by Valerian and has no real origins in the sense of "place." As Son cruelly reminds her at the end of the novel, "And you? Where have you lived? Anybody ask you where you from, you give them five towns. You're not *from* anywhere. I'm from Eloe" (266). Moreover, unlike Son, who had been sustained and nurtured by the ladies minding the pie table and by Francine and Rosa, Jadine had been orphaned at twelve and had never experienced communal nurturing.

In Eloe, when she dreams of the night women—the crowd of women that includes Son's mother as well as her own, Ondine, women from Eloe, Marie Thereze, and the African woman with the three white eggs, who all show her their breasts—Jadine is confused and frightened. Her response in this dream, which the narrator tells us she "thought" or "willed" is, "I have breasts, too. . . . But they didn't believe her. They just held their own higher . . . revealing both their breasts except the woman in yellow. She did something more shocking—she stretched out a long arm and showed Jadine her three big eggs" (258–59). Jadine finally determines that these night women, who "spoil her love-making" and take away her sex "like succubi," are out to get her, to "grab the person she had worked hard to become and choke it off with those soft loose tits" (262). She does not understand that in offering her their breasts, these women offer nurturance and even the opportunity to reconnect, to reestablish the bonds of racial and gendered kinship she has denied and lost.[8]

But the rescue attempt does not go well. The certainty of the night women spoil the trip "back home," and Eloe becomes for Jadine "rotten and more boring than ever. A burnt-out place. There was no life there. Maybe a past but definitely no future and finally there was no interest" (259). Representing a past and a folk culture from which Jadine is irrevocably disconnected, to which Son is just as irrevocably linked, Eloe is the place that directs the course of their relationship and their development as individuals. After they return to New York, the differences between this woman, who has denied her "ancient properties," and the "son" of Africa, who embraces his, become irreconcilable.

> Each was pulling the other away from the maw of hell—its very ridge top. Each knew the world as it was meant or ought to be. One had a past, the other a future and each one bore the culture to save the race in his hands. Mama-spoiled black man, will you mature with me? Culture-bearing black woman, whose culture are you bearing? (269)

Son finally likens Jadine to the tar baby in the folktale, to something "made" by the farmer to attract and entrap. And the text intends for us to see her as that, for ultimately the characterization of Jadine is not a sympathetic one.

The tar baby archetype and the adhesive quality of tar itself, however, inform the work on another level. In Jadine's room at Isle des Chevaliers, Son tries not only to press images of Eloe into Jadine's dreams, but he also tries to "breathe into her the smell of tar and its shiny consistency" (120). The African woman has "skin like tar" and

Gideon relates that the swamp women from Sein de Veilles had a "pitchlike smell." Morrison's statement of intent for the novel offers a clue. After she discovered there was a tar lady in African mythology, Morrison explains, "I started thinking about tar. At one time, a tar pit was a holy place, at least an important place, because tar was used to build things. It came naturally out of the earth; it held together things like Moses's little boat and the pyramids."[9]

In this novel, the tar motif complements and develops Morrison's two views of the world as briar patch. It is, as Angelita Reyes discerns, a metaphor for both bonding and entrapment.[10] Tar as a metaphor for entrapment is presented in the episode in which Jadine nearly sinks into the tarlike substance near the swamps. Jadine's efforts to extricate herself from the pit are overseen by women in the trees.

> The women looked down from the rafters of the trees and stopped murmuring. They were delighted when they saw her, thinking a runaway child had been restored to them. But upon looking closer, they saw differently . . . they wondered at the girl's desperate struggle down below to be free, to be something other than they were. (183)

Rendered metaphorically, the dilemma of black American women like Jadine Childs, a woman jaded by materialism, a woman who is ultimately no one's "child," as Morrison presents it, is near tragic. To claim relationship to the women in the trees and accept her primal relationship to nature, Jadine must sink into the tar pit and become like these women, the swamp women who smelled like "pitch" and mated with the tribe of blind horsemen. To the swamp women hanging from the trees, Morrison attributes the bonding properties of tar. Mindful of their "value," of their "exceptional femaleness," these women knew "that the first world of the world had been built with their sacred properties; that they alone could hold together the stones of the pyramids and the rushes of Moses's crib; knowing their steady consistency, their pace of glaciers, their permanent embrace . . ." (183).

In attributing the bonding properties of tar to the swamp women, Morrison presents another view of the tar baby archetype and makes it into something other than the doll used to lure and trap the rabbit. With regard to this second view, the writer explains, "'Tar baby' was a name that white people call[ed] black children, black girls as I recall. . . . For me, the tar baby came to mean the black woman who can hold things together."[11]

Though she is likened to the tar baby in the folktale where the adhesive quality of tar represents entrapment, Jadine fails to become a tar baby in its richest sense: that is, a true daughter of the African tar lady who represents the bonding property of tar, an "ancient property" strong enough to bond together a people's tradition. A complex novel, *Tar Baby* is a seminal example of how the art of folklore crosses into the art of fiction and how one tale from the African American folk matrix informs this writer's aesthetic.

As the values and traditions that ensure continuity and mark identity are denied, threatened, and finally salvaged in *Tar Baby*, in Marshall's *Praisesong for the Widow* they are overlooked, forgotten, and finally reclaimed. In this novel, as Barbara Christian discerns, Marshall balances the tension that inheres in black people's need to survive and develop in America and their even more important need to sustain themselves culturally.[12] This balance is reflected in one of the novel's thematic developments, that of progression from loss and displacement to spiritual regeneration and balance. Like Morrison, Marshall effects literal and metaphorical crossings, using the journey as a structural device and orchestrating a journey within a journey. And like Morrison, this writer mediates the crossings by situating a fictional rural community in the south, Tatem, South Carolina, as part of the "rich nurturing ground" from which her protagonist had sprung and to which she "could always turn for sustenance." But unlike the sudden retreat to myth in *Tar Baby*, the journey to the "source" in this novel is achieved slowly and with difficulty. In each of the novel's four sections, Marshall's protagonist confronts challenges to her values, her physical strength, and her spirit before she is able to complete the return to the African source.

The spiritual return of diasporic black women to the African homeland is a recurring thematic concern in Marshall's fiction, evidenced in her first novel, *Brown Girl, Brownstones*, and in *The Chosen Place, The Timeless People*. In commenting on this aspect of her work, and how, for her, Africa was both a "concrete destination and a spiritual homeland," Marshall explains,

> You could say that Africa was an essential part of the emotional fabric of my world. . . . The West Indian women around me

when I was a young girl spoke of Garvey's "back to Africa" movement in which they were active participants.... When I began to write my first novel, ... I experienced a necessity to make a spiritual return to my sources.... I think that it is absolutely necessary for Black people to effect this spiritual return.... I consider it my task as a writer to initiate readers to the challenges this journey entails.[13]

In *Praisesong for the Widow*, to "initiate" readers to the challenges of this journey, Marshall selects as protagonist a sixty-four-year-old, upper-middle-class black woman, Avatara Johnson, and situates her in first-class accommodations on a Caribbean cruise. To emphasize that Avey's journey is a spiritual one, the writer begins the novel with her psychic dislocation. Nervous, perspiring, and straining to pack her six suitcases, "blindly reaching and snatching at whatever came to hand," Avey has decided to leave her traveling companions and to desert the cruiser, the *Bianca* [white] *Pride*. She is irrational, fearful, and anxious. The source of her anxiety is a dream she has had two days earlier, a dream in which her great-aunt Cuney, the woman with whom she spent her childhood summers in Tatem, issues her a "patient summons."

Dreams, memories, and hallucinations assail Avey throughout the novel. Jolted by the first dream, she insists on returning to New York, but after leaving the cruiser where already she had begun to hallucinate, she is stranded on the island of Grenada. With her consciousness altered further by another dream in her Grenada hotel room, she undertakes a midday trek on the beach, which intensifies her physical and emotional exhaustion. Barely reaching a closed rum shop, Avey is rescued and given sustenance by the shop proprietor, Lebert Joseph, who convinces her finally to join him in the annual excursion to Carriacou.

Suffering through a physical purging en route to Carriacou, the embarrassment of vomiting and excretion, she is in a trancelike state when she reaches the tiny island. There she undergoes a ritual of healing and cleansing performed by Lebert's daughter, Rosalie Parvay. After she is physically and spiritually cleansed, Avey's disjointed states of mind are brought together in spiritual and psychic wholeness when she joins in the Nation Dance, the ritual through which she discovers and reconnects to African traditions and customs, the "source" of her being.

While the technique of juxtaposing dreams, memories, and hallucinations with external reality advances the theme of progression from fragmentation and dislocation to spiritual wholeness, this technique also enables Marshall to link past to present and develop the more compelling theme of continuity and identity for people of African descent in the Americas. The first dream of Avey's Aunt Cuney, which constitutes all of chapter 3 in part 1 of the novel, is the first link to the past. In this extended description of Tatem, Marshall consciously includes the storytelling, folk customs, and beliefs reflecting African survivals to give concrete expression to the theme of cultural continuity. The fictional island, Tatem, on the South Carolina tidewater, is much like the actual Tatemville, Georgia, a coastal community profiled in *Drums and Shadows*. As Marshall describes it, Tatem, South Carolina, much like the actual Tatemville, Georgia, is a community in which memories of slavery, emancipation, and "pure-born" Africans are very much alive. This community, in which the dance ritual, the "ring shout," makes up a part of regular church services, includes a practitioner of curative roots and herbs, "Doctor" Bernitha Grant; an artisan-craftsman known for his carved walking sticks, Mr. Golla Mack; and Avey's own Great Aunt Cuney, whose grandmother had been African. Twice weekly, Aunt Cuney takes her grandniece to Ibo Landing, to recount the story her own grandmother had told her of Ibos who walked on water "like solid ground" back to Africa.[14] Like Morrison's tale of Shalimar's flying home in *Song of Solomon*, Aunt Cuney's tale of Ibos walking on water is a touchstone of black folklore in the New World. With this story, people of African descent emphasized their own power, however mystical, fantastic, or irrational, to determine their own destiny. Though their bodies were enslaved, they could recall Africa as a spiritual homeland, as the source of their being.[15] Marshall's own understanding of the function of this tale is expressed by Aunt Cuney's African grandmother. At the end of her recounting of the story, the African woman always reminded her granddaughter that though "her body . . . might be in Tatem . . . her mind was long gone with the Ibos" (39). In *Praisesong*, as in *Song of Solomon*, the use of a black American folktale that situated a return to Africa affirms identity in specific relation to continuity.[16] First of all, in this novel, the tale is linked to ritual, which itself embodies an essential quality of continuity. More important, it survives through generations. As Aunt Cuney's grandmother tells her this story, she tells it to Avey, who in turn recounts "the whole thing almost word to word" to her brothers and later to her husband, Jay. Passed on from one generation to the next, tales like these mark and preserve cultural identity through continuity and thereby signal the importance of both.

Aunt Cuney, Marshall tells us, understands the vigilance needed to safeguard both identity and continuity. As she insists on giving her grandniece the name of her African grandmother, "Avatara," the old woman safeguards continuity in another, more vital way. As the narrator explains, "Moreover, in instilling the story of the Ibos in the child's mind, the old woman had entrusted her with a mission she couldn't even name yet had felt duty-bound to fulfill" (42).

But in the intervening years of marriage, three children, and a relentless pursuit of material success, Avey forgets the story recounted at Ibo Landing; she likewise rids herself of the notion of a mission. So when she first dreams of Aunt Cuney, she does not understand the old woman's beckoning gestures toward the landing and considers them "ridiculous business." She refuses to take a single step forward. What follows is a silent tug-of-war between the two, with the old woman trying to pull her forward and Avey steadfastly resisting. In the dream, the silent tug culminates in a physical battle in which Avey delivers blows to Aunt Cuney's face, neck, shoulders, and breasts, with her "striking the flesh that had been too awesome for her to even touch as a child" (44).

This dream sequence is as important to the temporal structure of the novel as it is to Marshall's characterization of Avey. With this sequence, Marshall foreshadows a future episode in which Avey wages a similar battle with another Old Parent. The sequence also enables Marshall to characterize Avey as an elderly matron deeply entrenched in materialistic, middle-class values. A great part of Avey's refusal to take the step forward hinges on the fact that she is wearing a "new spring suit," hat, and gloves. To respond to her aunt's beckoning would mean traversing scrub, rocks, and rough grass, which would make "quick work" of her stockings and the open-toed patent leather pumps she's wearing. The great difficulty and challenge of responding to the "call back" for middle-class black Americans like Avey, this scene suggests, inhere in a "shameful stone of false values" (201).

Avey's resistance to being "called back" in the dream as she is being "dragged forward in the direction of the Landing" illuminates also how the text dismantles and reframes temporal borders. Marshall's fusion of past and present, though achieved through dreams and memory, is a conscious adaptation of the concept of time in the African worldview. In that view, time is cyclical but centered on the past. Just as there is a profound and necessary connection between present activity and the past, the future is conceived only with reference to the past. As Dominique Zahan explains, "what is" and "what will be" achieve meaning only as they blend into "what already was."

> Being oriented towards the past, the African finds the justification and meaning of his actions not in the future but in time already elapsed. . . . "I do this because my forefathers did it. And they did it because our ancestor did it." The profound and necessary connection between present activity and the past thus appears. The aim is to trace the present from the past and thereby justify it.[17]

Thus, while Avey is "dragged forward" to a future, to the fulfilling of the mission entrusted to her by Aunt Cuney, she is dragged in the "direction of the Landing," that is, to the past, to her familial, communal, and ancestral past.

As the journey back is initiated by Avey's family ancestor calling her back to Ibo Landing, the final return is achieved by Lebert Joseph, a communal ancestor, who the narrator describes as one of those "old people who have the essentials to go on forever." The "essentials" Lebert represents, in the scheme of this novel, are the fundamentals of continuity: the vigilant safeguarding of the customs and traditions that mark identity along with a vital concern for human regeneration and healing.[18] Recognizing and understanding Avey's spiritual and psychic dis-ease, Lebert Joseph, from the first drink of coconut water and rum he gives her in his shop, undertakes the responsibility of helping her to "cross over." But as Avey resists her Aunt Cuney's call back, she also resists Lebert's invitation to join the excursion. The resistance to Lebert's call is ineffectual, for like the Ibos, Lebert has "special powers of seeing and knowing." He intuits and meets Avey's objections before "they were even born in her thoughts." And she is weary. "She felt exhausted as if she and the old man had been fighting—actually, physically fighting, knocking over the tables and chairs in the room as they battled with each other" (184).

Marshall fully characterizes Avey, stressing the similarity between Avey's encounters with her elders (just as Avey "fights" Lebert Joseph psychically, in her dream she fights Aunt Cuney physically). Though Avey has learned to control her high-strung behavior, this sixty-four-year-old matron has maintained a certain feistiness. And it is this spiritedness primarily that sustains her through the journey. As Lebert Joseph discerns, Avey was not the "kind to let a little rough water get the better of her" (248). At the same time, in stressing the similarity between her struggles against Lebert and Aunt Cuney, Marshall indicates the degree to which Avey has lost track of another, more essential spirit, how the "shameful stone of false values" has so separated her from her cultural values that she resists and disrespects the "Old Parents." In much the same way Ondine reminds Jadine in *Tar Baby* of the need and obligation "to feel a certain way, a certain careful way about people older than you are" (281), Lebert Joseph reminds and cautions Avey about respect for the Old Parents.

> I tell you, you best remember them. . . . They can turn your life around in a minute, you know. All of a sudden everything start gon' wrong and you don't know the reason. You can't figure it out all you try. Is the Old Parents, oui. They's vex with you over something. Oh, they can be disagreeable, you see them there. Is their age, oui, and a lot of suffering they had to put up with in their day. We has to understand and try our best to please them. (165)

As understanding the Old Parents insures an awareness of continuity, honoring and trying to please them is a safeguarding of continuity. It is Avey's lack of this understanding and respect for which she must "beg pardon." Soon after the description of Lebert Joseph's ritual of kneeling and singing in the communal Beg Pardon, Marshall structures Avey's private enactment of this ritual. "Over by the tree Avey Johnson slowly lifted her head. And for an instant as she raised up it almost seemed to be her great aunt standing there beside her . . . *Pa'doné mwê*" (237).

While the whole of the novel, in a sense, is preparation for the Beg Pardon, this ritual, like so many others in the novel, is finally a simple thing. Like the Sunday morning rituals of gospel music and poetry and the late afternoon rituals of jazz and dance Avey had shared earlier with her husband, the *pa'doné mwê* shapes her life and destiny.

> Moreover (and again she only sensed this in the dimmest way), something in those small rites, an ethos they held in common, had reached back beyond her life and beyond Jay's to join them to the vast unknown lineage that had made their being possible. And this link, these connections, heard in the music and the praisesongs of Sunday: "...*I bathed in the Euphrates when dawns were / young* ...," had both protected them and put them in possession of a kind of power. (137)

As a triumph of humility rather than humiliation,[19] Avey's Beg Pardon links and connects her again to that source of power, to that "vast unknown lineage" that had made her being possible. In the Nation Dance that follows, though Avey cannot call her "nation," she can and does call her name, the African name given to her by Aunt Cuney. With the metaphorical journey to the "source," the spiritual return to Africa complete, in the last chapter Marshall returns to the theme of continuity. The narrator tells us that Avey will return to Tatem and rebuild Aunt Cuney's old house to serve as summer camp for her own grandchildren and others. And to fulfill the mission, at least twice weekly, she will take the children to the Landing and recount the story of the Ibos. "'It was here that they brought them,' she would begin—as had been ordained. 'They took them out of the boats right here where we're standing ...'" (256).

In having Avey fulfill the "mission" at the end of the novel, the mission of preserving and passing on the story of Ibo Landing, Marshall characterizes Avey finally as a bearer of culture. In *Tar Baby*, Morrison attributes the same role to the night women, the women from Sein de Veilles, and Marie Thereze. Just as the women from Sein de Veilles and the night women offer Jadine the opportunity to reclaim the "ancient properties," it is Marie Thereze who finally guides Son to the "source." Moma and Nana in *The Wake and Resurrection* and the mother, Celia, in *The Bitter Nest*, are also culture bearers. And Betye Saar, resurrecting and actualizing in *Sambo's Banjo* the history of black women and antilynching crusades, sustains the tradition of a "woman's telling of events." In assuming themselves and/or assigning to other women the responsibility of "telling," of safeguarding and passing on the intangibles of culture, Morrison, Marshall, Saar, and Ringgold make manifest a collective sensibility. It is a sensibility that seeks to reclaim and re-create. It is the sensibility of the artist as border crosser, the double-voiced sensibility of those who inhabit the interstitial space between individual expression and collective goals.

NOTES

1. Elsie Clews Parsons, *Folklore of the Antilles, French and English*, 48–52.
2. Joanna Cole, *Best Loved Folktales*, 668.
3. Robert J. O'Meally, "Tar Baby, She Don't Say Nothin'," 197. O'Meally references Morrison's introductory comments for the Franklin edition of the novel.
4. Karla F.C. Holloway, "African Values and Western Chaos."
5. Morrison, *Tar Baby*, 206; all subsequent references are to the 1981 Alfred Knopf edition and will appear in the text.
6. Maroon communities were communities created by escaped slaves or never-enslaved Africans. They were concomitant with plantation slavery in the Americas and ranged from small bands that survived for a few months to powerful states with thousands of members that survived for centuries. For a brief history of the Suriname Maroons in South America, see Price and Price, *Afro-American Arts*, 14–15. For reference to maroon communities in the United States, see Angela Davis, "Reflections on the Black Woman's Role in the Community of Slaves."
7. Wilfred G.O. Cartey, "Africa of My Grandmother Singing: Curving Rhythms," 10.
8. Holloway, "African Values," 121. While Holloway sees the night women as offering the opportunity to recall and reconnect with "racial memory," my view is that these women offer symbolic nurturance as well.
9. Thomas Le Clair, "A Conversation with Toni Morrison: 'The Language Must Not Sweat,'" 27.
10. Angelita Reyes, "Ancient Properties of the New World: The Paradox of the 'Other' in Toni Morrison's Tar Baby," 25.
11. O'Meally, "Tar Baby," 197.
12. Christian, "Ritualistic Process," 78. Like Holloway's reading of *Tar Baby*, Christian's reading of this novel coincides with my own.

13. John Williams, trans., "Return of a Native Daughter: An Interview with Paule Marshall and Maryse Conde," 52.

14. Savannah Unit of the Georgia Writers' Project, *Drums and Shadows: Survival Studies among the Georgia Coastal Negroes*, 65–72 (hereafter referred to as *Drums and Shadows*). Ibo Landing on St. Simon's Island is referenced also in *Drums and Shadows*.

15. Christian, "Ritualistic Process," 76; see also Virginia Hamilton, *The People Could Fly: American Black Folktales*; Hamilton explains that there are numerous tales exemplifying this "wish-fulfillment motif" in black American folklore.

16. Christian, "Ritualistic Process," 76.

17. Zahan, *Religion, Spirituality, and Thought*, 89, 47.

18. Christian, "Ritualistic Process," 79.

19. Ibid., 83.

THE TEMPEST
(WILLIAM SHAKESPEARE)

"*The Tempest* and *A Midsummer Night's Dream*"
by Hermann Ulrici, in *Shakspeare's Dramatic Art: History and Character of Shakspeare's Plays, Vol. II* (1839)

INTRODUCTION

In this chapter from his 1839 philosophical study of Shake-speare's dramas, Hermann Ulrici examines the underlying view of existence suggested by the trickster figures that populate *The Tempest*'s fantastical world. Reading the play as an allegory of the struggle between good and evil, humanity and circumstance, Ulrici maintains that *The Tempest* is situated on the "boundary where the airy kingdom of the land of wonders and mystery looks into the reality of every-day life, and conversely is looked at by it." According to Ulrici, "Prospero's spirits are the personified resolves of fate," and Ariel, a kind of trickster, controls the "pulse" of events in the play.

Ulrici, Hermann. "*The Tempest* and *A Midsummer Night's Dream*." *Shakspeare's Dramatic Art: History and Character of Shakspeare's Plays, Vol. II.* Trans. L. Dora Schmitz. London: George Bell and Sons, 1908. 38–85.

INTRODUCTORY REMARKS

'The Winter's Tale,' forms, as it were, the point of transition to a couple of *purely* fantastic comedies, 'The Tempest' and 'A Midsummer Night's Dream;' both are internally and externally of the fairy-tale character, both also, as regards subject, are, as it seems, the poet's own invention.[1] As they are the only two purely fantastic comedies, and Shakspeare, so to say, first invented the whole species, they have attracted more attention than any others of his comedies, and, accordingly, must here also be submitted to a somewhat closer examination.

Every person of an imaginative or poetical turn of mind, probably knows from his own experience that peculiar state of mind, in which everything appears so strange, so mysterious and mystic that we can become wholly absorbed in the contemplation of a wild flower, of a murmuring brook, or of the hurrying clouds; a mood in which we feel as if, at every moment, something unheard-of must happen, or in which, at least, we long from the depths of our heart for some kind of wonderful occurrence, although in our immediate neighbourhood everything moves on in its usual course, nay although we ourselves feel perfectly content and happy in the everyday relations of our life and in our ordinary activity. There are, in fact, hours in which—illuminated only by single scattered stars—the deep darkness of the Mysterious and the Mystic struggles with the bright daylight of the well-known, for the possession of our soul,—hours, in which the dark, wonder-seeing eye of the imagination confronts the clear, sober look of reason, and man, as it were, beholds himself and the world around him from two entirely opposite points of view, as if he himself were two entirely different individuals. This state of mind forms, we may say, the psychological foundation of that fantastic, poetical picture which—as in the case of Shakspeare's 'Tempest' and 'A Midsummer Night's Dream'—blends into one, two perfectly heterogeneous and contradictory forms of existence, in order to shape them into a new, strange, half-known, half-unknown world. On the one side we are met by figures with which we are perfectly well acquainted—human faults and failings, feelings, passions and thoughts—all in the usual form of actual reality; we fancy we see ourselves and our surroundings but reflected in the mirror of poetry. On the other side, however, the magic power of the marvellous reveals its whole force, the laws of nature are set aside, the figures represented are at most but the imitations of common reality; their nature, and frequently also their appearance, is wholly different; everything contradicts the experience of every-day life, or at all events, exceeds its limit on either side. And yet we seem, nevertheless, to feel ourselves at home in this abnormal, unknown world of wonders. It is not pure illusion, for it touches a chord in our hearts, which forms an harmonious accompaniment to the mysterious sounds that reach us from that other world; we find ourselves possessed of a mysterious feeling that sympathises with the wonderful beings. The imagination of the true poet, in fact, only throws life into the unexplained wonder which is reflected in the heart of man. The world of wonders into which the poet leads us, does not contradict the laws and customs of common reality, but merely common, external reality; it is in perfect accordance with the higher laws of a reality which is indeed not common, but certainly general and ideal; the physical laws of *nature* are set aside, but they are replaced by the ethical laws of the *mind*. Both are, in fact, one in their origin and aim; we mentally perceive and feel this unity, and on this very account find ourselves equally at home in both spheres.

Shakspeare's fantastic drama is distinguished from the fairy tale by this double foundation, this double view of life which forms its basis. The fairy tale has but *one* world in which it moves, and this world is wholly wonderful, wholly a play of fancy. The fairy tale does not pretend to describe reality, but envelopes it in that gay, half-dazzling, half-transparent veil of haziness and mustiness, of light and colour, of which its own structure is composed. Its thoughts are but *assonances* of thought, so to say, but separate tones of a rich harmonious chord, the missing notes of which have to be discovered by the reader's own imagination. It does not *intend* to express one definite view of life, one idea, but to allude to the *whole* substance of thought and of life, to touch and to strike it every now and again, so that the bell (which is cast of a combination of all the different metals) gives back the separate sounds, which must harmonise among one another in spite of the looseness of their connection. It is this harmony alone, which, as it were, floats over the whole, that constitutes the general meaning and the truth of the fairy tale, because, in fact, it expresses the one side of real life. The fairy tale, accordingly has no desire to be explained, it does not wish to appeal to the reason but merely to the imagination. To presume to explain it, would be much the same thing as anatomically to dissect a flower to seek for its scent.

Plays like 'The Tempest' and 'A Midsummer Night's Dream,' however, are particularly in need of explanatory criticism, for, on the one hand, they possess the character of the fairy tale, which is apparently quite beyond explanation, but, on the other hand, this fairy-tale character of the representation is merely woven into common reality like a couple of fragrant, exotic flowers into a northern wreath of oak leaves. The Wonderful is so closely blended with the Natural and the Real, that the one cannot become clear if the other is not also explained. To leave the dramas uninterpreted would be to acknowledge them mere tales or fairy tales. But mere fairy tales they are evidently not. For while the fairy tale never expresses astonishment at what is wonderful—inasmuch as it does not consider it wonderful, but its own peculiar property—in 'The Tempest' and 'A Midsummer Night's Dream,' the Wonderful appears throughout rather as an actual wonder; the Magical, the Extraordinary and the Supernatural cause as much amazement as they would in our own everyday life. The dramas, therefore, evidently take their standpoint on the ideal boundary where the airy kingdom of the land of wonders and mystery looks into the reality of every-day life, and conversely is looked at by it. They here stand midway in connection with both, with a foot on either side; its centre of gravity, however, lies only on the one side, it rests, in fact, only upon the firm ground of *Reality*. But by the fact of the Wonderful *referring* only to the latter, and appearing interwoven only with actual life, it loses its independence, it exists only *for* reality; only in *connection* with Reality can it have any meaning and significance. And just because the Wonderful does not merely signify what it is itself, but at the same time denotes Reality, pointing to and embracing it, this *double* significance is obviously *symbolical* or *allegorical*. In other words, the Wonderful is and signifies, not merely that which it seems to be, but something else besides, to which it is connected as a part with its whole. The symbolical, however, by reason of its very nature, requires its significance to be explained; it is no symbol, if that which it denotes cannot also be recognised. In this case also explanatory criticism has not only to examine the unity of the conception upon which the play is founded, but has also to explain why, within this view of life, the Marvellous is so closely connected with the Real, and what is its symbolical significance in this connection.

[...]

If, in accordance with these preliminary remarks, we look more closely into the Shakspearian idea of comedy in general, and its affinity to the fantastic, it will, in the first place, lead us to discover the general significance of the Wonderful in his comedies. Man, in his folly and perversity, in his selfish arbitrariness and caprice loses the dominion over himself, and thereby over the outer world: caprice and arbitrariness are, in fact, but the consequences and expression of the want of self-control. Man, thereby, unavoidably falls beneath the sway of accident, and the unaccountable change of outward circumstances; he becomes a slave to a power foreign to himself, which soon he can no longer resist, because from the very first he had no wish to resist it. This power is, in reality, nature and its own natural condition; for in consequence of man's want of a just and true, *i.e.* of an ethical conception of things, and of a moral dominion over himself, he immediately becomes a slave to his natural impulses and passions, to the momentary conditions of his mind, inclinations and desires, and to his selfish resolves, ideas and fancies. This is no doubt what Shakspeare, in general, intends to intimate symbolically by making elves or spirits like Ariel and his fellows carry on their pranks only with fools or such persons as are decidedly immoral or excited by some violent passion,—whereas they not only spare those that are good and noble in character, but even appear subject to them. This, on the other hand, is the reason why Shakspeare's comic spirits are evidently but the personified powers of *nature*, as will be seen by a closer examination, and shall be proved more definitely in what we have still to say. For the present I shall content myself with drawing attention to the fact that, in consequence of the manner in which Shakspeare conceives and treats the Fantastic, the Wonderful, and what is like a fairy tale in character, the very improbability attached to these—and, therefore, to be avoided as much as possible in a drama—seems almost to vanish, because the spectator does not become clearly conscious of the improbability. Coleridge,[2] in his remarks on 'The Tempest,' justly maintains that there is a sort of improbability with which we are shocked in dramatic representation not less than in a narrative of real life, because it not only contradicts the latter, but also the *poetical* reality, or *that* reality which we—lost in the region of the imagination, as in a dream—unconsciously grant to the figures of poetry, and which constitutes the so-called illusion. The result of this is that in a simple tale or fairy tale, for instance, the ordinary, natural course of an event would be an improbability. In fact it is not only in nature and history, but also in poetry, that the poetically true is not always probable, and the probable not always true. For the probable is founded entirely upon experience and custom, it is only the effect of presupposed causes, *usually* resulting from given circumstances, and, therefore, an effect anticipated by the imagination. The psychological probability will, therefore, in many respects be wholly different under different circumstances, for instance, very different among the negro tribes of Africa, or among Indians and Chinese, from what it is to Englishmen or Germans. Truth alone is eternally the same.

If we bear this in mind, it is self evident that if the poet can only contrive, from the very beginning, to draw and to keep us within the view of life or within the poetical world in which he places his characters, much, in this world, will appear to us probable that in everyday experience would be utterly improbable. If, therefore, the scene of the poem is placed upon the above described ideal boundary between reality and the land of wonders, if the poet has made the fantastico-comic view of life the foundation of his drama—which, in accordance with its spiritual and ethical character, is perfectly correct although formally in absolute contradiction with reality—then, it only depends upon his describing this region to us from the outset, in the most vivid manner possible, in definite, sharp outlines and in fresh and powerful colours. He will thus have the satisfaction of seeing that all the marvellous things which he presents to us do not in the remotest degree disturb our illusion, in other words, that we find the really improbable perfectly probable.—With what consummate skill Shakspeare has contrived to lay this foundation for the structure of his fantastic dramas, and how powerfully and irresistibly he has contrived to draw our imagination over to his standpoint, will become clearly evident if we recall the subject of 'The Tempest,' and more particularly examine the first scenes somewhat more closely.

1. THE TEMPEST

[...]

The very first scene contains an unusual occurrence, even though it still lies perfectly within the sphere of common reality. But far more unusual, although still by no means supernatural or unnatural, is the form in which the occurrence is represented. No wailings and lamentations, no cries of deathly terror and despair are heard, as might have been expected, but in the midst of the confusion, danger and distress, there runs an under-current of humour and wit which makes sport with the obvious danger to life and pending death. We, therefore, not only feel that there is nothing very serious in the danger represented—and accordingly are far from being affected by fear and pity, the state of mind which tragedy would call forth—but we are, at the same time, transported into the centre of the comic view of life, which evidently constitutes the basis of the drama. We are challenged to laugh where otherwise we should weep. And yet that which we see is the most ordinary experience, men such as are met with every day, great and small, noble and common, according to the usual standard and cut. This alone is also shown, that the real world of folly, of moral weakness and mischief which we see in every-day experience is, in truth, rather the perverted, unreal side, and that accordingly, when light is thrown upon it, it is frequently most ludicrous where it apparently manifests the greatest misery.

The second scene introduces us to Prospero's cell, where we have the old man, a noble and dignified figure, with his magic mantle and magic wand, accompanied by his daughter of rare beauty and charming girlhood, in the midst of romantic scenery—all this must make upon us the impression of something unusual and strange, and yet still remains within the pale of nature. We have but advanced one step further into the poetical world whither the poet intended to lead us. Prospero then begins his story; with ever-increasing attention we listen to the exceedingly well-told narrative which, it is true, still does not exceed the bounds of real life, and yet, by reason of its extraordinary substance, already verges very closely upon the domain of the wonderful. Even Prospero's frequent questions during his narrative, as to whether Miranda is paying attention and whether she is not asleep, etc., must surely awaken her profoundest interest, and according to her own assurance, actually does; but these very questionings (about which critics have in vain puzzled their brains) are, in my opinion, but an artistic means of increasing the impression of the strangeness which the scene is intended to create, and of introducing Miranda's actual falling asleep, which is subsequently induced by Prospero's magic. We are thus already so far prepared that the appearance of Ariel and Prospero's magic arts—which, moreover, are at first introduced gently and noiselessly—no longer cause astonishment. The poet has succeeded in his object: our imagination is already *in his* poetical world, is unconsciously pervaded by *his* intention, and, accordingly, follows him willingly wherever he chooses to lead us.

[. . .]

The second act shows us the King of Naples—surrounded by Sebastian, Antonio, Gonzalo and the two courtiers Adrian and Francisco—in deep grief at the loss of his son whom, at the time of the shipwreck, Ariel had separated from the others, and who, as the King supposes, has met his death in the waves. Antonio and Sebastian form the plan of murdering the King in his sleep, but are thwarted in their design by Prospero's magic arts. Disturbed and dismayed, they all forsake the place, in order to make further investigations concerning the lost Ferdinand. In place of the refined and dignified intrigues of the servants of aristocratic ambition and arrogance, we now have, in an effective contrast, the common coarse fellows, the slaves of plebeian drunkenness and covetousness; in a droll parody, we find that the same creeping plants of evil also grow up among the lowest rabble, only in a different form, and thus prince and subject are tethered to the same yoke. Trinculo, the jester (as he is called in the list of characters, but evidently the representative of the clown), and Stephano, the drunken butler, accidentally meet Caliban. This scene is dipped in the inexhaustible well of Shakspearian humour; a keen sense of irony, goaded on by its wounded and delicate feeling for what is beautiful and noble, and by its vexation with what is ugly and low, makes game of human weaknesses and perversities, exhibits them in their entire nakedness, and yet, at the same time, treats man himself with affection and sympathy.[3] The dignity which is exhibited in Stephano and Trinculo as compared with the half-demoniacal, half brute-human hybrid Caliban, possesses something of the sublimely comical and comically sublime; the manner in which the former deport themselves gives evidence of deep moral degradation, it is true, but at the same time we perceive the glimmer of a certain good-nature, a concealed germ of humanity; their behaviour remains invariably human, without any distortion or any admixture of brutality. Even coarseness and immorality lose their depressing weight when they make themselves ridiculous and are coupled with folly and mischief, in other words, when they appear to spring less out of evil intention than from a want of judgment and of mental culture; thus, in place of exciting contempt and indignation, we rather feel a certain amount of interest in their representatives. Stephano and Trinculo are evidently the mimics of Antonio and Sebastian; for, as the latter brood upon murder for the sake of princely possessions that are entirely beyond their horizon, so

the latter allow a Caliban to pay them divine honour, and take possession of an island of which they as yet know nothing. The parodying
tendency is unmistakable; and although the whole scene seems still to
be foreign to the complicated plot of the dramatic development, still it
not only puts us into the best of humours, but we do not feel ourselves
at all offended by the apparent inappropriateness. It also serves to
efface the serious and revolting impression—inconsistent with the
nature of comedy—which Antonio's and Sebastian's treachery has
left upon us, and to prepare us for the lovely sight offered by the first
scene of the third act.

Ferdinand and Miranda confess their love while Prospero watches
them at some distance. A short space of time has sufficed indissolubly
to unite the two hearts which were destined for one another. In fact,
love, in the narrower sense of the word, is always the birth of an
instant; long acquaintance, mutual esteem and affection, may or may
not precede it—this is a matter of indifference to love; it does not grow
out of these like a bud from its *calyx*, acquaintance and affection are,
so to say, but the fuel which the flash of love has first to strike before
fire and flame are produced. Ferdinand and Miranda form the loveliest
companion-piece to Romeo and Juliet, with this difference, that here,
in comedy, love has exchanged the tragic *cothurnus* for the comic *soccus*.
In place of the melancholy, devouring heat of immoderate passion
which in 'Romeo and Juliet' tears everything along with it in its head-
long course, overcasting the horizon as with a thunder-cloud ready to
burst forth into destruction, and bearing within itself the full weight
of the tragic pathos, we here also behold the fire of passion, but the
passing of two tender obedient hearts, child-like in their gentleness; a
passion which, like a mild and yet far-reaching light, clothes all objects
in the brightest colours. In the former case all is thunder and lightning,
the forked light that shines and illuminates but which also destroys; in
the latter, it is the first rays of the morning sun which, in announcing
a lovely spring day, looks down timidly and blushingly over the mountain top into the valley. And nevertheless we feel that this delicate
germ, which has just begun to shoot forth, possesses a force unequalled
by any power on earth. Even Prospero's magic, which has made
thunder, lightning, and tempest its tools, and which guides all the
other personages like children in leading-strings, has no power here, it
cannot even restrain or retard, much less prevent or destroy. It is indeed
Prospero's wish that Miranda and Ferdinand shall be united—this

wish even forms the point to which all his desires and intentions are directed—but he, at the same time, would like to see their blossoming love keeping exact pace with the maturing of his own plans. For he does not know what will be the effect of the extraordinary occurrences of his magic arts, and of the supposed loss of the king's beloved son, or whether the king will yield and consent to the marriage of Ferdinand and Miranda. This is his reason for wishing to control their love; he would like to see the spark ignite, but not to see it burst at once into flame; this is doubtless the principal reason why he at first treats Ferdinand with so much unfriendliness and condemns him to work like a common servant. However, even in the form of a servant, love finds its kindred heart and contrives to ennoble its common state of servitude and its most menial work; unceasingly does the magnet exercise its invisible power, and Prospero is ultimately obliged to consent to that which all the magic in the world could not have prevented.

When conceived from this point of view, the first scene of the third act again stands in a deeply significant contrast to the two following, where Prospero's magic arts display their full power. This power is exhibited first of all playfully and deridingly upon the fools of the piece, upon those who are the slaves to their sensual desires, that is, upon wickedness in the form of stupidity and coarseness, which is not sufficiently great to be treated seriously because it is of itself harmless. I allude to the scene in which Caliban persuades the half-drunken Stephano to rob Prospero of his books and magic instruments, and then to kill him, so that he himself, as king of the island, may obtain possession of the fair Miranda. This scene, which is made an amusing farce by the interference of Ariel, is succeeded by the more serious play of aristocratic, refined wickedness in the higher spheres. Antonio and Sebastian—as we learn in the following scenes—have not yet relinquished their plan of murdering the King, they are only waiting for a more favourable opportunity. The King's heart also remains untouched and has no remembrance of his wrong-doing. This is why Ariel, in the form of a harpy, enters so suddenly amid thunder and lightning and gives the 'three men of sin' a terrible rebuke, by reminding them of Prospero and their crime. Nay, Prospero's sorcery proves itself so powerful here, that it even produces madness, the three men all quit the scene in a state of mental derangement and are anxiously followed by Gonzalo, Francisco and Adrian. These two scenes again obviously stand in contrast to one another. In the first case the ludicrous plan of the fools for murdering Prospero is only ridiculed and frustrated in quite an external manner, just as they are about to carry it out. In the latter case, the hardened criminals, who are already deep in crime and plotting fresh wickedness, meet with a most severe punishment which touches them to the very quick. The action almost threatens to take a tragic turn, and the last scene would, in fact, leave too deeply affecting an impression, had not the poet taken care to exhibit it so hurriedly and suddenly, and to give the colours, the outlines, light and shade in such light touches, that we can scarcely be said to have witnessed the madness and its horrors. On the other hand, it had to receive a certain degree of emphasis, because it is the climax of the dramatic complication; the knot is tied and all that the two following acts have to do is to unravel it skilfully and happily.

The fourth act, therefore, begins at once with this work. Prospero takes off his mask towards Ferdinand, begs to be forgiven for the trials he put upon him, and with paternal affection places Miranda's hand in his. In celebration of their betrothal, Prospero's spirits give an ingenious masque, in which Juno and Ceres congratulate the young couple. [. . .] The masque is followed directly by the merry chase after Caliban, Stephano and Trinculo. The high *cothurnus* upon which Juno, Ceres and Iris had walked about, falls again suddenly into the *soccus* of low comedy. This wavering to and fro between the two extremes is a characteristic feature peculiar to this piece, to which I draw attention, as it essentially belongs to that special view of life which, as I think, is expressed in the play.

When the plot has, in this manner, been unravelled from two points, the fifth act has only to solve the main complication. The unravelling, however, follows as rapidly and smoothly as was the case with the ravelling. Prospero's magic, which, so to say, tied the knot, is also the means of loosening it; 'heavenly music,' played by his spirits, drives off the madness it had produced. The king, upon recovering self-consciousness, appears deeply affected and filled with genuine contrition. Even Sebastian and Antonio cannot resist the mysterious power which captivates both heart and mind, at least, they remain silent and agree to the arrangements made by Prospero and Alonzo. The King willingly consents to the marriage of Ferdinand and Miranda, who when united are to rule over Naples and Milan. Stephano, Trinculo and Caliban are likewise pardoned. And in the end it is also found that the ship had not gone to pieces, but had been preserved by Prospero's magic, and was lying in a bay at the other end of the island. When Prospero, in this manner, has attained all that he desired, and has commissioned Ariel to arrange a favourable journey back his magic, too, has finished its work; therefore, after giving his obedient servant—who has carried out all his wishes so well—his promised freedom, he casts his magic books and staff into the depths of the sea. All is dissolved in peace and happiness; the tempest has worn itself out, calmness and cheerfulness have returned, and with these the ordinary, regular state of reality, the old sweet, habitual course of existence, such as all desire.

[...]

It is obvious, at a first glance, that in 'The Tempest' heterogeneous elements are intentionally brought together and placed in contrast. Happiness and unhappiness, virtue and vice, crime and good deeds, sudden wickedness and an equally sudden contrition, the summit of human greatness and dignity together with deep degradation, the highest purity and innocence by the side of almost brutal coarseness and sensuality, tragic seriousness and exuberant laughter, the sovereignty of princes and the state of common servitude, magic and marvels in the midst of every-day reality—in short, the two extremes of humanity seem here bound up together into one knot. We are, accordingly, for a moment in a state of dilemma, and look around for outward help. And, as [... the] titles of Shakspeare's comedies, (such as 'The Winter's Tale,' 'As You Like It,' 'Twelfth Night,') in spite of their strangeness, have nevertheless not been chosen without some intention and significance, our eye involuntary turns to the heading of this piece; we presume that, in this case also, the title of 'The Tempest' must stand in some kind of internal connection with the ideal substance of the play. We are confirmed in our supposition when we see that—as already intimated—the drama throughout exhibits a peculiar hurry and flurry, a rising and falling between the utmost extremes, not only as regards events, fortunes and situations, but also as regards the characters and their arrangement; and this internal restlessness affects the reader or spectator as well as the personages of the play. Elements so heterogeneous and so absolutely contradictory as we have them here, must, when encountering one another, inevitably produce a violent state of agitation. At the very commencement, therefore, we have life and death engaged in conflict with each other; the crew of the stranded ship, apparently on the point of meeting an unavoidable death, are indeed saved, but some, at least, are led into new struggles and perplexities. Prospero's conversation with Miranda, where he narrates the story of his fortunes, receives a restless form, corresponding with its substance, from those perpetual questions of which we have already spoken; but it, at the same time, is a proof of the deep inward emotion in Prospero's own mind. The real action begins immediately upon Ariel's appearance; he is evidently the fly-wheel which, urged on by a higher power, puts the whole machinery in motion. And yet Ariel himself is excited and affected by a burning thirst for freedom; he grumbles at the state of servitude to which he has been half-compelled to submit and has half voluntarily (out of gratitude) taken upon himself, but after a warning from Prospero, endures it with patience and dutiful obedience. Thus, he forms a contrast to the diabolical and brutal Caliban, whom wickedness, hatred and animal savageness provoke to rebel against Prospero, and whose cursing spirit is forced to wander about without rest. Then under Ariel's direction the shipwrecked persons are thrown into the same state of internal and external agitation. Ferdinand, who, upon seeing Miranda forgets all his sufferings, is cast out of the heaven of his bliss by Prospero, and degraded into a common servant. Alonzo, who is oppressed with grief at the loss of his son and wanders about the island in search of him, suddenly falls into a deep sleep; Antonio and Sebastian who are spurred by their ambitious designs, find them thwarted at the very moment when they are to be carried into effect; all three, just when they are a little at ease, and about to refresh themselves with the enjoyment of a repast, fall into a kind of madness and fly off from one another in terror. It is much the same with the comic heroes of the drama, the prince of drunkenness Stephano and his subjects; they are perpetually made uneasy, teased and tormented, and stroll about the island, which, with its bogs and morasses, is the equally insecure scene of all this disquietude. They, in place of acquiring sovereignty by the intended murder, only act as common thieves, and in place of rising to be princes and lords are more like the animals of the forest, hunted by dogs; however they are finally pardoned, and put back into their respective places. In the same way the princes and lords also get safely out of their deep misery and perplexity, and on to the right track; they recover not only their consciousness, but son and daughter, as well as ship and kingdom. The end is as surprising to them all as was the beginning and the middle; it is only at the close of the play, on the return home, that quiet and peace are fully restored. And all this abundance of incidents and events, as the poet expressly states, is played out with hurrying rapidity in the short space of four hours!

The drama has been censured for being devoid of real action. And the action certainly does consist almost entirely of *inward* hurry and pressure; outwardly it is generally expressed only in resolves and plans which come to a stand-still when but half accomplished, and lead to entirely opposite results. Prospero's wishes alone are realized. And yet these very thwartings, this fruitless striving and struggling, might be regarded as fully corresponding with the poet's intention. At least, when we perceive this constant surging, when we find that the characters also not only represent the most extreme contrasts, but that all are tossed hither and thither by the most abrupt change of outward good or bad fortune, as well as by the states of their own minds, and lastly, when we see that the diction too—in the change from the sublime to the comic, from the comic to the serious—manifests the same rise and fall,[4] we cannot well doubt that this restless motion of the inner and outer life was *intentional* on the part of the poet, and a result of the depth of his fundamental view of life.

In fact there are, perhaps, in the life of everyone, days and hours in which we cannot succeed in anything, in which we seem driven about by some invisible demon, and strive and struggle without attaining our object, in which we waver and hesitate between conflicting impulses, tendencies and purposes, in which we apparently lose ourselves in some internal and external contradiction, until at last we suddenly and unexpectedly find ourselves in our right place. This strange hurry and worry does not merely depend upon the play of accident, or upon the change of external circumstances and relations; contingencies rather form but the one side; these correspond, on the other, with an internal ferment of the mind, a budding and sprouting of new resolves and half unconscious wishes, hopes and fears, a restless state of the whole soul. Both sides act in correlation with one another, the one being but the echo of the other. Such times are generally the days of those secret throes of birth where the inmost depths of life struggle to come forth in a new form, and where the old matter begins to drop off chaotically, but is gathered together again by hidden forces and formed into new structures. We are no doubt conscious of this struggle of coming into being, this restlessness and pressure, but we are not aware from whence it comes and whither it tends. It is only when our minds are again at rest, and we look back upon what has come to be, that we recognise the various motives and forces which called it forth. In history, these days are those dark, incomprehensible times in which men, without knowing why, feel themselves restless and uncomfortable; times of ferment, when the old edifice is tottering and threatening to fall in, and there is as yet no material for the construction of a new one; periods of transition in which the ship of history is driven on by some invisible power, apparently without rudder or compass, in which are formed those new tendencies, new motives of development, the embryos of creative ideas, that are hidden from the eyes of the present, and in which are sown the seeds of a rich and significant future: times which of necessity are somewhat obscure and mysterious and in which therefore we find the rank weeds of mysticism, the love of the marvellous and superstition shoot forth by the side of the ordinary business of life and by the side of the current interests of every-day life. In short, there are times—as when the tempest agitates the sea and we know not whence it comes or whither it goes—in which the mysterious powers, which direct our fate and shake the old rotten pillars of life, impregnate the fruitful womb of history and stir up all existence to its very foundation, and the most distant and heterogeneous substances are brought into collision; and together with the new forms which are thus struggling for birth, old and even mystic shapes rise up again, half-forgotten dreams become reality, and that which was apparently dead rises up into fresh life.

I mean to say that the poet who wrote 'The Tempest' has conceived life and history from that side which is especially prominent in such restless times, but which belongs as much to the usual and general state of human existence. He represents life as agitated by a *tempest*—agitated by heterogeneous and conflicting elements, which have come into collision, seemingly by accident—agitated by its own sap and forces, which have been put into a state of ferment—agitated by the mysterious power which men call chance or fortune, but which, in fact, is the magic power of fate, that is, by the spirit or the creative forces of nature and history which are subservient to the great historical minds, to the geniuses of humanity, in order that by their help they may be the means of paving the way for the progress of life and history, and so accomplish the Will of Providence.

If we assume that it was this special view of life which Shakspeare meant to describe in 'The Tempest,' it not only explains the title of the drama but also the characterisation, the substance and the course of the action, but more particularly the nature of the magic and the marvellous which here everywhere exert their influence. It explains why all the characters, with the exception of Prospero, are not so much the bearers of their own existence, as rather borne by it, driven on by the tempest which unconsciously gathers round them, determining their fate and guiding their actions, the effects of which tempest they no doubt perceive, and its nature is not revealed to them, till all that was to be has actually come to pass; the misfortunes which befell them, the marvels that terrified them, they regard as strange matters of chance, as freaks of nature, peculiarities of the island and of its inhabitants. In truth, however, it is Prospero's magic arts which effect everything, Prospero's spirits which in reality control and shape earthly existence, inasmuch as they are the embodiment of the stirrings and movements of the secret psychical life of nature, so to say, the souls of plants, of stones and metals, of winds and clouds, the small yet powerful spirits which Prospero so beautifully describes, when in act v. 1, he exclaims:

> Ye elves of hills, brooks, standing lakes and groves;
> And ye that on the sands with printless foot
> Do chase the ebbing Neptune, and do fly him,
> When he comes back; you demi-puppets that
> By moonshine do the green-sour ringlets make
> Whereof the ewe not bites; and you, whose pastime
> Is to make midnight-mushrooms; that rejoice
> To hear the solemn curfew; by whose aid
> (Weak masters though ye be) I have bedimm'd
> The noontide sun, cull'd forth the mutinous winds,
> And 'twixt the green sea and the azur'd vault
> Set roaring war: to the dread rattling thunder
> Have I given fire, and rifted Jove's stout oak
> With his own bolt.

From this description it is clearly evident that the very introduction of the elves and magic is but a fantastico-symbolical form given to the mysterious powers which prevail in *nature* and which so significantly influence human life. But these spirits, at the same time, boast of being the 'ministers of fate' who have 'to instrument this lower world and what is in 't.' And, in fact, the mysterious powers of nature—when the stream of life hurries onwards as when agitated by a tempest—are mighty instruments in the hand of fate; failure of the crops, famine, epidemics and pestilence can in such times become the levers of far-reaching revolutions, of wasting wars, of horrible cruelties; an unusually severe winter may occasion the downfall of an empire. In fact, Prospero's spirits are the personified resolves of fate, which not only direct the course of natural events, but also influence those wonderful coincidences which, in the superficial language of common-sense, are called accident or fortune. According to the usual view of things, the storm which drives the King's ship on to Prospero's island, and thus proves the means of the latter's return and his reinstate-ment, would be called an accident; but here the storm appears raised intentionally in order to serve definite purposes. Prospero's previous rescue would usually be accounted an accident, here it is described as a wonder. The King awakening at the moment when his life is threatened by Sebastian and Antonio, would generally be considered a special piece of good luck; here it is Ariel, who rouses the sleepers and frustrates the criminal design. Even the sudden madness and the equally sudden conversion of the three 'men of sin' would, at most, be regarded as a remarkable psychological phenomenon induced by peculiar circumstances, whereas it is here the work of Prospero and his spirits. Lastly, the mistakes and perplexities into which Stephano, Trinculo and Caliban fall, would usually be given out to be the mere bantering play of accident in league with their own folly, drunkenness and coarse desires, whereas here it is Ariel who makes them the play-balls of his whims, and thus thwarts their foolish intentions.

And yet the mysterious powers which direct the course of the action, which thwart and confound the designs of the fools and the wicked, do not, as already said, possess any control, or at least, only an external power over Ferdinand and Miranda. Gonzalo also is spared by them. For it is only on account of the disturbing power of evil that these agitated times are full of dark turmoils and wild restlessness. Without it the life of the individual as well as the history of humanity would indeed be agitated, nay, perhaps might flow along in a more rapidly advancing movement, but the movement would never assume the form of restless-ness, of surging and heaving, of uncomfortable hurry and confusion. This is called forth only by the struggle between good and evil. This struggle, therefore, forms the centre of the action in the present drama. Prospero is, so to say, the personification of the power of good; he here represents the place of one of the great spirits, one of the geniuses of humanity who are entrusted with the guidance of history. Accordingly, he is master of the elements of nature, master of those wonderful coincidences of apparently unimportant accidents and natural events, which are nevertheless often followed by the most serious consequences; he is master of the small, weak little spirits which are nevertheless capable of darkening the light of the sun and of shaking the earth to its very foundations. At the same time we have the significant intimation that, after all, it is only the power of *thought*, of understanding and knowledge, directed by *ethical* motives, which, in the first instance produces the new forms of individual life, in fact, precisely as the great evolutions of history are brought about; Prospero's profound studies are the sole means by which he has risen to the height from which he now has control over the fate of his powerful adversaries.

Opposed to him, and at the extreme limit of the contrast, stands Caliban, the climax of wickedness and brutality, the very personification of the evil Will. He is only momentarily tamed by outward constraint and inward powerlessness; his will remains evil, and in him we have a proof of the irrefutable truth that evil, even though, by its own acts, it invariably annihilates itself and serves the purposes of what is good, still evil as Will cannot become converted either by any affliction or punishment, or by the clearest conviction of its helplessness. This seems to me to be the meaning, the poetical, because ethical, significance of this most strange of all the creatures ever formed by the poetical imagination—a creature in whom devil, animal and man, are equally blended, and who, in spite of his wholly fantastic abnormity, rises up before us with the vividness of actual reality. Caliban is no mere creation of a passing poetic fancy, no chance addition to the substance of the drama; for although he may have originated in Shakspeare's imagination from the fantastic and wondrous reports about the wild inhabitants (the cannibals) of the newly discovered continents, and although grotesquely formed and humorously exaggerated—so as to suit the fantastico-comic colouring of the whole—still he is a necessary member in the artistic organism of the piece. And as Prospero's mind is evidently one of more than ordinary endowments, and, like every historical leader of men, represents the higher idea of what is general, so Caliban, his organic opposite, is likewise no mere individual, but also the representative of what is general, the personified idea of human wickedness; in him, in his defiance and arrogance and his blind, coarse sensuality, the demoniacal meets the brutal. Of a kindred mind are Stephano and Trinculo, the representatives of folly and perversity, and of the want of mental and moral culture. In the case of the latter, the evil does not consist in the evil Will but in the unconsciousness and indeliberateness with which they indulge their natural desires. In this they differ from the deliberate and conscious wretches, Antonio and Sebastian, in regard to whom the poet leaves it undecided whether they are ultimately converted, or whether they persist in their evil ways. They thus form the transition to the indeed morally polluted, but in itself nobler and merely misguided, character of the King, who is in the end purified from sin by his sincere repentance. Miranda and Ferdinand, and honest old Gonzalo, on the other hand, follow the power of the good and join Prospero. Between them we have those that are indifferent, lukewarm, neither black nor white, but who turn about, like weather-cocks, as the wind happens to be blowing; these are the courtiers Adrian and Francisco. They are the dummies, and represent that large indifferent class, which seems to exist only in order to fill up the gaps between good and evil, so that no space is left unoccupied on the stage of history. Thus all the characters are arranged into harmonious groups between the great contrasts which run through the whole drama.

[...]

What I have called the ideal point of unity, the fundamental motive, the leading thought of the piece, is expressed by old Gonzalo—not indeed in the form of reflecting thought, but still as a simple statement—when at the close he says:

> Set it down
> With gold on lasting pillars: In one voyage—
> Did Claribel her husband find at Tunis;
> And Ferdinand, her brother, found a wife
> Where he himself was lost; Prospero, his dukedom,
> In a poor isle; *and all of us, ourselves,*
> When no man was his own.

Indeed the very fact of all the characters losing and recovering not only their outward fortune but their *own selves*, forms the actual substance of the drama. This utterance is the strongest proof of the effect which a general state of excitement and stormy commotion in life must exercise upon individuals. But in reality, our life is perpetually threatened by this influence; the storms, at times, place it in a violent state of agitation perceptible to everyone, they do not arise from without but from within, from internal discord, from the perennial struggle between good and evil. And life itself is, in fact, but like a passing wave in the surging ocean of time, set in motion by some higher mysterious power. This thought which must arise in the mind of every thoughtful reader, when viewing the course of the action, is emphatically expressed by Prospero when, in the celebrated lines that adorn Shakspeare's monument in Westminster Abbey, he says:

> Like the baseless fabric of this vision,
> The cloud-capp'd towers, the gorgeous palaces,
> The solemn temples, the great globe itself,
> Yea, all which it inherit, shall dissolve;
> And, like this insubstantial pageant faded,
> *Leave not a rack behind*: we are such stuff
> As dreams are made on, and our little life
> Is rounded with a sleep.

Rack signifies much the same thing as gossimer cloud, a light, flakey little cloud, the so-called wind-clouds or *cirrus* of modern science which are drifted across the sky by the wind. The meaning, accordingly, is that our life with all its glittering splendour will disappear as if swept off by a *tempest*, not a *rack* being left; for life resembles the feathery clouds that arise from vapours and damp, and are carried along by the wind; it is woven out of the same perishable material as that of which our dreams are composed, a solitary, bright spot encompassed by the darkness of uncertainty and unconsciousness, by a deep terrestrial sleep which holds all earthly existence within its embrace. This is why *Ariel*, the airy spirit, is described as the pulse of the action, and that, from beginning to end, it is directed by him. This is why everything appears in so restless and unsettled a motion, why events appear as rapidly as they vanish—in short, why the drama is pervaded by that wondrous hurry which flits past our soul like a fleeting vision.

Notes

1. Oberon and Titania, and the whole elf tribe who are derived from the old northern religion and legends, had, indeed, been

long known to the English, partly from popular superstition, and partly from the old French romance of *Theon and Auberon*. The legend of the love potion is also ancient. Chaucer's *Knight's Tale* and his *Tysbe of Babylone*, or Golding's translation of Ovid's *Pyramus and Thisbe* have therefore probably been regarded as the sources of *A Midsummer Night's Dream*. (Compare Halliwell: *An Introduction to S.'s Midsummer Night's Dream*. London, 1841, p. xi. f. xxiii. f.) And yet what these sources offered could at most act as suggestions; they in reality do not at all contain the substance and invention of the play. Of *The Tempest* also, most commentators have assumed that the substance was Shakspeare's own invention. And certainly no safe source has yet been discovered from which he might have drawn his materials. For Tieck's conjecture (*Deutsches Theatre*, s. xxii.) that it is remodelled from an old English Play, is a mere conjecture; there is no trace of any such piece, and J. Ayrer's play *Die schöne Sidea*, which exhibits some similarities with *The Tempest*, is no adequate support for Tieck's supposition. Nevertheless it is very doubtful whether Shakspeare did not draw from the old ballad (discovered by Collier), or from an earlier source (common to him and to the author of the ballad, perhaps also of Ayrer, the Nürenberg poet), it may be from an old Spanish novel. It is true that no such novel has yet been discovered, in spite of zealous investigations; but after reading the ballad (in Collier's *Farther Particulars regarding the Life and Works of S.*, and printed herefrom in the *Quarterly Review*, No. cxxx., 1840, p. 478), it must be admitted that the substance in the simpler form in which it is there given, has quite the character of one of those novels of which Shakspeare made such various use, by dramatising them in his own fashion, that is, not only by furnishing them with new characters, and placing these in different circumstances, but also by giving a deeper significance to the ideal substance of the action, as well as to the various characters. At all events, it is inconceivable why the ballad-poet (if he drew from Shakspeare) should have so curtailed the matter, and entirely omitted many significant incidents. Moreover he had no conceivable reason for changing the dramatic personages from Italians into Spaniards, whereas Shakspeare, owing to the political relations between England

and Spain in 1610–11, and King James' love of peace, and
his endeavours to bring about a good understanding with
Spain, might have found pressing occasion to convert the
Spaniards of the ballad or novel into Italians. He, however,
it may be intentionally, gave them Spanish names, to remind
the spectators that the personages were real Spaniards, and
that, accordingly, the political allusions interspersed were to
be referred to Spain. The fact, that the printing, as well as
the diction of the ballad, speak in favour of a somewhat later
date than 1610–11, cannot matter much, partly because new
editions of ballads thus handed down traditionally, were always
changed in accordance with the language and character of the
time, partly, also, I think, because even the ballad followed an
earlier Spanish novel, and, accordingly, may have been known
to Shakspeare from an earlier lost print. As long as this novel
remains undiscovered, the question must remain undecided.

2. *Literary Remains*, ii. 92.

3. This is a peculiarity of Shakspearian wit, to which I cannot
refrain from drawing attention at this opportunity. Shakspeare
is ironical, it is true, and, perhaps, also occasionally satirical, but
in so objective and so moderate a manner that his comic figures
never become caricatures. He treats them, so to say, with a certain
kind of humanity, as if they were his brothers; the real man in his
original dignity and majesty we always see peering forth from
beneath the cap-and-bells. Even the clowns from the lowest
classes, the representatives of the common vices of the rabble,
never degenerate in barbarous coarseness and brutality. We can
never actually despise them, but feel ourselves in a state of mind
similar to that of the poet, and, I might almost say, feel our hearts
filled with a similar kind of irony of affection and sympathy.

4. I will only draw attention to the celebrated passage in act iv.
1, "*these our actors are melted into air,*" etc.; there is, in all of
Shakspeare's works, scarcely any passage more sublime than this.
Ariel's rebuke to the three royal sinners (iv. 3) is likewise written
in the grandest style, and forms a most striking contrast to the
jokes of Stephano and Trinculo.

A Thousand and One Nights

"Seven Times a Trickster: The Tale of Sindbad"
by Monique Dascha Inciarte
University of California, Berkeley

"Sindbad the Seaman and Sindbad the Landsman," included in the collection of stories *A Thousand and One Nights,* contains many of the qualities of a trickster tale. First compiled between the twelfth and fourteenth centuries in Persia, *A Thousand and One Nights* was first translated into a European language by Antoine Galland in 1704. The translation that will be considered here is Sir Richard Burton's "unexpurgated" English version of 1885. Burton's translation keeps some Arabic words, uses some archaic phrases that convey a somewhat foreign and medieval flavor, and includes comic and idiosyncratic footnotes that pretend to be anthropological in nature. Such play is indicative of Burton's trickster-like translation, but it is also appropriate for a self-reflexive narrative that contains tales within tales, much like Boccaccio's *Decameron* or Chaucer's *Canterbury Tales.* In keeping with this tradition, we are introduced to Sindbad (often spelled "Sinbad" by other writers) the Seaman through a frame story told by Sindbad the Landsman, a hardworking porter resting by the gate of the Seaman's sumptuous house. The Landsman smells a "delicious fragrance" and "the savoury odours of all manner meats rich and delicate, and delicious and generous wines." He hears the seductive sound of "lutes and other stringed instruments, and mirth-exciting voices singing and reciting . . . glorifying Almighty Allah in various tunes and tongues" (Burton 386). The reader learns a great deal from this preliminary description. Sindbad the Seaman is a voluptuary who surrounds himself with sensuous delights: music, perfume, meat, and drink. His environment includes exotic elements (perfumes, sounds). Finally, all this excess and delight do not exclude God but, rather, are used as an instrument of spirituality. Sindbad the Landsman, overcome by this scene, which is more akin to the courts of kings and sultans than to the homes of merchants, praises God and reflects on fortune, reciting: "Each morn that dawns I wake in travail and in woe, / And strange is my condition and my burden gars me pine: / Many others are in luck and from miseries are free, / And Fortune never loads them with loads the like o'mine." He deduces from what he witnesses that he himself is unlucky whereas others, like his lucky counterpart the Seaman, "live their happy days in all solace and delight; / Eat drink and dwell in honour 'mid the noble and the digne" (387).

Sindbad the Seaman hears the lament and is "delighted." He sends for the porter and asks him to sing it again and to sit, eat, and drink with him, exclaiming:

> "Know, O [Porter], that my story is a wonderful one, and thou shalt hear all that befel me and all I underwent ere I rose to this state of prosperity and became the lord of this place wherein thou seest me; for I came not to this high estate save after travail sore and perils galore, and how much toil and trouble have I not suffered in days of yore!" (389)

Deploying itself like a dizzying Chinese box, the story of Sindbad becomes a miniature of the central frame story of *A Thousand and One Nights*, a collection of stories about storytelling. Just as Shahrazad tells her stories to King Shahryar over many nights in intense episodes replete with monstrous creatures and spine-chilling cliff-hangers, Sindbad the Seaman will tell his stories over seven evenings, seven riveting tales of voyage.

The desire and need to tell his story is one of the chief characteristics of the trickster Sindbad. Trickster myths often describe someone who justifies himself in his obsessive retelling. Tricksters have, above all, great rhetorical skill, and the retelling of their experience is often tailored to suit the audience and the need. The Seaman's retelling of his adventures for the listening pleasure of the Landsman highlights the ways in which fortune seems adverse to him (he appears unlucky), and yet by dint of cleverness, improvisatory élan, and outright trickery, he outwits fate. As Sindbad explains, "I deserve my riches since I suffered and survived." Of course that begs the question as to whether his ultimate or true fate was indeed to outwit the outward manifestations of a false fate (all those shipwrecks!), giving credence to the reflections of the Landsman. We will discuss this a bit later. Suffice it to note here that Sindbad the Seaman wishes to convince Sindbad the Landsman of something. His retelling is a response to the landsman's perception of a wheel of fortune guided by predestination; through his storytelling, the Seaman argues for a form of free will, the only possible *de facto* philosophical position for a trickster, a man who lives by his wits.

Complicating the mirror effect of the overall story-within-a-story structure, Sindbad tells how he recounted elements of his story to the people he met on his travels. Sindbad's performances are often selective retellings of his journey, stories designed to help him obtain what he wants. Such rhetorical skill attests to this trickster's ability to manipulate people and exploit their inherent fascination with stories. At the end of the Fourth Voyage, for example, after being rescued by a ship, Sindbad tells the captain only the first part of his adventure on the island, "but acquainted him with nothing of that which had befallen [him] in the city and the cavern, lest there should be any of the islandry in the ship" (430). What Sindbad wants, of course, after each of his seven shipwrecks, is to survive. He wants food, shelter, and the means to return to Baghdad.

TRAVELING AND ETHNOLOGY

A trickster is always "on the road" (or, for our purposes, "on the sea"); he is an inveterate traveler who cannot stay put. Seven times Sindbad describes his blissful existence in Baghdad in similar terms: "I was living a most enjoyable life" (398); "[I lived] in utmost ease and prosperity and comfort and happiness" (407). And seven times this comfortable delight is interrupted by his yearning for the open sea, for the possibility of "traveling about the world of men and seeing their cities and islands" (398). Sindbad's appetites drive his wanderings. His greatest pleasure is to discover "strange countries" (418) where "strange folk dwell" (443). Seven times he leaves his home to seek adventure.

Sindbad knows about many cultures, as befits an avid traveling man, and he intersperses the retelling of his exploits and adventures with ethnological details. For example: "when the folk have a mind to get camphor, they bore into the upper part of the bole with a long iron; whereupon the liquid camphor, which is the sap of the tree, floweth out and they catch it in vessels, where it concreteth like gum" (404). During the first voyage, when Sindbad is saved by King Mihrhan's groom, the first question Sindbad asks after telling his own story is "who thou art and why thou abidest here under the earth and why thou hast tethered yonder mare on the brink of the sea" (392). After food and water, Sindbad next needs stories that satisfy his ethnological curiosity. Oftentimes the plausible ethnological details one would expect from a travel narrative (the information about the camphor tapping) are mixed in with tall tales about fantastic animals (a rhinoceros that impales elephants on its horn and wanders around the island while the fat of the elephant runs into his eyes, or a gigantic Rukh bird that plucks the rhinoceros off the beach to feed his young [405]). When Sindbad arrives in a new city, he is a stranger, observing foreign customs. His cleverness gains him patrons (as Joseph in Egypt), and he enters the new society. In two instances (during his Fourth and Seventh voyages) his marriage to a patron's daughter sanctions his integration, and yet he never completely assimilates (reminiscent of the stories of Moses and King David).

Sindbad the trickster is perpetually in-between states and places: When he is in Baghdad he fancies the sea; when he is at sea he yearns for land; when he arrives at an exotic locale, he wants to return to Baghdad. Lewis Hyde, in his book *Trickster Makes this World*, describes the mythic trickster as "the spirit of the doorway leading out, and of the crossroad at the edge of town. . . . [h]e is the spirit of the road at dusk, the one that runs from one town to another and belongs to neither" (Hyde 6). Not only does the trickster move around in space (from land to ship, from island to island), but he can also move between the living and the dead, as we shall see when we look at the Fourth Voyage.

At some point during every voyage, someone who hears Sindbad's story, saves his life, or recognizes him after his near-death escapades proclaims that Sindbad has accomplished a feat that no one ever has before. At the end of the Third Voyage, for example, after a hair-raising adventure during which Sindbad discovers a Rukh egg, tethers himself to the parent Rukh, becomes stranded at the top of a serpent-and-diamond-laden mountain, and then daringly hides in a Rukh nest disguised under a carcass, a merchant familiar with the land exclaims: "none ever reached yonder valley and came off thence alive before thee" (Burton 404). This becomes a mantra repeated from episode to episode: Sindbad survives where others die. Although Sindbad attributes his survival in every instance to Allah, it is clear in the narrative that the reason Sindbad prevails is because he is extraordinarily clever.

In episodes reminiscent of *The Odyssey*, Sindbad demonstrates that one of the ingredients of his cleverness is his memory: He remembers the stories he has been told by all the people he has met on his travels. When he sees a "huge white dome rising high in air and of vast compass," he remembers "a story I had heard aforetime of pilgrims and travelers, how in a certain island dwelleth a huge bird, called the 'Rukh'" (400). This retained piece of information saves his life. By comparison, in the Fifth Voyage, the crew of his ship does not recognize a similar egg for what it is, and the men ignore his advice not to touch it: "They paid no heed to me and gave not over smiting upon the egg" (433). The Rukh parents destroy the vessel and only Sindbad survives by catching the plank of the ship and washing up on an island. Many times Sindbad's wit and improvisatory brilliance save his life and the lives of others. During his Third Voyage, when a group of survivors seek shelter in the house of a Polyphemus-like giant, Sindbad's suggestion that they "carry some of this firewood and planks down to the sea shore and make us a boat wherein, if we succeed in slaughtering him, we may embark" temporarily saves them all (410). Later in the same episode, Sindbad constructs a box from pieces of wood that enclosed him "like a bier," protecting him from being eaten by a huge serpent that devours the last two of his companions (413).

At the beginning of his Fourth Voyage, Sindbad evinces another sort of cleverness when he refuses to eat the food fed to him and his companions by a tribe of cannibals, victuals that "no sooner had [his] comrades tasted . . . than their reason fled and their condition changed and they began to devour it like madmen possessed of an evil spirit" (420). While his comrades are fattened and pastured like cattle, he "wasted away and became sickly for fear and hunger and [his] flesh shriveled on [his] bones" (421). Finding his body undesirable, the savages allow Sindbad to flee. Once again, only Sindbad survives.

Sindbad is aided by an old herdsman and later by men gathering pepper. One of the latter asks, "But how didst thou escape from these blacks who swarm in the island and devour all who fall in with them; nor is any safe from them, nor can any get out of their clutches?" Sindbad tells his story and is guided by them to a wealthy and populous city. Here, he rises in the ranks, later boasting: "I became more in honour and favour with them and their king than any of the chief men of the realm" (423). Sindbad knows other cultures, whose artifacts he has collected during his travels. In this case, he builds smooth leather saddles for the king and the nobles, for which Sindbad is handsomely rewarded. In his Fifth Voyage, he saves himself by tricking the Old Man of the Sea (about whom "none ever felt his legs on neck and came off alive but thou ..." [437]) into drinking an unfamiliar beverage (wine). In his First Voyage, his counseling skills lead him to become an "intercessor for the folk and an intermediary between them and [King Mihrjan]" (394).

Sindbad's Fourth Voyage is the central episode of the set of seven. Like many tales that owe their gestation to ancient oral traditions, this story is organized in a ring composition. Episodes align in mirror-like fashion on either side of a central point. Voyage One has many elements in common with Voyage Seven; Voyage Two has many elements in common with Voyage Six; Voyage Three has many elements in common with Voyage Five. The center, Voyage Four, represents a turning point in the narrative, although the episode begins like all the rest:

> After my return from my third voyage and foregathering with my friends, and forgetting all my perils and hardships in the enjoyment of ease and comfort and repose, I was visited one day by a company of merchants who sat down with me and talked of foreign travel and traffic, till the old bad man within me yearned to go with them and enjoy the sight of strange countries, and I longed for the society of the various races of mankind and for traffic and profit. (418)

Let us note that Sindbad has "forgotten" his previous hardships, is tempted to travel again to foreign places, and, for the first time, refers to the "old bad man within me," frankly admitting that his uncontrollable need to be on the move endangers him and verges on evil.

Just as in the previous three episodes in which Sindbad is ship-wrecked, the craft he travels on is again torn apart in a furious squall. There follows the episode with the cannibals and the (over)feeding of his companions. When Sindbad finally arrives in the city, ingratiates himself with the king, and gains "high honour and great favour," he is invited to settle down. The king says, "Know thou, O such an one, thou art become one of us, dear as a brother, and we hold thee in such regard and affection that we cannot part with thee." The king offers to marry him to a wife "so thou mayst be naturalised and domiciled with us." The woman he marries is "a lady of a noble tree and high pedigree; wealthy in moneys and means; the flower of an ancient race; of surpassing beauty and grace, and the owner of farms and estates and many a dwelling place" (424). By this point Sindbad has remarked many times upon man's evil desire for "traffic and lucre and emolument" (407). Content with this "choice wife" and comfortable life, he "forgot everything which had befallen me of wariness and trouble and hardship" (424). Will this be another *mise en abime*, in which Sindbad's story within a story reflects the frame tale? (Sindbad is, after all, not at home, not in Baghdad, but in an adopted home, an exotic land with exotic traditions.) In fact, the episode turns into an ethnological nightmare when Sindbad discovers a foreign custom that chills him to the bone: When a subject's spouse dies, he or she is interred along with the corpse "so that neither may enjoy life after losing his or her mate" (425). He witnesses the custom firsthand when a friend's wife dies and his friend is dropped into a cavern along with his wife's body. Sindbad runs to the king and pleads that this fate should not be his (if his wife were to die) given that he is a foreigner and so not subject to the laws of the land. For the first time in the course of his tale, Sindbad feels trapped by his own initial cleverness and chameleon-like ability to improvise and assimilate: "I felt as if in a vile dungeon; and hated their society." Of course, the marriage that has "naturalized" him has also made him subject to these laws, and soon enough his wife dies.

The people bind Sindbad and drop him into the cavern with his wife and seven cakes of bread and some water. Sindbad cries, "Almighty Allah never made it lawful to bury the quick with the dead! I am a stranger, not one of your kind; and I cannot abear your custom, and had I known it I never would have wedded among you!" (426). This time Sindbad curses himself: "By Allah, I deserve

all that hath befallen me and all that shall befal me! . . . As often as
I say, I have escaped from one calamity, I fall into a worse. Would
I had been drowned at sea or perished in the mountains!" (427).
This episode is different for the strength of his self-reproaches ("I
kept blaming my own folly and greed of gain") but also for what
happens next. He manages to survive until the next pair is let down
into the cavern and kills a surviving woman with a leg bone. He
subsists in this way for a long time, "killing all the live folk they let
down into the cavern and taking their provisions of meat and drink"
(428). Once again, Sindbad demonstrates that, where everyone else
is content to die, he will fight, all tooth and nail and cleverness,
to survive. As with other tricksters in folklore who transgress the
boundary between life and death, the episode recounts a trip to the
Underworld where Sindbad is left for dead, inhabits for some time
this land of death, ultimately rejects the fate designed for others, and
survives to tell the tale.

Eventually, Sindbad finds a way out by following an animal's
tracks to a crevice in the rock and, true to cunning form, he manages
to bring out of the cavern all the treasures that were buried with the
bodies since "time immemorial" (426). He makes camp on a beach,
returning to the cavern every day to murder and avail himself of his
victims' provisions, waiting to be rescued. Sindbad saves no one from
the cavern. A merchant ship appears in the distance.

In the midst of the greatest difficulties, Sindbad always invokes
Allah, and perhaps this is the real tale that Sindbad tells when he
finally leaves the cavern. Although in previous episodes he attributes
his salvation to Allah, the emphasis seems rather to be on his own
cleverness. While in the cavern, he never ceases "to ban the Foul
Fiend and to bless the Almighty Friend" (427). He implores Allah to
help him in his despair. During his Seventh and final voyage, while
clinging to the planks of yet another destroyed ship, Sindbad insists
on his need to repent: "O Sindbad, O Seaman, thou repentest not
and yet thou art ever suffering hardships and travails; yet wilt thou
not renounce sea-travel . . ." (454). Here Sindbad acknowledges that
he deserves all that has befallen him and repents the cause of all his
woe: "Never will I again name travel with tongue nor in thought"
(455). The episode ends with his finding himself again in a city where
he is taken under the wings of a shaykh who takes him home, helps

him integrate in to society, and offers him his daughter in marriage. It is a mirror version of the Fourth Voyage except that this one ends very differently. As in the Fourth Voyage, Sindbad stumbles upon a foreign custom: The men fly off once a month disguised as birds. With the strength of his rhetoric, and still as ethnologically curious as ever, he convinces them to take him along. When he "hear[s] the angels glorifying God in the heavenly dome," he wonders and exclaims, 'Praised be Allah! Extolled be the perfection of Allah!'" A fire comes out of heaven, and the company curses him and leaves him alone on a high mountain. He has flown, in a sense, on this ultimate ethnological trip with pagans and has remained true to Allah even so, saving himself one last time. Eventually he is rescued and returns to his wife. They decide to leave the land and return to Baghdad. This had been his longest trip, twenty-seven years and, again like Odysseus, his people back home "had given up all hope of [him]" (461). This time, however, it would seem that Sindbad's accumulated experiences have made him learn his lesson: "Then I forswore travel and vowed to Allah the Most High I would venture no more by land or sea, for that this seventh and last voyage had surfeited me of travel and adventure." For the seventh and last time Sindbad returns, and, although he does not say so this time, we can well believe that, as he has done all the previous times, he gives alms to beggars and widows and orphans, one of the more important pillars of Islam.

Sindbad's travels showcase his superior cleverness and demonstrate how he exploits opportunity, as he "regularly bumps into things he did not expect" (17). The last thing that needs to be said about Sindbad, and about all tricksters, is that they are exceedingly vital creatures. Their supernatural urge to save themselves and survive what would kill any other being attests that they are in love with life. In his third voyage, when Sindbad realizes that he cannot protect himself from being eaten by a snake except by building a bier, he gives voice to this fundamental drive: For "verily life is dear" (413). It is the intensity of this categorical proclamation that forces him over and over again to devise tactics by which to survive—strategic storytelling, bribery, trickery, brilliant improvisation—and instigates others to repeat "none ever came off alive but thou . . ." (437). As we have seen, Sindbad is such a trickster, a character who derives creative intelligence from his appetite for life.

WORKS CITED

Burton, Richard F., Trans. "Sindbad the Seaman and Sindbad the Landsman." *Tales from the Arabian Nights*. Ed. David Shumaker. Random House: New York, 1977.

Hyde, Lewis. *Trickster Makes this World: Mischief, Myth, and Art*. Farrar, Straus and Giroux: New York, 1998.

Uncle Remus
(Joel Chandler Harris)

"Tricksters in *Uncle Remus: His Songs and Sayings*"
by Robert C. Evans,
Auburn University Montgomery

Brer Rabbit, the main animal character in the "Uncle Remus" tales by Joel Chandler Harris, is so obviously a trickster that there almost seems no point in discussing the matter—partly because the matter has already been so much discussed. Hardly a year has gone by, especially recently, in which scholars have failed to examine or at least mention Harris's rabbit as a trickster in some connection or another. Harris himself, in the immensely popular first book of the "Uncle Remus" series (*Uncle Remus: His Songs and Sayings*), never explicitly calls Brer Rabbit a trickster, nor does he even use the verb or the noun "trick" when presenting him in that collection. Nevertheless, the rabbit's trickery is so blatant and so frequent that scholars of Harris almost always call Brer Rabbit a trickster, while scholars of tricksters almost inevitably mention Brer Rabbit (see, for example, the index to Bickley and Keenan).

A more interesting question has been the subject of some recent critical discussion: To what extent (if at all) is it reasonable to interpret Uncle Remus himself, as well as Joel Chandler Harris, as tricksters? In other words, to what extent are both Remus and his creator more complex characters—more clever, more deceptive, more ironic and sly and manipulative—than they might initially seem? There was a time when most interpreters confidently assumed that Remus was a simpleton and racial stereotype and Harris was a simple-minded racist (or at least a naïve defender of plantation-style paternalism). More recently, however, both Remus and his creator have sometimes been depicted as more complicated figures. The issue is still a matter of controversy, and for that reason alone it merits further investigation.

One of the first critics to suggest a more complicated view of both Harris and Remus was Raymond Hedin, who argued in a 1982 article that Remus "uses the tales and his own power as a storyteller to serve his own ends rather than anyone else" and that "Remus's innocence is more strategic than pastoral; he is never as guileless as he seems." According to Hedin, "Remus is at his most powerful through his ability to conjure the tales or withhold them, to explain them or not." Meanwhile, in a far more lengthy and substantial article published in 1990, Wayne Mixon made a very strong case for seeing both Harris and Remus as extremely complex figures. Mixon suggested that the experiences of Harris's youth probably "did much to engender" a "sympathetic understanding of the plight of blacks" (458) and that his "ambivalence toward the white South caused him to engage only rarely in glorifying the Lost Cause of the Confederacy" (459). "Perhaps the most withering attack" of Harris's journalistic career (according to Mixon) "was directed at Jefferson Davis because he thought Davis was trying somehow to resurrect the Old South of slavery" (460).

Mixon's main argument is that "sufficient evidence exists both within the Remus tales and in Harris's other writings to justify the conclusion that a major part of his purpose as a writer was to under-mine racism" (461). Mixon provides abundant evidence to support this view, contending that Harris "fought the almost hopeless battle against racism in the only way he could—subversively, through fiction" (465). Mixon believes that Uncle Remus himself "is an exceedingly complex figure who recognizes a stereotype when he sees one and whose personality includes none of the traits, such as immaturity, exuberance, and laziness, that are commonly ascribed to the happy inferior" (467). "Although Remus regards a few whites highly, he is" (in Mixon's view) "nobody's lackey. His attitude toward the whites who seemingly control his life serves his own interests" (469). "Like Brer Rabbit" (Mixon contends) Remus "is intelligent, sly, and proud" (473). All in all, Mixon provides plenty of evidence to suggest that Harris deliberately created Remus—and wrote the Remus tales—with the intention of undermining white racist prejudices.

Mixon's view found influential support in a massive and important 1993 book by Eric J. Sundquist titled *To Wake the Nations: Race in the Making of American Literature*. Sundquist began by conceding that there "is no question that Harris's attitudes toward blacks were very complicated. . . . Even though his essays show him to be an unapologetic paternalist, when measured against the southern demonology of his day Harris was often and obviously liberal. But his views are hardly predictable" (339). By the end of his discussion, however, Sundquist concludes that Harris sometimes speaks as a "double-voiced trickster": "Brer Rabbit is a trickster disguise for Remus, who in turn is a trickster disguise for Harris himself" (343). This view has found emphatic recent support in a significant article from 2004 by Robert Cochran. There is a very strong likelihood, Cochran asserts, that Harris

> constructed his tales and their framing narratives with consummate skill and deliberate cunning, that multiple ironies were not only not lost upon him but were in fact something of his stock-in-trade, and that he was, in short, something of a Brer Rabbit among authors. Uncle Remus, by such an approach, is revealed as a secret hero of Harris's work, a figure worthy of comparison with Brer Rabbit himself. . . . Fundamentally, Harris's strategy as a writer is of a piece with that of Remus the storyteller and Brer Rabbit the character. (24)

It would be inaccurate to suggest that the views of Hedin, Mixon, Sundquist, and Cochran now represent anything like the critical orthodoxy concerning Harris and his "Uncle Remus" tales. Many critics and readers still find these works quite unsavory in their explicit and implicit racism and paternalism, and many readers and critics are far from sympathetic to the view that either Harris or Remus can be seen as a cunning, clever, and finally sympathetic trickster who sought to undermine racist assumptions. Mixon and Cochran offer the most substantial support for such a view, but much more investigation obviously remains to be done. Over the course of his lengthy career, Harris published scores of "Uncle Remus" tales in a succession of different collections; the standard edition of the complete tales runs to more than eight hundred pages. Only after careful, detailed study of all the tales in their historical and biographical contexts may it ever be possible to say with any certainty how persuasive the view of Harris and Remus as "tricksters" ultimately seems, and, even *after* such study, controversy will probably still abound. In the space remaining, however, I wish to focus on the animal tales printed in the first and most influential of the "Remus" volumes—*Uncle Remus: His Songs and Sayings* (1880; new and revised edition 1896)—in order to explore the ways and the extent to which Harris, and especially Remus, might be viewed as narrative "tricksters."

One of the most obvious and least controversial ways in which Remus is a trickster involves the various methods he actually uses to tell his tales. Thus, at the very end of the first part of "The Wonderful Tar-Baby Story"—perhaps the most famous of all the tales—Remus deliberately concludes on a note of suspense. When the seven-year-old white boy (son of the owners of the plantation on which Remus lives) excitedly asks whether the fox ate the rabbit that the fox had so cleverly trapped, Remus tantalizingly replies, "Dat's all de fur de tale goes. . . . He mout, en den again he moutent. Some say Jedge B'ar come 'long en loosed 'im—some say he didn't. I hear Miss Sally [the boy's mother] callin'. You better run 'long" (11). Cunningly, then, Remus intentionally delays the much-desired ending of the story, postponing it for at least two evenings, until the little boy asks him to take up the tale again (16). The first volume of Remus stories is full of such narrative wit, indirection, and evasiveness; Remus obviously knows what he is doing and enjoys his position of storytelling power. He is highly aware of his audience and of the impact he is having on the boy. Thus, after telling the child a hilarious story titled "Mr. Rabbit Grossly Deceives Mr. Fox," Remus once more cleverly ends on a note of suspense, leaving both the boy and the reader hungering for more: "'Is that all, Uncle Remus?' asked the little boy as the old man paused. 'Dat ain't all, honey, but 'twon't do fer to give out too much cloff fer ter cut one pa'r pants,' replied the old man sententiously" (29). Here, as throughout the tales, Uncle Remus is fully in control of the pace, structure, content, and meaning of the narration. And, of course, Harris is in control of Uncle Remus. Both men obviously enjoy spinning clever and tantalizing yarns; both storytellers clearly relish their roles as narrative tricksters.

Numerous examples of this kind of narrative trickery—by both Remus and Harris—abound. Repeatedly, for instance, Remus leaves his seven-year-old listener in suspense, causing him to assume what

Harris calls "the anxious position of auditor" (47). Harris thereby produces the same kind of anxiousness in his readers: Both we and the boy are constantly left wanting more. At one point, for example, Remus tells the boy, "Brer Wolf mighty smart, but nex' time you hear fum 'im, honey, he'll be in trouble. You des hole yo' breff 'n wait" (58). At another point, a tale begins as follows: "When the little boy ran in to see Uncle Remus the night after he had told him of the awful fate of Brer Wolf, the only response to his greeting was: 'I-doom-er-ker-kum-mer-ker!'" (68). Of course the little boy is puzzled and intrigued by this mysterious outburst—and so are we. Only after some effective delay by Harris, in which the puzzling phrase is repeated twice more, does Remus explain: "Dat's Tarrypin talk, dat is" (69). Remus thus plays with the boy as auditor in the same way that Harris plays with us as readers, and indeed part of the delight of reading the Remus tales comes from our sense, as readers, that we are once again in the position of small children—of being played with, teased, and affectionately tricked.

Remus's manipulation of the boy, however, goes beyond mere narrative trickery and often serves very practical purposes. At one point, for example, the youngster offers to steal some tea-cakes for Uncle Remus as a way of making amends for some boyish misbehavior Remus has just rebuked. Instead of objecting to such theft on moral grounds (as might have been expected from his recent condemnation of "bad chilluns"), Remus says of the cakes, "Seein' um's better'n hearin' tell un um" (30). And when the boy returns a few minutes later loaded down with cakes for the old man, Remus simply jokes that the boy's mother will blame the theft on rats (31). Moreover, in a nice example of Harris's own skills as a narrative trickster, he reports how Remus immediately deals with the cakes: "'Deze,' he continued, dividing the cakes into two equal parts—'dese I'll tackle now, en dese I'll lay by fer Sunday'" (31). The part of this sentence that precedes the hyphen might lead us to expect that Remus is about to share the tea-cakes with the small boy; the part of the sentence that follows the hyphen, however, makes his real intentions clear. Once more, then, Harris plays the kind of trick on us as readers that Remus repeatedly plays on the boy and that Brer Rabbit constantly plays on his various victims.

Some nice examples of the ways in which various kinds of trickery are blended are provided when Harris describes Remus's efforts to get access to Christmas gifts from the boy's family. Thus, at the conclusion of one tale, Remus speaks to the boy "in a confidential tone" just before the youngster is about to return to the "big house":

> "Honey, you mus' git up soon Chris'mus mawnin' en open do do'; kase I'm gwinter bounce in on Marse John and Miss Sally, en holler Chris'mus gif' des like I useter endurin' de farmin' days fo' de war, we'n ole Miss wuz 'live. I boun' dey don't fergit de ole nigger, nudder. W'en you hear me callin' de pigs, honey, you des hop up en onfassen de' do'. I lay I'll gave Marse John one er dese yer 'sprize parties." (36)

Here the old man quite explicitly manipulates the boy, making him a confederate (no pun intended) in a scheme to get what the old man wants. Later, when the boy steals Remus some pie from the big house, Remus even commends and justifies the boy's own trickery: "'Chris'mus doin's is outer date, en dey ain't got no bizness layin' roun' loose. Dish yer pie,' Uncle Remus continued, holding it up and measuring it with an experienced eye, 'will gimme strenk fer ter persoo on atter Brer Fox en Brer Rabbit en de udder creeturs w'at dey roped in 'long wid um'" (53–54). The boy's sympathy for Remus—a sympathy Harris not only seems to share but also encourages in his readers—causes the lad to steal from his own parents, and neither he, Harris, nor we seem bothered by Remus's justifications of such trickery.

Perhaps the most intriguing examples of trickery by both Harris and Remus, however, involve those places in the tales where the stories about animals seem to reflect quite clearly on the positions of blacks in pre-war and post-war Southern society. Harris had already suggested, in his "Introduction" to the volume, that the "story of the Rabbit and the Fox, as told by the Southern negroes," might "be to a certain extent allegorical," and he had remarked that "it needs no scientific investigation to show why he [i.e., the negro] selects as his hero the weakest and most harmless of all animals, and brings him out victorious in contests with the bear, the wolf, and the fox" (xiv). Harris had thereby subtly invited his readers to interpret the tales as reflections on race relations, and some of the tales make it almost impossible to read them in any other way. Repeatedly, for instance, Remus refers to fear of "patter-rollers," a phrase Harris defines in a note as follows: "Patrols. In the country districts, order was kept on the plantations at night by the knowledge that they were liable to be visited at any moment by the patrols. Hence a song current among the negroes, the chorus of which was: 'Run, nigger, run; patter-roller ketch you—/ Run, nigger, run; hit's almos' day'" (32). This explanation explicitly links the experiences of the mythical animals to the experiences of real Southern blacks, and the note implies strong sympathy for the victims of such "patter-rollers."

Continually, throughout the tales, Harris craftily uses Remus to suggest ideas that seem applicable to the injustices suffered by oppressed peoples. When the boy, for example, objects that Brer Possum dies because of thefts that were in fact committed by Brer Rabbit, Remus replies: "In dis worril, lots er fokes is gotter suffer fer udder fokes sins. Look like hit's mighty onwrong; but hit's des dat away. Tribbalashun seem like she's a waitin' roun' de cornder fer ter ketch one en all un us, honey" (86). Clearly the suffering of Brer Possum seems to reflect on the sufferings of blacks, and although Remus's explanation might strike modern readers as too accepting and compliant, perhaps that was part of the effect Harris intended: We, like the boy, are repelled by the injustice of Brer Possum's gruesome death, and Remus's explanation seems partly realistic (in describing how the world really does often work) but also finally inadequate (in suggesting how the world ideally *should* work). In fact, Remus's final statement here may be taken to imply that prosperous whites may not always enjoy their presently privileged positions and that some whites may suffer for racial sins that they themselves did not commit. (Indeed, that it is Brer Rabbit—the most obvious symbol of blacks in the tales—who unfairly triumphs in this episode makes this interpretive possibility all the more intriguing.)

A similarly suggestive and unsettling exchange between the boy and Uncle Remus occurs later, after Remus has just described how a turtle (Brer Tarrypin) used deception to defeat Brer Rabbit in a contest. When the boy protests against the cheating, Remus responds: "De creeturs 'gun ter cheat, en den fokes tuck it up, en hit keep on spreadin'. Hit mighty ketchin', en you mine yo' eye, honey, dat somebody don't cheat you 'fo' yo' ha'r git gray ez de ole nigger's" (91). This passage might easily be taken as a reflection, by an old black man, on the experiences of American blacks, but it might also be read as a veiled warning (as in the earlier anecdote) that "what goes around comes around." Uncle Remus implies a world in which little white boys may grow up to be cheated just as old black men have been—probably (Remus would seem to imply) by other whites.

At times the phrasing used by both Harris and Remus can seem positively disturbing in its racial overtones. Thus, during the course of telling one tale, Remus has promised to give the little boy a whip he has been making for him. At the end of the tale, Remus presents his gift, but he does so in a way that can seem unsettling to any reader familiar with the lynchings of blacks that were rampant in the South during the era when these tales were published: "'Now den, honey, you take dis yer w'ip,' continued the old man, twining the leather thong around the little boy's neck, 'en scamper up ter de big 'ouse en tell Miss Sally fer ter gin you some un it de nex' time she fine yo' tracks in de sugar-bair'l'" (103). Surely the old man has no intention of truly threatening the young boy, but the imagery and phrasing have the effect of disturbing any adult reader with qualms about lynchings. Equally ominous is the beginning of another tale, when Uncle Remus explains not only why Brer Rabbit was sometimes defeated in wit contests with other creatures but also why it was advantageous that he sometimes lose: "Hit's des like I tell you, honey. Dey ain't no smart man, 'cep' w'at dey's a smarter. Ef ole Brer Rabbit hadn't er got kotch up wid, de nabers 'ud er took 'im for a ha'nt, en in dem times dey bu'nt witches 'fo' you could squinch yo' eyeballs. Dey did dat'" (104). Uncle Remus implies that irrational beliefs—such as the assumptions of the "nabers" that a completely fortunate Brer Rabbit might possess malign supernatural powers—could easily lead to persecution and death. Here as so often elsewhere in the tales, Remus instructs the boy about the dangerous and often deadly injustices and illogical prejudices that often determine how creatures live and how they sometimes die.

Throughout the "Remus" tales, Harris inserts moments that are potentially disturbing and unsettling for anyone familiar with abuses of power—abuses of the sort suffered by blacks both before and after the abolition of slavery. One of those moments, for instance, comes when Brer Bull-frog, having been falsely accused of deception, is about to be eaten by his accuser, Brer B'ar [i.e., Bear]. The frog pleads frantically and repeatedly, "Oh, pray, Brer B'ar! I won't never do so no mo'! Oh, pray, Brer B'ar! Lemme off dis time!" (118). These pleas go on for several paragraphs and are increasingly painful to read, especially since we know that the frog is innocent. Moments such as this remind us of how easy it was for a powerless person in Harris's era to be falsely accused of a crime, how quickly and summarily accusers might impose justice (or injustice), and how little hope the desperate victim of any such accusation could realistically possess. Eventually, after the frog does manage to escape the bear by outwitting him, he sings what seems a nonsense song—a song the boy finds "mighty funny." To this comment, Remus replies: "Funny now, I speck, . . . but 'twern't funny in dem days, en 'twouldn't be funny now ef folks know'd much 'bout de Bull-frog langwidge ez dey useter" (119). Such comments are tantalizingly suggestive, implying that there are more unsettling meanings in Remus's stories than might at first be obvious. Thus, Remus later lulls the little boy to sleep by singing a song of his own—a song set right before the Civil War and one that clearly seems to imply the longing of blacks for freedom:

> Hit's eighteen hunder'd, forty-en-eight,
> Christ done made dat crooked way straight—
> En I don't wanter stay here no longer;
> Hit's eighteen hunder'd, forty-en-nine,
> Christ done turn dat water inter wine—
> En I don't wanter stay here no longer. (156)

Perhaps the most intriguing of all the tales, however, at least for anyone interested in the possibility of racially subversive innuendo in the stories, is one of the last and one of the briefest—a tale simply titled "Why the Negro is Black." In this tale, Remus patiently explains to the boy that "dey wuz a time w'en all de w'ite folks 'uz black—blacker dan me" (163). "Niggers is niggers now," Remus continues, "but de time wuz w'en we 'uz all niggers tergedder" (163). "In dem times," Remus explains, "we 'uz all un us black; we 'uz all niggers tergedder, en 'cordin' ter all de 'counts w'at I years fokes 'uz gittin 'long 'bout ez well in dem days es dey is now" (164).

That last comment—implying that "fokes" have *never* gotten along very well together—is typical of the sly insinuations of which both Remus and Harris, as trickster-narrators, are so often capable. Remus explains how whites managed to wash off their blackness in a special pond, but the really memorable message of the tale is the one he emphatically repeats: "de time wuz w'en we 'uz all niggers tergedder." One implication of this statement—an implication borne out by the undeniable emotional power of the tales themselves—is that blacks and whites, despite their superficial differences, share a deeper bond than they might imagine. Another implication is that although whites at present enjoy greater power than blacks, they may someday find themselves (either individually or as a group) returned to their original status as powerless "niggers." It seems entirely fitting that almost the last tale of the original batch of Uncle Remus stories should slyly remind readers (mostly whites) of their original kinship with blacks—a kinship (it might be argued) that the stories themselves, through subtle narrative trickery, cleverly help revive and strengthen.

WORKS CITED OR CONSULTED

Bickley, R. Bruce, Jr. and Hugh T. Keenan. *Joel Chandler Harris: An Annotated Bibliography of Criticism, 1977–1996, With Supplement, 1892–1976.* Westport, Conn: Greenwood, 1997.

Cochran, Robert. "Black Father: The Subversive Achievement of Joel Chandler Harris." *African American Review* 38.1 (2004): 21–34.

Harris, Joel Chandler. *Uncle Remus and His Sayings.* 1896. New York: Appleton-Century, 1938.

Hedin, Raymond. "Uncle Remus: Puttin' on ole Massa's son." *The Southern Literary Journal* 15.1 (1982): 83–90.

Mixon, Wayne. "The Ultimate Irrelevance of Race: Joel Chandler Harris and Uncle Remus in Their Time." *Journal of Southern History* 56 (1990): 457–480.

Sundquist, Eric J. *To Wake the Nations: Race in the Making of American Literature.* Cambridge, Mass.: Harvard UP, 1993.

"The Wife of Bath's Tale"
(Geoffrey Chaucer)

"Transforming the Trickster in Chaucer's *Wife of Bath's Tale*"
by Dean Swinford, Fayetteville State University

The pilgrims of Chaucer's *Canterbury Tales* display a depth that anticipates the literary realism of the nineteenth-century novel. At the same time, the tales they tell use genres indebted to the allegorizing tendency of myth and legend. Chaucer uses familiar archetypes such as the trickster and the hero but often obscures fixed character identities. Determining the identity of the tricked and the trickster is not always an easy task. Likewise, the identity of the trickster often depends on the conventions of the genre used to tell the tale. Chaucer's Wife of Bath tells a tale discernible as a romance of the type popular in thirteenth-and-fourteenth century England. The romance as a genre has this unstable identity of the tricked and the trickster at its core. As William Paton Ker notes in *Epic and Romance*, "Romance means nothing if it does not convey some notion of mystery and fantasy" (4). To this extent, it lacks the direct statement of warlike virtue encountered in the epic. The genre is typified by a tension resulting from the quest for a heroic ideal that remains, ultimately, unattainable. At the same time, this genre, built on quests, battles, and declarations of loyalty, or "troth," also revels in betrayal, games, and impossible challenges. Often, the token exemplifying the tale serves to remind characters and readers alike that the "rules'" governing a quest or game have, in fact, been broken and, simultaneously, fulfilled. The green girdle that Sir Gawain receives at the end of another romance, *Sir Gawain and the Green Knight*, is "the sign of sore loss" as well as a token "taken by the Table Round" that "honored [he who] had it" (lines 2506, 2519).

Chaucer's *Wife of Bath's Tale* takes advantage of this discrepancy, ultimately presenting a take on the "war of the sexes" that ironizes the quest motif at the heart of the romance. The Wife presents a quest for the answer to a question. In the first part of this tale, the knight must seek the answer to a tricky question. The knight, a member of King Arthur's court, is convicted of rape. The law of the court demands his head, but "the quene and othere ladies mo" ["the queen and other ladies as well"] (*Bath* 900) spare his life on the condition that he can tell them "What thing is it that wommen most desyren" ["What thing it is that women most desire"] (911). He has a year to complete his quest but finds no conclusive answer until he comes across an old woman in the woods. She promises to give him the answer, whispering this secret message in his ear, on the condition that he pledges to do "The nexte thing that I requere thee" ["The next thing that I require of thee"] (1016). They return to the court, which is presided over by the queen and filled with women of various stages of life: "Ful many a noble wyf, and many a mayde,/ And many a widwe" [Very many a noble wife, and many a maid,/ And many a widow"] (1032–1033). He provides the correct answer, telling the queen that "Wommen desyren to have sovereyntee" ["Women desire to have sovereignty"] (1044). The court grants him freedom, ending the quest.

At this point, the old woman reveals her role and demands that the court "do me right" ["do me justice"] (1055) by forcing the knight to take her "unto thy wyf" ["as thy wife"] (1061). The knight resists marrying a woman so "foul and old and pore" ["ugly, and old, and poor"] (1069) yet soon finds himself in bed with her after the wedding. She doubts his virility until he reveals his obvious concerns: She is "loothly" ["loathsome"], "so old," and "of so low a kinde" ["from such low-born lineage"] (1106–1107). In response, she details the advantages of these qualities, starting with an estimation of the Christian virtue of poverty, moving to the honor due the aged, and concluding with the most important point, namely that her lack of beauty means she will never betray him. Then she offers the knight the choice "To hay me foul and old" ["To have me ugly and old"] (1226) or "yong and fair" ["young and fair"] (1229). The knight, having learned what women really want, tells her to "Cheseth youreself" ["Choose yourself"] (1238) and puts himself in her "wyse governance" ["wise governance"] (1237). She transforms herself so that she is "bothe fair and good" ["both fair and good"] (1247), and the pair lives "In parfit joye" ["In perfect joy"] (1264).

The Wife of Bath's tale allegorizes the relationship between men and women, using fantastic elements such as the court of women, a heroic quest, and a magical transformation to comment on, as she repeatedly declares, the "wo that is in mariage" ["woe that is in marriage"] (3). She claims authority as the teller of this tale from her personal experience through five marriages. Indeed, she has been on multiple "pilgrimages," in a literal and figurative sense. Besides traveling to a number of places, including "Rome [. . .] Boloigne [. . .] Galice [. . .] and [. . .] Coloigne" ["Rome . . . Boulogne . . . Galicia . . . and . . . Cologne"] (*Prologue* 465–466) as a religious pilgrim, she has also journeyed to the "chirche dore" ["church door"] (460) five times, leading the narrator to conclude that "she coude of that art the olde daunce" ["she knew the old dance of that art"] (476). These characteristics help to establish the Wife of Bath as well traveled in all senses of the word. This is important because Chaucer never loses sight of the relationship between words and the character who speaks them.

The first line of her prologue establishes an important opposition that drives her self-representation as well as her depiction of male and female roles in the tale. She distinguishes two ways of knowing and ordering the world, one offered by "experience" and the other by "auctoritee," or the written authority of secular law, holy scripture, and ecclesiastical interpretations.

The Wife of Bath constantly repudiates the misogynistic logic of classical authorities. Scholars have attempted to uncover Chaucer's complex views on gender and the power struggles that ensue in relationships, but they have been unable to conclusively prove that the Wife of Bath "speaks" his views directly or obliquely. What we do know, however, is that the tale achieves its enduring power by eliding simple identifications and conclusions. In the same way that the romance privileges paradox, Chaucer's connection of the characters in the romance, the imaginary audience of pilgrims wending their way toward Canterbury, and the reader prohibits any easy identification between these levels. The message, or "pistel" (*Bath* 1027), at the heart of the tale changes meaning depending on who is doing the telling.

Any consideration of Chaucer's tales must take into account the relationship between the speaker of the tale and the tale itself. The Wife of Bath is justifiably famous as Chaucer's most elaborate and complex character, a woman representative of her age who, at the same time, reveals a complex personality grounded in the daily appetites of the body. She is a woman who would seem equally comfortable on a fourteenth-century pilgrimage as she would on the set of a contemporary daytime talk show.

Chaucer first introduces the Wife in the *General Prologue*, setting her amid the other pilgrims, men identified chiefly by profession. The wife, too, has an important skill: "Of cloth-making she hadde swiche an haunt, she passed hem of Ypres and of Gaunt" ["She had such a skill in cloth-making/ She surpassed them of Ypres and of Ghent"] (*Prologue* 447–448). Sheila Delany sees this reference to Dame Alice's trade as a way of marking her place in the world: "The Wife of Bath belongs to the petty bourgeoisie; she is a small-time entrepreneur in the textile trade, which, already by the thirteenth century, had come to dominate the English economy and its international trade" (Delany 72). At the same time, this reference to her skill in weaving may be intended to undercut her authority. First, the fabrics from the Wife's city, Bath, actually had a poor reputation. John Manly describes Chaucer's meaning here as "perhaps ironical" (Manly 527). In fact, this poor reputation resulted in the threat of violence: "a statute of Richard II notes that some of their cloth was so bad that English merchants abroad were in danger of their lives" (*Riverside* 818n.). Second, as a profession filled primarily by women, the Wife of Bath's weaving may have been read by Chaucer's principal audience as unimportant women's work, a profession suggestive of the gap between experience and authority she rails against in the prologue.

After the *Tale of Melibee*, another weaver, the Host's wife, curses her husband by telling him to take "my distaf and go spynne" ["my distaff and go spin"] (*Monk* 1907). The distaff, an elongated stafflike spool around which thread is wound, represents the feminine and the trivial. In medieval thinking, this image also marked a contrast with the pen as a symbol of the kinds of authority that the Wife is most interested in overturning. Heloise, an abbess who is the lone female mentioned by the Wife as an "authority," "explain[s] that women are separated from clerical pens by their need to wield distaves" (Holloway 27). While Heloise achieved renown as "an admirable embodiment of spiritual femaleness," she gained this status through a life lived "in the enclosure of the Paraclete" (Cazelles 79). However, Heloise most likely appears as an authority because, having been "socialized into anti-feminist attitudes," she often "regurgitate[d], with passionate conviction, all the commonplaces of anti-feminism used to discourage clerics from marriage" (Barratt 12). The Wife of Bath, by contrast, resists this encapsulation of the female voice to show, instead, that the distaff is mightier than the pen. The Wife of Bath contends directly with the wisdom of the pen in her prologue, refuting or overturning the patristic condemnation of multiple marriages and the enjoyment of sex while demonstrating the equally virtuous nature of clerical celibacy and her drive to "bistowe the flour of al myn age/ In the actes and in fruit of mariage" ["bestow the flower of all my age/ In the acts and in fruit of marriage"] (*Bath* 119–120).

The noble world of Arthur's court would have been encountered by female weavers through songs, tales, and embroidered tapestries rather than through written texts. Indeed, "So far as medieval culture is scriptless or non-literate, there is a natural overweight of the visual and pictorial" (Meier 45). Of course, we cannot forget that the Wife is a fictional character, and it would be equally fictitious to suppose that she speaks to or for an audience of equals. Instead, Chaucer speaks through the Wife: "Romance promised a code of courtliness resulting from nurture as well as from birthright, an education of the soul available to the 'free' and 'gentle' man, who finds in the tales a mirror to his aspirations" (Allen 46). The romance, then, serves as a counterpoint to authority for a number of audiences.

In keeping with the order of tales found in the Ellesmere manuscript, the *Norton Anthology of English Literature* and other modern editions position the *Wife of Bath's Tale* after the *Man of Law's Epilogue*. These editions also enhance the continuity between these tales by representing the Wife of Bath as the speaker who interrupts an argument between the Host and the Parson. The Host proclaims that "this lollere heer wil prechen us som what" [this Lollard here will preach something to us"] (*Law* 15) and names the preferred genre of the Parson's tale: "we schal han a predicacioun" or a sermon (14). While the Wife of Bath cites a uniformity of faith among the pilgrims, who, by her reckoning at least, "leven alle in the grete god" ["all believe in the great God"] (19), she questions the motive underlying any "predicacioun" coming from the Parson, who, to her understanding, seems all too eager to "sowen som difficulte,/ Or springen cokkel in oure clene corn" ["sow some difficulty,/ Or sprinkle weeds in our clean grain"] (20–21). This exchange in the *Man of Law's Epilogue* marks a transition to a new kind of authority, indicative not of a disembodied moral law but of a philosophy of the senses guided by the Wife's "joly body" ["jolly body"] (23).

In the same way that the order and arrangement of tales transforms the fluid identities of Chaucer's pilgrims, the message at the core of the Wife's tale shapes our perception of its central characters. There is no single trickster in the tale; instead the form of the romance subverts customary character roles through a process that begins when the king cedes the administration of justice to the queen. In this way, we should give equal weight to the derivation of the word *trick* from *triccare*, which denotes deception and robbery, as well as additional meanings of *trick*, such as illusory appearances, alteration, and transformation. The effect of the trick depends as much on its perceived reception as it does on the trickster.

As an archetype, the trickster is characterized in two important ways: The most well known and obvious is that the trickster subverts authority. The less frequently considered corollary is that, in order to subvert authority, the trickster must somehow also lay claim to authority and the privileges and powers it bestows. Examples from myth, for instance, show characters like Loki undercutting the authority of the gods and promoting the chaotic incursions of the giants while remaining firmly delineated as a god. The Arthurian cycles display a similar logic of character roles, so that the "Trickster Mordred—playing the Loki role—[. . .] brings on the climax and downfall of Camelot" (Fox 94), and this despite Mordred's familial link to King Arthur. In both types of example, the trick or deception has a connection to the kinds of alteration or transformation that are so central to the magical qualities of myth and romance.

Trickster characters like Loki in Norse myth or Raven in Native American folklore are also shape-shifters. Mordred's deception comes, in various versions, from the crime of his conception. Several tales configure Mordred as Arthur's illegitimate son by his sister Morgause either directly, through rape, or indirectly, through deception. In this case, Mordred's identity as trickster embodies Arthur's capacity for treachery and, hence, the treachery underlying law and authority.

Mordred literally causes Arthur's death and the downfall of his kingdom; Mordred's existence signifies the rot at the root of chivalry.

Who plays the role of the trickster, then, in the Wife of Bath's tale? A list of possibilities extends outward from the center of the tale, eventually implicating the teller, the audience, and the vast weight of authoritative texts compiled in the books of the Wife's husband, Janekin. At first glance, the role of trickster seems to fall to the "olde wyf" ["old wife"] (*Bath* 1006), the crone who provides the answer the knight seeks but exacts the terrible price of marriage. Indeed, the initial appearance of this "wyf" ["wife"] sitting on the "grene" ["green"] in a forest through which "heerforth ne lyth no wey" ["there lies no road out"] (1004, 1007) suggests the "fayerye" ["supernatural creatures"] (865), who "Daunced ful ofte in many a grene mede" ["Danced very often in many a green mead"] (867), mentioned at the beginning of the tale. As an "elf-queen" (866), her supernatural justice is, by definition, based on illusion and magic. However, the knight's initial reference to the wife as "My leve mooder" ["My dear mother"] (1011) shows a deference to female authority that doesn't quite match his actions thus far. His initial characterization reveals a "lusty bacheler" ["lusty bachelor"] (889) who uses "verray force" ["utter force"] (894) to deprive a maiden of "hire maydenheed" ["her maidenhood"] (894) when he encounters her in a lonely forest. In this sense, his show of respect to the crone is an ironic reversal of his previous actions, leading us to question whether he says what he means. Beyond that, a consideration of the situation surrounding the knight's temporary escape from justice reveals the possibility that the knight's indiscretions may not be limited to the situation that sets the events of the tale in motion.

The knight's "oppressioun" ["wrong"] (895) runs counter to the clearly established order of King Arthur's court: The "cours of law" ["course of law"] (898) declares that "dampned was this knight for to be deed" ["this knight was condemned to be dead"] (897). The method of death is as specific as it is severe. As a result of his trespass, the knight "sholde han lost his head" ["should have lost his head"] (898). At this point, and for reasons not made entirely clear, "the quene and othere ladies mo" ["the queen and other ladies as well"] (900) beg for contrition from the king. Beyond releasing the knight, however, the ladies of the court ask that the knight's fate be determined by the queen's "wille" (903). The Wife of Bath uses striking imagery to depict the queen's alternatives. She may choose to "save or

spille" ["save or put to death"] (904) the knight; in this line, the word
"spille" evokes the gory consequences accompanying a justice that has
been transferred from the clearly definable code of masculine law to
the capricious, perhaps unstable, authority of the queen's will.

The structure of this part of the tale echoes that of the Arthurian
romances popular in the court and in the kinds of tapestries alluded to
in the lines of the *General Prologue* that introduce the Wife. In particular,
the specifics of the queen's challenge parallel those of the phantasma-
goric giant whose Yuletide game mocks the supposed virtue of King
Arthur's court in *Sir Gawain and the Green Knight*. First, the penalty
for both is the same. In *Sir Gawain*, the giant challenges the court to
a "beheading game." Whoever is brave enough to behead the Green
Knight must submit to equal treatment at the end of a year and a day.
Similarly, the queen warns the knight to "keep thy nekke-boon from
yren" ["keep thy neck-bone from the axe"] (912) by providing an answer
within "A twelf-month and a day" ["A year and a day"] (915) to a seemingly simple question: "What thing is it that wommen most desyren?"
["What thing is it that women most desire?"] (911). Second, a woman
helps the quester to achieve his mission. Gawain receives a green girdle
that supposedly has the power to resist weapons, opening the possibility
that he may "escape unscathed" (*Gawain* 1858) from his meeting with
the giant in the Green Chapel. However, Gawain comes to see the
girdle as a sign of "my falsehood" (2378), because Bertilak's wife tricks
him into accepting the gift.

The crone of the Wife's tale also offers a gift that saves the knight.
This gift, however, is a message, not an object. This message filters
through the numerous levels of the tale, the resonances of its meaning
influenced by its speaker. The content of the message is not revealed
when it first appears in the tale. Shortly after the knight grants her
his "trouthe" ["pledged word"] (*Bath* 1019), she whispers something
in his ear that we can presume is the answer to the queen's riddle. The
narrator recounts that the hag "rouned she a pistel in his ere" ["whispered a message in his ear"] (1027), then moves the story forward to
the moment of reckoning in the court at the end of the year. The word
pistel, while often glossed as *message*, also suggests a specific kind of
message, the epistle. The word *epistle*, beyond referring to any kind
of message, is also used to describe instructive letters, particularly
those written by the apostles and appearing in the New Testament. In
effect, the unstated message at the center of the text has some kind of

connection, ironic or otherwise, to the authoritative epistles, including those of St. Paul to the Corinthians, the Ephesians, and Timothy, that the Wife of Bath argues against in the prologue to her tale.

After this transmission, the knight possesses and assumes responsibility for the authority of the message. When he appears in the court, he "stood nat stille as doth a best" ["stood not silent as does a beast"] (1040) and, instead, addresses the queen "With manly voys" ["With manly voice"] (1042). The adjective *manly* in this phrase serves to develop the plot in a direct way and signifies that he elevates his voice so that he can be heard. The word also conveys an important quality of the message he transmits. His manly authority gives credence to the distasteful illogic of his message. Women, considered inferior in religious teachings, classical philosophy, conceptions of natural order, and the eyes of the law, "moste desyr" ["greatest desire"] (1047) a masculine prerogative, namely "sovereyntee" ["sovereignty"] (1044). The second part of the knight's "quest," a pilgrimage to the "chirche door" ["church door"] (*Prologue* 462) not unlike the Wife's, forces him to internalize the message he has just validated. While he has "tricked" the court through a skillful performance that earns him his life, he only puts himself under the "wyse governance" ["wise governance"] (1237) of his "humble wyf" ["humble wife"] (1227) when he realizes he has no other alternative.

Of course, his acceptance of her authority results in her bodily transformation, a development that seems to signify a parallel metamorphosis in the knight's morals and ethics. When considered from this perspective, the knight's "manly" declaration of female authority foreshadows the tale's happy ending and, as a statement by a character in a narrative, serves the purposes and goals surrounding the Wife of Bath's telling. The Wife creates an effective illusion only inasmuch as her fellow pilgrims deem her tale "believable."

While the pilgrims, and Chaucer's courtly audience, may affirm the patriarchal authority of Janekin's book of wicked wives, they also value the Wife's tale. The Friar, who follows the Wife in the Ellesmere arrangement, tells her she "han seyd muche thing right wel" ["has said many true things"] (*Friar* 1273). This apparent contradiction should come as no surprise, however, as "romance stories, sketched briefly as *exempla*, could comfortably stand adjacent to rather than in opposition to religious material" (qtd. in Allen 46). This characteristic of the romance becomes even more important for the Wife, and women like her, as she represents the knight in a process of change that mirrors the crone's metamorphosis. The knight's transformation succeeds at "tricking" the Wife's (and, by extension, Chaucer's) audience as long as they perceive this as a likely conclusion representative of a "coming into his true self," a process Marina Warner identifies in her analysis of Apulius's *Golden Ass* as "the ultimate goal of such a concept of metamorphosis" (Warner 89). To this extent, the crone's message, first whispered in the knight's ear and then filtered through layers of listeners, tricks all who hear it and, perhaps momentarily, moves them to affirm that it is the right answer to the queen's question as well as a suitable penalty for the knight's initial transgression.

Works Cited

Allen, Valerie. "Medieval English, 500–1500." *English Literature in Context*. Ed. Paul Poplawski. New York: Cambridge University Press, 2008. 1–109.

Bal, Mieke. *Narratology: Introduction to the Theory of Narrative*. Trans. Christine van Boheemen. Toronto: University of Toronto Press, 1994.

Barratt, Alexandra. *Women's Writing in Middle English*. New York: Longman, 1992.

Bloch, R. Howard. *Medieval Misogyny and the Invention of Western Romantic Love*. Chicago: University of Chicago Press, 1991.

Cazelles, Brigitte. *The Lady as Saint: A Collection of French Hagiographic Romances of the Thirteenth Century*. Philadelphia: University of Pennsylvania Press, 1991.

Chaucer, Geoffrey. *Canterbury Tales by Geoffrey Chaucer*. Ed. John Manly. New York: Henry Holt, 1928.

———. *Chaucer's Poetry: An Anthology for the Modern Reader*. 2nd ed. Ed. E.T. Donaldson. New York: Scott Foresman, 1975.

———. *Reading Chaucer: An Interlinear Translation of Selections in* The Norton Anthology of English Literature. 8th ed. Trans. Larry D. Benson. New York: W.W. Norton, 2006.

———. *The Riverside Chaucer*. 3rd ed. Ed. Larry D. Benson. Oxford: Oxford University Press, 1987.

Copeland, Rita. *Rhetoric, Hermeneutics, and Translation in the Middle Ages: Academic Traditions and Vernacular Texts*. New York: Cambridge University Press, 1995.

Delany, Sheila. "Sexual Economics, Chaucer's Wife of Bath and the Book of Margery Kempe." *Feminist Readings in Middle English Literature: The Wife of Bath and All Her Sect.* Ed. Ruth Evans and Lesley Johnson. New York: Routledge, 1994. 72–87.

Fox, Robin. *Conjectures and Confrontations: Science, Evolution, Social Concern.* New Brunswick: Transaction Publishers, 1997.

Holloway, Julia Bolton, Joan Bechtold, and Constance S. Wright. "Women and the Distaff." *Equally in God's Image: Women in the Middle Ages.* Eds. Julia Bolton Holloway, Joan Bechtold, and Constance S. Wright. New York: Peter Lang, 1991. 27–29.

Ker, William Paton. *Epic and Romance.* London: Macmillan, 1908.

Meier, H.H. "Writing and Medieval Culture." *Writing and Culture.* Ed. Balz Engler. Tübingen: Gunter Naar Verlag, 1992. 33–52.

Radice, Betty. Introduction. *The Letters of Abelard and Heloise.* By Abelard and Heloise. Trans. Betty Radice. London: Penguin, 1974. 9–55.

Sir Gawain and the Green Knight: A New Verse Translation. Trans. Marie Boroff. New York: W.W. Norton, 1967.

Warner, Marina. *Fantastic Metamorphoses, Other Worlds: Ways of Telling the Self.* Oxford: Oxford University Press, 2002.

❧ *Acknowledgments* ❧

Billingslea-Brown, Alma Jean. "The Journey as Crossing." *Crossing Borders through Folklore: African American Women's Fiction and Art*. University of Missouri Press, 1999. 67–83. © 1999 by The Curators of the University of Missouri. Reprinted by permission.

Brodtkorb, Paul, Jr. "*The Confidence-Man*: The Con-Man as Hero." *Studies in the Novel* 1.4 (Winter 1969): 421–435. Reprinted by permission.

Le Bossu, René. "A General View of the Epic Poem, and of the *Iliad* and *Odyssey*; Extracted from Bossu." *The Odyssey of Homer, A New Edition*. Vol. 1. Trans. Alexander Pope. London: printed for F.J. Du Roveray by T. Bensley, Bolt Court, 1806. 5–39.

Lincoln, Kenneth. "Futuristic Hip Indian: Alexie." *Sing With the Heart of a Bear: Fusions of Native and American Poetry, 1890–1999*. Berkeley, Calif: University of California Press, 2000. 267–276. © 2000 by the Regents of the University of California. Reprinted by permission.

Lindberg, Gary. "Faith on the Run." *The Confidence Man in American Literature*. London: Oxford UP, 1982. 259–279. © 1982 by Oxford University Press, Inc. Reprinted by permission.

Manzoor, Sohana. "The Prometheus Myth in the Novels of William Golding." *BRAC University Journal* 4.2 (2007): 105–111. © BRAC University. Reprinted by permission.

Mazzotta, Giuseppe. "Games of Laughter." *The World at Play in Boccaccio's Decameron*. Princeton, N.J.: Princeton UP, 1986. 186–212. © 1986 by Princeton University Press. Reprinted by permission.

Ulrici, Hermann. "*The Tempest* and *A Midsummer Night's Dream*." *Shakspeare's Dramatic Art: History and Character of Shakspeare's Plays, Vol. II*. Trans. L. Dora Schmitz. London: George Bell and Sons, 1908. 38–85.

Warde, Frederick. "The Grave Diggers in 'Hamlet.'" *The Fools of Shakespeare: An Interpretation of their Wit and Wisdom*. 1915. Los Angeles, Calif: Times-Mirror Press, 1923. 153–173.

Index